Autobiography, Politics
and Sexuality

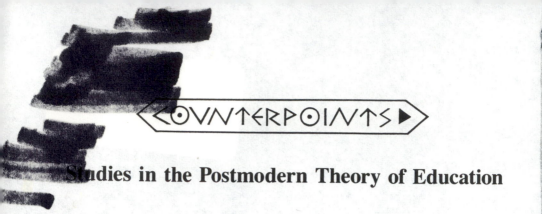

COUNTERPOINTS

Studies in the Postmodern Theory of Education

Joe L. Kincheloe and Shirley R. Steinberg
General Editors

Vol. 2

PETER LANG
New York • Washington, D.C./Baltimore • San Francisco
Bern • Frankfurt am Main • Berlin • Vienna • Paris

William F. Pinar

Autobiography, Politics and Sexuality

Essays in Curriculum Theory 1972–1992

PETER LANG

New York • Washington, D.C./Baltimore • San Francisco
Bern • Frankfurt am Main • Berlin • Vienna • Paris

Library of Congress Cataloging-in-Publication Data

Pinar, William.
  Autobiography, politics and sexuality: essays in curriculum theory
1972–1992 / William F. Pinar.
     p.   cm. — (Counterpoints: studies in the postmodern theory of
education; vol. 2)
  Includes bibliographical references.
  1. Education—Curricula. 2. Education—North America—Curricula.
3. Education—Biographical methods. I. Title. II. Series: Counterpoints
(New York, N.Y.); Vol. 2.
LB1570.P55   1994   375—dc20   94-132
ISBN 0-8204-1849-8   CIP
ISSN 1058-1634

Die Deutsche Bibliothek-CIP-Einheitsaufnahme

Pinar, William F.:
Autobiography, politics and sexuality: essays in curriculum theory
1972–1992 / William F. Pinar. - New York; Washington, DC/Baltimore;
San Francisco; Bern; Frankfurt am Main; Berlin; Vienna; Paris: Lang, 1994
  (Counterpoints; Vol. 2)
  ISBN 0-8204-1849-8
NE:GT

The front cover photograph entitled, "Rolf Duerig in Rome," by
Herbert List has been reproduced with the kind permission of the
Herbert List Estate.

Cover design by George Lallas.

The paper in this book meets the guidelines for permanence and durability of
the Committee on Production Guidelines for Book Longevity of the
Council on Library Resources.

Printed in the United States of America.

Table of Contents

Editors' Introduction.. vii

Introduction.. 1

I: Working from Within (1972)... 7

II: Mr. Bennett and Mrs. Brown (1973)............................ 13

III: The Method of *Currere* (1975)................................. 19

IV: The Trial (1976)... 29

V: What is the Reconceptualization? (1978)..................... 63

VI: Notes on the Curriculum Field (1978) 77

VII: The Abstract and the Concrete in Curriculum
Theorizing (1979) 101

VIII: The Voyage Out: Curriculum as the Relationship
between the Knower and the Known (1979)............... 117

IX: Understanding Curriculum as Gender Text: Notes
on Reproduction, Resistance, and Male-Male
Relations (1981) 151

X: The Corporate Production of Feminism and the
Case of Boy George (1983) 183

XI: Death in a Tenured Position (1984)............................ 191

XII: Autobiography and an Architecture of Self (1985)...... 201

XIII: A Reconceptualization of Teacher Education
(1988).. 223

XIV: "Dreamt into Existence by Others:" Curriculum
Theory and School Reform (1991)............................ 235

XV: The Lost Language of Cranes:
Windows and Mirrors in the Regressive
Phase of *Currere* (1992)................................... 253

Name Index... 269

Subject Index... 273

Credits

Working from Within (1972). *Educational Leadership*, 29:4, 329-331.

Notes on the Curriculum Field (1978). *Educational Researcher*, 7:8, 5-12.

What is the reconceptualization? (1979). *The Journal of Curriculum Theorizing*, 1 (1), 93-104.

The voyage out: Curriculum as the relationship between the knower and the known (1980). *The Journal of Curriculum Theorizing*, 2 (1), 71-92.

The Trial, from Life History and Educational Experience, *The Journal of Curriculum Theorizing*, Vol. 2, No. 2 (Summer 1980), pp. 159-212.

The Abstract and the concrete in curriculum theorizing. Fragment from H. Giroux, A. Penna, W. Pinar (Eds.), *Curriculum and Instruction* (1981). Berkeley, CA: McCutchan.

Curriculum as Gender Text: Notes on Reproduction, Resistance, and Male-Male Relations, *The Journal of Curriculum Theorizing*, Vol. 5, No. 2 (Winter 1983), pp. 26-52.

The Corporate Production of Feminism and the Case of Boy George, paper read to undergraduates on the campus of the University of Rochester, 1984.

Death in a Tenured Position, *Curriculum Perspectives*, Vol. 4, No. 1, pp. 74-76, May 1984.

Autobiography and the Architecture of Self, *The Journal of Curriculum Theorizing*, Vol., 8, No. 1, 7-36.

A Reconceptualization of Teacher Education. *Journal of Teacher Education*, 40:1 (January-February 1989), 9-12.

Dreamt into Existence by Others: School Reform and Curriculum Theory. *Theory Into Practice*, Vol. XXXI, No. 3 (Summer, 1991), pp. 226-235.

The Lost Language of Cranes, paper presented to the Bergamo Conference on Curriculum Theory and Classroom Practice, October 14, 1992.

Editors' Introduction

Shirley R. Steinberg
Joe L. Kincheloe

No one writes like Bill Pinar. This book is a conversation that Bill began over twenty years ago and is now sharing with us—we would like merely to introduce the conversation.

I met Joe at Bergamo in 1989—it was instant attraction. However, he was on his way to have pizza with Bill Pinar and excused himself. The pizza postponed our eventual intimate moments for at least a day. Two days later, (after Joe and I had finally gotten together), Joe introduced me to a tall, light-haired, dare I say, patrician-like man. Bill was warmly elegant and obviously very fond of Joe. As he sat down, he leaned back on his chair, folding his arms peacefully over his chest—sort of watching what was happening around him. He was funny, very funny, yet he didn't seem to need to wait to see if anyone else heard his comments. Understated—yet, a presence.

Shreveport, Louisiana is described by political scientists as the most conservative urban area in America. Not only one of the most racially segregated cities in America, Shreveport has more Southern Baptists per square mile than any other city in the world. Southern Baptist evangelists still are allowed in the public schools, sometimes preaching the Holy Word to trapped students via a police bullhorn (no kidding). Many of my students' autobiographical analyses of their educational experiences in Shreveport were reminiscent of a Southern-fried *Handmaiden's Tale*—Margaret Atwood meets Jimmy Swaggart in Dogpatch. It was in Shreveport that I met William Pinar. Having read his work in Reconceptualism, I already understood that he was an important influence in my life. Little did I realize how significant a role he would come to play in the years that followed.

Meeting Bill was exciting—as a graduate student I discovered that Pinar made curriculum breathe after the suffocation I experienced with the early theorists. I like to think of the reconceptualization of curriculum as the Salon de Beaux Arts of education. Attacked, ignored and minimized by the curriculum status quo-keepers, the reconceptualists have managed to create light and movement through autobiography, feminist theory and intuition interwoven with theory.

Restoring the "living" into the curriculum field, Bill taps a pulse so vital that technicists squirm in discomfort. "You're too close, Bill, sometimes too close for your own good." *Currere* was/is such a good idea. I watch my teacher education students encounter it term after term. It seems so strange to them at first reading, after their close encounters with Bloom, Maslow, Hunter, lesson plans, and behavioral objectives. They are disturbed by *currere's* humanity and subjectivity. They have learned that sensation has so little to do with education that they are flustered by the notion of private experience, the public analysis of the private sphere of life. They have often learned to hide their private faces in public places; their culture dictates that they indulge their feelings only in solitude. It is with Bill's help that we bring them out, slowly and respectfully, but *out* just the same. For the majority, professional education will never be the same.

*Reading this collection of essays has been like a "happening" for me. Listening to Bill develop his curriculum throughout the last twenty years is the epitome of praxis. Avoiding the typical criticisms of much autobiographical work, Bill's essays avoid any scent of self-indulgence—*other autobiographical pedagogues take heed! *We are able to find our own place within Bill's place and expand and elasticize our own agendas with his ideas. Bill uses literature as the linseed oil in which to mix his colors—he creates new insights and vision for us as readers and as teachers of teachers. Our students seek their own subjectivities as they write autobiographical pieces—they are Hansel and Gretel picking up the crumbs as they follow the trails that constructed their own consciousness.*

Bill's "voyage out" resonates at a variety of levels, his identity shakes our faith in the certainty—the groundedness and boundedness—of modernist identity. Humility is an interesting concept that rarely finds expression in the proclamations and communiqués of the vanguard. But in the recesses of my Appalachian sense of self, it means something very important. Bill's genius is intertwined with a humility that always takes me by surprise. As he fans the flames of the festival, Bill retreats to the shadows leaving others to carry the torch. The sensitivity that produces the insights is quite demanding and draining. I watch him watch the world from the shadows.

Joe and I spent sparkling week with Bill in New Orleans this year. We laughed too much as well as ate too much. He is the consummate host—I honestly don't know anyone easier to be around. We shared stories about our sons—laughed at our own embarrassment at discovering that we had indeed, against all vows made in the sixties, turned into our parents. Joe told his (lengthy) southern tales, Bill's mid-Western—nee, New York observations pronounced wry epithets upon the unreal conditions of reality and my caustic, Jewish expectations of universal collapse and failure blended into an ethnic collage—I actually suffered from separation anxiety when we left.

My parodies of male-male relations delight Bill. His descriptions of the sadomasochistic patriarchal order have always moved me to another plane, forcing me to go on. Just when I think my syntheses start to resonate, Bill gently deconstructs them with the type of insight he always visits upon me. Shirley's presence fans the flames of the festival. Watching her interaction with Bill is one of my greatest joys. A feminine panache emerges that envelops all involved in a paganistic rite of passage to no *man's* land. If they only knew, the Gender Police would overreact.

We took three stellar undergraduate students this year (1993) to Bergamo with us—Elena, Jeff and Leila. They could hardly wait to attend Bill's session with Margo Figgins from University of Virginia. Elena Chinea wrote to Bill and Margo after she returned home to Miami:

Dear Bill and Margo:

    I am stealing this moment just before my next class because you are very much present in my thoughts. I have not written a letter in quite a long time. Your reminded me of that special feeling you get when you sit and compose your thoughts. You can control the conversation without worrying about the other person's reaction. Yet you must patiently wait your turn as you read the response. Oh, the excitement of going to your mailbox and finding a fresh one waiting for you, the chance to steal forbidden moments in the chaos of your daily life to read it! It is a wonderful way of sharing. The distance is good, and yes, sometimes bad. But overall it enhances many relationships because it gives you your physical freedom while reinforcing the emotional parts of the relationship. It provides a good tool to reflect on a relationship.

I was there at the dance in North Carolina. It was magical. I too became lost in the music. Oh, you read it so beautifully! It was so vivid and mesmerizing. I thank you for sharing the romance, the intimacy between you, with me. I cried hard and deeply for the friendship that you shared, for the longing, the uncertainty, the sincerity, and the passion. When you finished I had to leave. Not because I was ashamed to let you see me crying, but because the moment was too intimate for small talk.

Elena's recall of Bill and Margo's presentation speaks to our memory and impressions of this book—this conversation. We appreciate the romance, the intimacy and the friendship that Bill has shared through metaphor, literature and autobiography. Thank you Bill for this book, for this dance.

Introduction

While the public schools labor to convert from factories to corporations [see Fiske, 1991], the North American field of curriculum studies has been reconceptualized from a bureaucratic support system to an intellectually exploratory academic discipline. Nowhere are these developments clearer than in the work of those of us who, in the early 1970s, worked to reconceive the field in which we found ourselves. Entering the openings created by the work of James B. Macdonald, Dwayne Huebner, Paul Klohr, and Maxine Greene, we insisted on doing business very differently. At the University of Rochester twenty years ago, Madeleine Grumet and I worked to elaborate a way of studying and teaching curriculum that honored the immediacy, specificity, and complexity of the concretely-existing student and teacher. That way incorporated aspects of phenomenology, psychoanalysis, and theater, but came to form through autobiography. Our initial formulation of autobiographical study was published in 1976 in *Toward a Poor Curriculum*, a book which fell on deaf ears and quickly went out of print. Madeleine Grumet [and Janet Miller who worked at Rochester in 1972-1974] moved to feminist theory and I explored male gender theory while continuing to suggest directions for the reconceptualization of the field.

In the 1990s we find a very different situation. Autobiography has become sufficiently important to the field that the *Cambridge Journal of Education* devoted a special issue to the topic.

At least four major projects employing autobiography in some form are underway on the North American continent: F. Michael Connelly and D. Jean Clandinin's work on "personal practical knowledge," William Schubert and William Ayers' "teacher lore" and "student lore" projects, Richard Butt and Danielle Raymond's elaboration of collaborative autobiography, and Margo Figgins exciting theatrical work at the University of Virginia. Robert Graham (1991) recently reviewed the burgeoning literature in curriculum studies. However, the interest in autobiography has hardly been confined to curriculum studies. Recent work in teacher development, teacher thinking, and teacher education shows influence of autobiographical theory. [For a review of autobiographical scholarship in education, see chapter 10 "Understanding Curriculum as Autobiographical/Biographical Text," in Pinar, W., Reynolds, W., Slattery, P. & Taubman, P. (in press).]

My work did not begin in autobiography. It began teaching high-school English on Long Island, trying to respond as sensitively and intelligently as I was capable to the situation there in the late 1960s. It was clear to me that traditional schooling was more than inadequate for this generation, it was maddening (Pinar, 1975). Could it be otherwise? As the first piece indicates, all I knew in 1972 was that it was necessary to "work from within."

From that first step I stumbled my way toward autobiography. The second piece moves from Jackson Pollock to Virginia Woolf as I searched for a method which might offer the possibility of authentic educational experience in a thoroughly bureaucratized school establishment. The method seems to me now a bit "metaphysical" at times, and perhaps too starkly a method, but I sketch my initial sense of it in the third piece. Certainly the mainstream of the field found the method of *currere* [the infinitive form of curriculum to indicate an emphasis upon experience] difficult to appreciate, and so I made some effort to speak to what I took to be its importance. For this work I turned to Kafka's *The Trial*.

By the mid-1970s the movement to reconceptualize the field was well underway, framed at the one end by autobiographical theory and the other by political theory. The early success of the movement led quickly to power struggles within it, and from the start the Marxists fought for ascendancy, which many would say they achieved. I attempted to speak to these "internal" disputes in "What is the Reconceptualization?" while in that same year attempting to explain the movement generally to the mainstream field in "Notes on the Curriculum Field 1978." As the end of the decade approached, it was clear that the field would indeed be reconceived, and I returned to autobiography. In "Abstract and the Concrete" I defended autobiography against the Marxist misunderstanding of it as "bourgeois narcissism" (I omit the second section, the "concrete," as that autobiographical work is described in the following piece, "The Voyage Out," where, once again relying on Virginia Woolf, I played with the relations between curriculum and one's "life situation").

By the late 1970s my life situation had changed. Sexual identity occupied center stage; no longer could it taken for granted. Feminist theory had been instrumental in helping me frame this issue, both as theory and as it had transformed the lives of the women who had been important to me. In December 1981, while visiting my son and his mother in Berkeley, California, I wrote the "male-male" piece in the public library there. That seemed to say it for me, although I sketched an implication or two in the "Boy George" talk to Rochester undergraduates two years later.

By 1984 the situation in the United States and in the education field was bleak. I enrolled in Colgate-Rochester Divinity School, but theology could not erase the grimness of the time, which I characterized as "death in a tenured position." The move from Rochester to Baton Rouge provided the jolt I needed to think again about what might be after this dark age had passed. I returned to autobiography in 1985, attempting to rethink earlier assumptions in light of initial readings in poststructuralism.

The LSU Department chairmanship required that I participate in debates which had not engaged me before, and in "A Reconceptualization of Teacher Education" I attempt to sketch for a mainstream audience why curriculum theory might endorse, provisionally, the Holmes Group proposals regarding teacher education. That piece is followed by a reflection on school reform, emphasizing my ambivalence toward it. The final essay recapitulates earlier work on autobiography and points me to what I hope will be a next phase.

The essays vary in formality. Several were written to be read, for instance "What is the Reconceptualization?" [at the 1978 Rochester Institute of Technology Conference], and "The Lost Language of the Cranes," which I read to the 1992 Bergamo Conference. Of course, "Notes on the Curriculum Field 1978" was also written to be read, but as the first annual [and now no longer] "state of the art" address at AERA, my language was more formal than it would be for papers given to friendly audiences, such as "Cranes."

Generally I chose essays that while previously published had not been reprinted in books. For instance, while "Notes on the Curriculum Field 1978" drew considerable attention, it has not been reprinted in any reader. Other essays, such as the "Boy George" fragment and "Cranes," have not been published before. "Death in a Tenured Position" has been published only in Australia. The dates listed below the titles indicate when the piece was written, not when it was published which, in more than one occasion, was several years after the writing.

As a student of autobiography, I wanted essays for this book which traced my history, beginning in 1972 in a fascination with Jackson Pollock and trying to think about high-school teaching as "working from within," to what I hope is not the end in 1992 to recover "lost languages," a piece which links my reading, my friends, and my family in ways which illustrate the autobiographical method I developed nearly twenty years ago. This tracing I hope will be of encouragement to beginning students of education, whom I hope will take heart in the modest beginnings of my skepticism toward lesson plans, and the twenty-year movement to a more extensive view of what living without lessons plans might entail.

I wish to thank Joe Kincheloe and Shirley Steinberg for inviting me to publish in their series. There are many others to thank, and many of these are named in the essays themselves. In particular I want to acknowledge my son Mike and his mother Denah. Denah and I were together when I was formulating the autobiographical method, and she has always been lovingly supportive of my work. Her achievements in feminist psychotherapy have been influential for me. Our son has also taught me much. Mike, your presence in my life has always made me feel it was worth living. To you and to Denah this book is dedicated.

W.P.

References

Cambridge Journal of Education (1990). Special issue: Biography and Life History in Education, 20 (3).

Fiske, E. (1991). *Smart schools, smart kids.* New York: Simon & Schuster.

Graham, R. (1991). *Reading and the writing the self.* New York: Teachers College Press.

Pinar, W. (1975). Sanity, madness, and the school. In W. Pinar (ed.), *Curriculum theorizing: The reconceptualists* (359-383). Berkeley, CA: McCutchan.

Pinar, W. & M. Grumet (1976). *Toward a poor curriculum.* Dubuque, IA: Kendall/Hunt.

Pinar, W., Reynolds, W., Slattery, P. & Taubman, P. (in press). *Understanding Curriculum.* New York: Peter Lang.

I
Working From Within
(1972)

In a 1950 interview, Jackson Pollock was asked: "Then you don't actually have a preconceived image of a canvas in your mind?" He replied: "Well, not exactly—no—because it hasn't been created, you see. Something new—it's quite different from working, say, from a still life where you set up objects and work directly from them. I do have a general notion of what I'm about and what the results will be." The interviewer continues: "That does away, entirely, with all preliminary sketches?" Pollock replied: "Yes, I approach painting in the same sense as one approaches drawing.... I don't make sketches ... into a final painting. Painting, I think, today—the more immediate, the more direct—the greater the possibilities of making a direct—of making a statement" (Wright, 1950, quoted in O'Connor, 1967).

One way I view teaching is similar to the way Pollock approached painting. Regularly I walk into class without a preconceived lesson plan. Although I have a general notion of what I am up to, I make no preliminary sketches. This last year, for example, in a ten-week introductory course on Existentialism I taught as part of a senior elective program, I walked in, sat at a student desk, and asked if there were any comments or questions concerning the film we have viewed the day before. There were, and some time was spent in exchanging observations, questioning each other's conclusions, and wondering aloud about the film's symbolic import. Finally, some moments of silence persuaded me that no one had anything more to say about the film. I began reading from Kierkegaard's *Either/Or*, but interrupted myself soon after to ask for comments, of which there were many. We did some textual analysis, but primarily students explained how a particular passage affected them, what it meant to them. One such explanation intrigued me; I responded, referring to my life history to express agreement with the student's observation. In the remaining time, various individuals responded to that particular point, and to each other, most disclosing elements of their life histories in doing so.

Prefigurative content

Margaret Mead has urged that we learn to use the existential knowledge of the young in what she calls the prefigurative realm. What does such a commitment mean for the teacher? How are we to translate this into teaching style? For me, in a course in American and English fiction for high school juniors, it meant that I walked into the room and, first of all, listened to their talk. Among the numerous conversations, I heard a student describing what he termed the senselessness of his parents' lives. They arose at 5:30 a.m.: father to catch a 7:15 train to New York, mother to prepare breakfast for him, then to awaken the children for school.

During this description, other students stopped their talk and began to listen to the speaker. As he finished his account of a typical working day at his house, another responded by giving a brief but similar description. Most of the class was involved in the discussion, some marveling over the grueling ritual of adult life, others expressing contempt that their parents would choose to lead such lives. I intervened at this point. We had been reading Thoreau's *Walden,* and I quoted from it: "The mass of men lead lives of quiet desperation." I asked if Thoreau might legitimately make such an observation now, one hundred years later. Most believed he might. Thinking associatively, I suppose, a student wondered aloud if that might be one criterion of fine writing: it rang true now as it did when it was written. Discussion ensued. Books we had read earlier in the year were mentioned, usually either to contradict or to corroborate the hypothesis. As the bell rang ending the period, we were discussing what life in Thoreau's America must have been like to prompt him to make such a disquieting observation.

These two examples are illustrative of the way I often teach. I have knowledge of my discipline, some knowledge of my students, and some self-knowledge which I am willing to share on occasion. As well, I come ready to respond, not only as a student and teacher of literature, but as a person. In fact, I must be willing to disclose my thoughts and feelings if I am to hope for similar disclosures from students. I must be willing to explain, at times I intuit as "right," how and why a certain literary piece affects me. I must be so willing if I am to hope that the discipline that is significant for me will also be significant for my students. So, although I make no preliminary sketch, that is, a lesson plan outlining material to be covered, I do have a general notion of what I'm about and what the results will be.

I think there is value to this approach. As Pollock remarked in regard to his painting, it is direct. I "be" with my students in a direct way; there is no lesson or sense of authority to make our conversing indirect; as a result, we often make cognitive and emotional contact. The class becomes more immediate; we tend to become immersed in the moment. I find that students tend to speak what they are thinking and feeling at the movement, and they come to make honest, direct statements—to each other and to me. I sense, and many have explicitly reinforced my belief, that most feel no pressure, however subtle, to say things that they think I might like to hear.

Working from within

Returning to the Pollock interview helps me further explain why I value this approach more than other strategies. At one point, the interviewer asked: "Mr. Pollock, the classical artists had a world to express and they did so by representing the objects in that world. Why doesn't the modern artist do the same thing?" Pollock replied: "Hm—the modern artist is living in a mechanical age and we have a mechanical means of representing objects in nature such as the camera and photograph. The modern artist, it seems to me, is working and expressing an inner world—in other words—expressing the energy, the motion, and other inner forces." From another section of the interview Pollock reiterates: "The thing that interests me is that today painters do not have to go to a subject matter outside of themselves. Most modern painters work from a different source. They work from within."

We teachers have the mechanical means to present the material we deem important to present. Many approaches are open to us. I often do it by simply typing on stencils whatever I judge might be helpful in explaining the literature we read. Each student receives a copy of this information, and he or she is free to pursue it at his or her convenience. Class time is freed and I can work to create an atmosphere in which students feel free to express, in Pollock's phrase, their "inner worlds." Like some modern painters, my students and I have come to feel that we rarely need to go to subject matter outside ourselves. We work from a different source. We work from within.

Reference

Wright, William (1950, 1967). An interview with Jackson Pollock. Printed in
O'Connor, Francis V. *Jackson Pollock*. New York: The Museum of Modern
Art.

II

Mr. Bennett and Mrs. Brown
(1973)

But, you may ask, what have these names to do with curriculum theory? For an answer let us return to Virginia Woolf's essay of that title.

Perhaps you recall that Mrs. Woolf begins by describing a train ride. The particular night in question she was late and jumped into the first compartment she came to. In it sat an elderly woman, a Mrs. Brown, and a middle-aged man, a Mr. Smith. Judging by the flushed and annoyed look on his face, and by the relieved expression on hers, their conversation had been interrupted. They then begin a safe, obviously substitute one, and the newcomer speculates about what had transpired before her entrance, and about their relationship. After some time Mr. Smith gets off, a little later so does Mrs. Brown, and the story ends.

The essay continues. Mrs. Woolf tells us that all novels begin with a "lady in the corner opposite." That is, novels begin with character and in fact that is what novels are about: the expression of character. They are not meant to argue doctrines or even tell stories primarily. They are to express character and, she notes, on this point Mr. Bennett, novelist and critic, is in agreement. It is on the question "what does it mean to express character" that they disagree. For example, an English version of Mrs. Brown would focus on her personality and its peculiarities. A French writer would blur the fine edges in order to give a more abstract, general view of human nature. "The Russian," she continues, "would pierce through the flesh; would reveal the soul—the soul alone, wandering out into the Waterloo Road, asking of life some tremendous questions which would sound on and on in our ears after the book was finished." Mr. Bennett has insisted that novel be expressive of character, and of character that is real but which version, Mrs. Woolf, asks, of reality is real?

The point is taken further. We are asked to imagine the train compartment again, and in it a changed and enlarged party. With Mrs. Brown this time are three Edwardian novelists: Mr. Bennett himself, Mr. Galsworthy, and Mr. Wells. Each studies Mrs. Brown and each attempts to express her character. Mr. Wells, observing her poor dress, her small size, and her harassed and anxious state, would decry the unsatisfactory condition of England's primary schools. His eyes would quickly leave Mrs. Brown, peer out the carriage window, and see a new day coming, when proper primary schools and intelligent economic planning will eliminate poverty and misery. Suitable housing, child-care, and income distribution will create a Utopia in which there are no Mrs. Browns. In his rush to correct the conditions which make her what she is, Mr. Wells spends little time thinking about her as she is. As for Mr. Galsworthy, he would immediately reflect on factory conditions and the exploitation of the working classes. Only Mr. Bennett, we are told, would remain in the carriage. He would carefully note the condition of the carriage, the advertisements on the wall, the way the cushions bulged out from the buttons, the quality of Mrs. Brown's brooch and gloves. He would observe that this train is a nonstop from Richmond to Waterloo which calls at Windsor, a middleclass suburb, he notes, whose residents are moneyed enough to go to the theater but not moneyed enough to hire their own motor car. So goes Mr. Bennett's description.

Where is Mrs. Woolf taking us? I think it is an important place, in literary history and, analogously, in the history of curriculum inquiry. She writes:

> With all his powers of observation, which are marvellous, with all his sympathy and humanity, which are great, Mr. Bennett has never once looked at Mrs. Brown in her corner. There she sits in the corner of the carriage—that carriage which is travelling, not from Richmond to Waterloo, but from one age of English literature to the next, for Mrs. Brown is eternal, Mrs. Brown is human nature, Mrs. Brown changes only on the surface, it is the novelists who get in and out—there she sits and not one of the Edwardian writers has so much as looked at her.

They have looked very powerfully, searchingly, and sympathetically out of the window; at factories, at Utopias, even at the decoration and upholstery of the carriage, but never at her, never at life, never at human nature. And so they have developed a technique of novel-writing which suits their purpose; they have made tools and established conventions which do their business. But these tools are not our tools, and that business is not our business. For us those conventions are ruin, those tools are death.

The parallel between the literary situation to which Mrs. Woolf was speaking in 1924 and the situation in educational research in 1974 is striking. As one reflects on this research, one notes that we look at programs, at materials, at teaching styles and techniques, at objectives, at evaluation. We say we look at the the "individual," but that too, is usually just a word, an abstraction, and not the embodied spirit behind the world. These words are conceptual tools and not the reality to which they refer, but for those of us who wish to study the human experience of education, these words are distortions outside the carriage window. To get underneath the old words we must abandon them. We must devise new methods of research that help us keep our gaze steadily inside the carriage, on Mrs. Brown.

Mrs. Brown is ourselves, and to say we have lost track of her and spend our time looking elsewhere is to say we have lost track of ourselves. Many of us are lost in "thought," in the conceptual. Having spent 6 hours a day, 5 days a week, for 12 to 20 years in classrooms dominated at least by words if not by thought, seated in chairs sufficiently uncomfortable to keep our attention off both the chairs and the discomfort, in rooms sterile enough to keep us away from noticing it, and disciplined to keep our thoughts to ourselves, made to listen to words which usually bear little if any relation to our immediate physical and existential situations, understandably we are trapped in thought. (I use "thought" in its psychoanalytic sense, connoting fantasy and other forms of associative thinking, as well as directed and critical thinking.) Further, it is thought uprooted from its preconceptual basis, from the reality to which it ought to refer. So it is we learn to live in thought tangentially and illogically related to our biographic situation. This process of estrangement has numerous psycho-social effects, including atrophy or hypertrophy of fantasy life, loss of self via modeling, thwarting of affiliative needs. Because we have become lost from ourselves we peer out the window rather than at Mrs. Brown. To bring our gaze back into the carriage is to look past words like "curriculum" and "instruction" and even ones like "the individual" and "humanization." It is to look inside ourselves as well as outside, and begin to describe, as honestly and concretely as we can, what our internal experience is.

To do so is not easy. It has taken years of programming and conditioning to take our attention away from our interior reality, to keep it fixed on the exterior world, both by suppressing problematic messages from within and by channeling those that do surface into socially preferred behaviors. (The process of "sublimation" is not necessarily damaging; in fact it can be integrating and liberating. But for it to be so it must be conscious and directed to some extent, not channelled unconsciously and manipulated as is typically the case.) What is necessary is a continual referring back to the reality underneath words, to our immediate experience, a perpetual placement of the attention to one's physical insides to attempt to discover what one's true emotional, cognitive—in short, psychic—state is. Persistence in this can effect a gradual turning inward (properly directed involving heightened, i.e. clearer, awareness of the public world), which after a time (years in most cases) will become autonomous. This is the first step, however: to return inside our carriage, where we live, and begin to observe Mrs. Brown.

Educational research as it presently conducted cannot perform this task. Its focus tends to be elsewhere, on the public, on the visible, and its methods of making sense of what it sees keep it outside the carriage, correlating that, counting this. I do not intend to dismiss the work that is being done by mainstream educational researchers; it does a certain kind of job well. But like the Edwardian novelists Mrs. Woolf discusses, it is caught in a vision of reality that while adequate in the past, and for many in the present, is not adequate for the future.

In brief, we have gone just about as far as we can go in understanding the nature of education by focusing on the externals. It is not that the public world—curriculum materials, instructional techniques, policy directives—has become unimportant; it is that to further comprehend their roles in the educational process we must take our eyes off them for a time, and begin a lengthy, systematic search of our inner experience.

There are few precedents for this kind of theorizing and research in the fields of education. Some of the work of John Dewey is still helpful, but on the whole, it is not. There are precedents in other fields, and I mention them not as models for our efforts, but because they aim, however esoterically, at the proper target. Existentialism is one such field. I emphasize that I am not suggesting, for example, that Sartre's view of the world is to be applied to the problems of education. What I am suggesting is that Sartre, as well as Kierkegaard, Nietzsche, Buber, and others, write from "levels of being" that are internal and deep, that have bracketed the taken-for-granted conceptual world. Similarly, some psychoanalytic theory is grounded in internal experience. Of course, it is quite arguable how truthful and useful psychoanalytic interpretations of experience are, but the point is that Freud, Jung, and now Laing (among others) were digging underneath the surface of their lives, trying to uncover the roots of what is experienced on the surface.

In imaginative literature I find the so-called stream-of-consciousness writers closest to what I am after. Joyce, Proust, Faulkner, and Sartre come to mind, but Virginia Woolf is my favorite. While the external aspects of her life and novels are very removed from my own, the internal realities she is able to portray artfully bring me back, again and again, to her work.

The order of inquiry I want shares the focus of these fields but not their methods of looking. We cannot solely rely on the imagination however artful its expression, or reports of psychological problems, or philosophic accounts of experience. Some synthesis of these methods needs to be formulated to give us a uniquely educational method of inquiry, one that will allow us to give truthful, public, and useable form to our inner observations. It is this search for a method I am now undertaking.

References

Pinar, William F. (1975). Sanity, Madness, and the School. In W. Pinar (ed.), *Curriculum Theorizing: The Reconceptualists* (359-383). Berkeley, CA: McCutchan.

Pinar, William F. (1975). Search for a Method. In W. Pinar (ed.), *Curriculum Theorizing: The Reconceptualists* (415-424). Berkeley, CA: McCutchan.

Woolf, Virginia (1924). *Mr. Bennett and Mrs. Brown*. London: The Hogarth Press.

III

The Method of *Currere*
(1975)

1.

It is regressive—progressive—analytical—synthetical. It is therefore temporal and conceptual in nature, and it aims for the cultivation of a developmental point of view that hints at the
transtemporal and transconceptual. From another perspective,
the method is the self-conscious conceptualization of the temporal, and from another, it is the viewing of what is conceptualized through time. So it is that we hope to explore the complex
relation between the temporal and conceptual. In doing so we
might disclose their relation to the Self and its evolution and
education.

2.

I want to try to understand the contribution of my formal academic studies make to my understanding of my life. I am taking as hypothesis that I am in a biographic situation, and while
in certain ways I have chosen it (and hence must bear responsibility for it), in other ways I can see that it follows in somewhat
causal ways from previous situations. I can look at my life in a
linear way, acknowledging its actual multidimensional character, but limiting my view to a linear one, to make it more man-
ageable, and I see that this has led to that; in that circumstance
I chose that, rejected this alternative; I affiliated with those people, then left them for these, that this field intrigued me, then
that one; I worked on this problem, then that one. And if I
chart these choices and circumstances on a time line, and then

begin to describe (as I remember it now), the transitions from that situation to the one that followed, I see that there is a certain coherence. Not necessarily a logical one, but a lived one, a felt one. The point of coherence is the biography as it is lived: the *lebenswelt*.

What role in this biography do my evolving intellectual interests play? In what ways do they contribute to an understanding of the dominant themes of this biography? In what ways have they permitted biographic movement, that is, freed one from interests whose life has gone out of them, and drawn one on into areas that excite? What is the relation of these interests and concomitant professional activities to one's private life? I must have not submerged agendas here; I must be willing to impartially describe the relation between my professional work and my personal work, not succumbing to popular attitudes, whether these insist the two must be connected or must remain separate.

There are many related questions, but the predominant one is: what has been and what is now the nature of my educational experience?

By taking as hypothesis that I do not know the answer to this question, I take myself and my existential experience as a data source. The method of data generation is like the psychoanalytical technique of free association. I take a particular question, like why am I involved in the research project which occupies me now? and I record, by pen or recorder, all that occurs to me, regardless how esoteric and hence unrelated the information apparently is. But I get ahead of myself.

My hunch is that by working in the manner I will describe, I will obtain information that will move me biographically, and not only linearly, but mutidimensionally. If I take my current perspective, and try to put parentheses around it (so to speak) by recording it, then I have moved to another vantage point. If I write about my biographic situation as I see it (not as I want to see, although this can be included), then it is as if I have escaped from it. It is there, on the paper in a way, and I am still here, at the typewriter, looking at the print and the conceptualization of the perspective that was mine, and so the place is new. In Sartre's language, I have totalized my situation, and the new sum is where I conceptually (and more inclusively, biographically) am now. Because the view is new, the old problem (say it was a research problem) is seen differently. But because the problem is inherently a partial product of my conceptual apparatus, and because this apparatus functions slightly differently since its operator has moved slightly, the problem itself poses itself differently, and hence the problem is different.

We use an analogous strategy sometimes without thinking about it. If something stumps us, we back off (we say) to do something else, then come at it again later. I am willing to guess that we do this, that is, we allow time to pass before we attempt to reconceive the problem, because we must move on to another level, from where the problem looks different and hence is different, and the solution may then become clear. We left the problem initially because we could not solve it on the conceptual level where we were at first. Perhaps formal studies, like literary theory, or physics, can be utilized to illuminate the myriad of surface ways, and subliminal ways, we evolve through time, how our intellectual interests evolve through time.

3.

Regressive. The first step of the method is regressive. One returns to the past, to capture it as it was, and as it hovers over the present. Let me illustrate.

Listening to this paper being read one can be said to be absorbed in the present. As soon as we have said that seemingly simple statement, we slip into complexity. In which present is one absorbed? Is it the concrete, literal present? That is, is one attending to the sight and sound of Pinar reading, of sitting in a certain chair in a certain room amid others? Or is the present where one dwells what we can call an abstract, conceptual present? Perhaps it is the conceptual reality created by the words that I read, perhaps it is a more private one, and thoughts, your own thoughts "what is this about?" or "who is it I'm to have lunch with today?" or "I must remember to phone home before too late tonight." A survey would probably reveal that the majority dwell in the conceptual present (rather than the concrete present), maybe mine (as I read), probably yours (your ideas of what it is I'm saying, your plans for the next day).

My guess is that to the extent one dwells in a conceptual present, and in the subjective present, is the extent to which one dwells in the past. Not just the literal past, as the memory of arrival last night, which like the literal present often is superficially apparent and just as superficially important.

The biographic past? It is usually ignored. Ignored but not absent. The biographic past exists presently, complexly contributive to the biographic present. While we say it cannot be held accountable for the present, the extent to which it is ignored is probably the extent it does account for what is present.

Unconsciousness perpetuates itself. Hence the formation of habit, of habitual responses to seemingly characteristic stimuli, responses that are to varying degrees (we say) adjustive, or not. The habitual is the surface is the public, the outer, and its strength or the force of habit, is probably positively correlated with unconsciousness and capture by the past. The present then becomes an acting out of the past, the superimposition of past issues and situations and persons onto the present. The complex of habitual responses is constitutive of the present personality. Its predictability is its habituality is its unconsciousness is its pastness.

In all likelihood one is in the past while in the present. The present is then veiled; the past is manifest and apparent, however, so transparently present that it is veiled, and one assumes oneself to be in the present when one is not. To ascertain where one is, when one is, one must locate the past. Locating means identification means bracketing the past. Bracketing means looking at what is not ordinarily seen, at what is taken-for-granted, hence loosening oneself from it. As the past becomes, the present is revealed. So it is we aim at freedom from the past, freedom in the present. Such objectives require entrance into the past as a first step.

One must regress. Not in the commonsensical fear of losing one's hard-won maturity, and becoming infantile. Nor not necessarily involving dramatic and painful character decrystallization, as in the Janovian approach to psychotherapy. [Although it is true that as one leaves the present to enter the past one detaches from one's acculturated character. This detachment is sufficiently subtle as to escape notice, but it does initiate a gradual process of decrystallization and accompanying disclosure of a nonstatic, nonarrested character always in transition.]

Re—back. *Gradi*—to go back. One goes back, and there one finds the past intact. The past is entered, lived in, but not necessarily succumbed to. Because one is not there concretely one is not necessarily vulnerable. One avoids complete identification with the self that was, and hence is able to observe.

That is the point of this phase of the method: to observe functioning in the past. Since the focus of the method is educational experience, one takes special notice of one's past life-in-schools, with one's past life-with-schoolteachers and one's past life-with-books and other school-related artifacts. Observe and record. Include present responses to what is observed.

It is suggested that one return to the schooled beginning, to the elementary years, to wherever one is able to reach. Enter again the classroom, watch the teachers, yourself and your classmates, what you did. More importantly how you did it. From the start did your attention adhere to the public program? To what extent did you absent yourself in fantasy? Did these absences coincide with particular lessons (like geography) and with particular teachers?

Do not attempt to interpret what you observe at this point. Interpretation interrupts presence in the past.

On through the primary grades into junior and senior high school, keeping the observer's focus on the self. The self, in this classroom, with that teacher, these subjects, this response to that teacher, the intervention of parents regarding that situation, and one's response. One's attachment to these subjects, to those teachers; one's disinterest in that field, one's dislike of this teacher.

Athletic and other extracurricular interests if any and their effects upon one's studies. Erotic interests as they impinged upon one's studies. The importance of public conceptions of status. This college or that? The self amidst it all, evolving this way, leaving those friends, taking on these, having these academic interests, then those.

Through the undergraduate years. These courses, those professors. These friends. What sequence?

Autumn. Winter. Spring.

Summer jobs. Building houses in the suburbs, reading Bertrand Russell during lunch breaks. What was on the subject's mind those months? What mood, not visible then perhaps, kept him encapsulated, blurring his view?

School again in the fall. Taking these courses. Studying in the library, trying to in the dormitory. This girl, that friend, the War, anger, hatred, becoming awake, rather thinking oneself awake and knowing but neither awake nor knowing, always thinking, one's physical body absent, mostly.

The major subject finally chosen. Onto graduate school. Graduation and a teaching job. Professional meetings. The present moment.

The subject's life, his or her educational life, also his or her life in schools (the disentangling of those terms to come later). It exists still; one re-enters it; one goes back; one regresses; it is there, here, present. Recording it via words; conceptualizing it.

Bringing the past to the present by printing it. The words coalesce to form a photograph. Holding the photograph in front of oneself, one studies the detail, the literal holding of the picture and one's response to it, suggestive of the relation of past to present.

Thus we conclude the first step of the procedure, the regression to the past and the return to the present.

4.

Progressive. Progressive derives from *pro* meaning "before" and *gradi* meaning "to step, go." In this phase we look the other way. We look, in Sartre's language, at what is not yet the case, what is not yet present. We have found that the future is present in the same sense that the past is present. It influences, in complicated ways, the present; it forms the present.

Sit alone, perhaps in a slightly darkened room, in a comfortable chair with a writing table and a pen. Close the eyes, place the attention on the breathing. Take a few slow deep breaths as these are comfortable. The point of these minutes is relaxation. After one is relaxed, one thinks of the future, of tomorrow, of next week, of the new few months, of the next academic year, of the next three years and so on. Since our interest is educational experience, gently bring the attention back to matters associated with your intellectual interests, and allow your mind to work free associatively. Record what comes. Try to discern where your intellectual interests are going, the relation between these evolving interests and your private life, between these two and evolving historical conditions. Perhaps you will being to see something of the interdependent nature of your interests and the historical situation. If you are a teacher, focus on your teaching, on your relationships to students and to colleagues, especially on the emotional content of these, as well as on the intellectual content. Discern where these appear to be going. You might imagine a future, perhaps a year hence or perhaps several years hence; describe it. (It is important in the progressive as well as the regressive moment to free associate, to avoid use of the rational, logical, and critical aspects. Don't, for instance, conclude that an imagined future state is unreasonable. At this stage allow usually buried visions of what is not yet present to manifest.)

Do this for as long as it is comfortable; when resistance occurs take note of its quality and content. Do not force the process.

Return to the chair and this dwelling in imagined future states several times on different days over a period of several days or weeks or months. Such elongation of the experiment reduces the possibility of distortion of temporary preoccupations. Increased is the likelihood that the photographs taken are reflective of more lasting anticipations.

This completes the progression.

5.

Analytical. One takes photographs, and sets them aside. What is left? Describe the biographic present, exclusive of the past and future, but inclusive of responses to them.

For many the present is woven into the fabric of institutional life. Within that historical form, embodied concretely in the building which houses your office and those who are your colleagues and students, what is your present? What are one's intellectual interests? What is one's emotional condition?

To what ideas, what areas of study, which discipline, is one drawn? From what is one repelled? List these. Describe, not interpret these attractions. Photograph the present as if one were a camera, including oneself in the present taking the photograph, and your response to this process.

Description via conceptualization is breaking into parts the organic whole.

Ana—up, throughout. *Lysis*—a loosening. Conceptualization is detachment from experience. Bracketing what is, what was, what can be, one is loosened from it, potentially more free of it, hence more free to freely choose the present, and future.

Study the three photographs. What are they; what is their individuality? What fundamental biographic theme(s) do they express? Why are they as they are?

Interpretation must make more visible what is lived through directly. Interpretation must not subordinate the lived present to an abstract, analytical grid. One's analysis is a constituent element of the present, like the brain a part of the body, not the body a thought in the brain. The biographic present is not part of a conceptual system; the system is an aspect of the present.

Juxtapose the three photographs: past, present, future. What are their complex, multi-dimensional interrelations? How is the future present in the past, the past in the future, and the present in both?

6.

Synthetical. *Syn* means "together" and *tithenai* means "to place."

Put them aside.

Then look at oneself concretely, as if in a mirror. Attention on the breath, to underline the biological concreteness of being.

Who is that?

In your own voice, what is the meaning of the present?

What is the contribution of my scholarly and professional work to my present? Do they illumine the present? Obscure it?

Are one's intellectual interests biographically freeing, that is, do they permit, in fact encourage, movement?

Do they point to increased conceptual sophistication and refinement, deeper knowledge and understanding, of both one's chosen field of study and that field's symbolic relation to one's evolving biography? Do they move one to enter new, higher levels of being?

What conceptual gestalt is finally visible? That is, what is one's "point of view?" Can one bracket and thus escape from the conceptual, take it into one's hands as it were, examine it, and see its relation to one's psychological, physical, biographic condition? See its relation to "one's form of life?" This includes one's public and private lives, one's externally observable behavior and the contents of one's stream-of-consciousness.

The physical body may be a concrete manifestation of all that occurs in and through it.

The Self is available to itself in physical form. The intellect, residing in physical form, is part of the Self. The Self is not a concept the intellect has of itself. The intellectual is an appendage of the Self, a medium, like the body, through which the Self and the world are accessible to themselves.

Mind in its place, I conceptualize the present situation.

I am placed together.

Synthesis.

IV

The Trial

(1976)

"Some one must have traduced Joseph K., for without having done anything wrong he was arrested one fine morning" (Kafka, 1968, p. 1). So begins Franz Kafka's *The Trial*.

K. has done nothing wrong, nothing at least that he or the reader knows. Yet, he is arrested, he is tried, and executed. What is the nature of his arrest? K. asks, but his warders disclaim authorization to answer. Further, he is advised that "I can't even confirm whether you are. You are under arrest, certainly, more than that I do not know" (p. 12). The warder then asks K. if he will be going to the bank today (where K. works), and K. wonders how he can go to work if he is arrested. The warder replies: "You have misunderstood me. You are under arrest, certainly, but that need not hinder you from going about your business. Nor will you be prevented from leading your ordinary life" (p. 14).

K. responds with anger. He calls the arrest "ridiculous" (p. 5). His concierge, Frau Grubach, responds with an almost sorrowful smile. Softly she tells him:

> ... and above all you mustn't take it too much to heart. Lots of things happen in this world!... You are under arrest, certainly, but not as a thief is under arrest. If one's arrested as a thief, that's a bad business, but as for this arrest.... It gives me the feeling of something very learned, forgive me if what I say is stupid, it gives me the feeling of something learned which I don't understand, but which there is no need to understand (p. 19).

It is the most direct advice K. will receive, but he does not hear it. He will do exactly what Frau Grubach warns against: he will take it very much to heart. In fact, his case becomes an obses-

sion with him. Relentlessly he demands to know the nature of
his arrest.

This case is his life, and K.'s questions concerning it, the
Court and the Law, are questions regarding the structure of
human existence. Thus K. is a kind of metaphysician, although
not the philosophical specialist the term ordinarily designates.
Rather, K. is an ordinary man, every person, every modern
individual (Rahv, 1969, p. 49). The kind of metaphysician he is
is the kind each human being is: one without training, one in
the midst of an "examination," a "trial," i.e., a life. He is one
who senses he must comprehend, however, primitively, the
meaning of what transpires. But many never consciously raise
such questions, and in this K., before his arrest, is one of the
many.

About K. Kafka tells us little, yet what he tells corresponds
with what one imagines of the many. "He had always been
inclined to take things easily, to believe in the worst only when
the worst happened, to take no care of the morrow even when
the outlook was threatening" (p. 4). Further: "That spring K.
had been accustomed to pass his evenings in this way: after
work whenever possible—he was usually in this office until
nine—he would take a short walk, alone or with some of his colleagues, then to a beer hall, where until eleven he sat at a table
patronized mostly by elderly men. But there were exceptions to
this routine, when, for instance, the Manager of the Bank, who
valued his diligence and reliability, invited him for a drive or for
dinner at his villa. And once a week K. visited a girl called Elsa,
who was on duty all night till early morning as a waitress in a
cabaret and during the day received her visitors in bed" (p. 17).
Importantly, Kafka tells us that "it was not usual with him to
learn from experience" (p. 4).

What is representative about K. is not so much the particular
details of his life, but the quality of them. They have a certain
automatic quality; they are habitual. K. is not a reflective man.
He does not examine the nature of his involvement at the bank,
or with his colleagues, or why he is attracted to the company
elderly men, or why he sees Elsa. It all happens. There is no
reason why it does; it simply does. K. is socialized, conditioned
being.

Of course, some of the details of this unexamined life are representative of many, especially of many men. The absorption in career is common enough. One's hours of relaxation are sometimes spent with colleagues, making such hours a kind of appendage to the working ones. They are not discrete; they continue, though more casually perhaps, the quality of thought, as well as the content of thought, typical at work. True, talk may turn to sex, but again it often bears the quality of "adjunct" to the working life. K. is a man buried in his work, and he is thereby identified with the particular version of social reality constructed at the place of his work. In part this accounts for the flatness of his character, and the parochialism of his vision. Discussing his arrest with Frau Grubach he transposes the event into the social reality of the bank: "my mind is always on my work and so kept on the alert, it would be an actual pleasure to me if a situation like that cropped up in the Bank" (p. 20). In fact, he continues: "if I had behaved sensibly, nothing further would have happened, all this would have been nipped in the bud. But one is so unprepared. In the Bank, for instance, I am always prepared" (p. 20). Interpersonal relations and events are predictable at the bank; such an arrest could not have occurred there without warning. It is that the arrest is unexpected and without precedent that seems to stun K. What infuriates him is the lack of access to the Law, the lack of explanations regarding his arrest. The laws by which judgments are made at the bank are knowable; explanations for actions taken are available. But it is not at the bank K. is arrested; it is at home.

At the bank K. is highly regarded, and in line for promotion. At home, where he lives, there is not such regard. He is alone. His private life, as we saw, is only a fragment of his working life. He experiences no love; he visits a prostitute to satiate his sexual need. His emotional needs are, we might say, repressed. In fact, he exhibits classic symptoms of such repression: rigid adherence to schedule, even after working hours, and irritation at interruption in that schedule. Interruptions threaten the social veneer which is the projected extension of his psychological encapsulation. If the veneer-capsule were to be punctured, as the arrest does, then the pressurized emotion explodes.

We observe an explosion when the warders first arrive to arrest him. K. insists "I shall neither stay here nor let you address me until you have introduced yourself" (p. 2). Later, when the warder explains he has made the arrest because it is his duty, K. snaps back that it is a stupid duty (p. 15). At the first interrogation K. is reminded that he is late. "Whether I am late or not, I am here now" (p. 39). Speaking to the examining magistrate, K. demands: "Listen to me. Some ten days ago I was arrested, in a manner that seems ridiculous to myself, though that is immaterial at the moment" (p. 43). His rudeness becomes patronizing and self-delusive: "I am quite detached from this affair, I can therefore judge it calmly, and you, that is to say if you take this alleged court of injustice at all seriously, will find it to your great advantage to listen to me" (p. 45). The result is unsurprising: "'I merely wanted to point out,' said the Examining Magistrate, 'that today—you may not yet become aware of the fact—today you have flung away with your own hand all the advantages which an interrogation invariably confers on an accused man.' K. laughed, still looking at the door. 'You scoundrels, I'll spare you future interrogations,' he shouted, opened the door, and hurried down the stairs" (p. 48).

K. has a right to explode, the reader might observe. My focus here is not the justice of the anger, but its quality. It is not anger conscious of itself. It is anger that is unfocused. K. aims at any moving target: the warder's duty, the magistrate's reminder of his tardiness. Whatever is said to him, he responds indignantly. There is little sense here that K. has choice, whether to express his anger or not, or how to express it. He is petulant. He is his anger.

K.'s reaction—to the warders, to the magistrate, to the priest during the cathedral scene—is exaggerated compared with the provocation. The warders are rather matter-of-fact. Not only the tone of their behavior is quiet and steady, their message itself, while a disturbing one, is not inherently a shattering one, precipitating panic. Yes, K. may go to work as usual, in fact he may continue his life has he has conducted it. K.'s response is nearly uncontrolled anger, refusing to talk with the warders until they "properly" introduce themselves, calling the magistrates scoundrels. His responses to others generally are not commensurate with the others' responses to him. In fact, his responses suggest little sensitivity to others. Frau Grubach's view of the arrest we noted, and K. seems not to have heard it at all (p. 19). He is encapsulated; he is dissociated from others. Regardless the complexity and subtly of that which confronts him, he responds with irritation, abruptness, rudeness. He seems to possess no options.

Joseph K. is stunted psychologically and socially. He is dissociated from his subjectivity, and consequently clings to outer character structure, i.e. social role. To perpetuate its dominance, the suppression of his subjectivity, he adheres closely to a social reality in which order and predictability are preeminent characteristics. He underlines social support for his psychological alienation by working long hours, and spending time with bank colleagues after hours. The reader is not told, but it is plausible that it is the quiet stability sometimes characteristic of the aged which may attract K. to the elderly men he visits at the bar.

One comes to understand the sense in which K. is in fact arrested. He is arrested intellectually, psychologically, and socially. It is quite true that such an arrest does not preclude going about one's business, leading one's life. One works and lives with others similarly arrested, and in collusion perpetuate the stasis.

At this point, however, K. becomes atypical. He will not settle for living with arrest, now that he is, in a sense, conscious of it. True, his motives are not high ones. In fact, he cannot be said to have motives, as these suggest some awareness of what moves one to act. K. is driven, evidently without choice or awareness, to comprehend his arrest. At this point he ceases being the unreflective "everyone" and becomes a metaphysician. For this he is admirable; for this the reader empathizes with him. For this insistence of his, to understand his "case," the reader urges him on, wishes for his success.

K. is inadequate to the task. He is stunted psycho-socially, and necessarily relatedly, he is stunted intellectually. His intellectual arrest is a familiar one. His rationality is a technical one only, capable of solving problems narrowly conceived, such as: where have I misplaced the car keys? Which tax deductions are most advantageous? K.'s is a rationality of procedure, of technique. The questions posed being "how," "who," and "what." "Who could these men be? What were they talking about? What authority could they represent? K. lived in a country with a legal constitution, there was universal peace, all the laws were in force; who dared seize him in his own dwelling?" (p. 4). Such questions typify his "intellectuality." He asks them throughout the trial. Early in the novel he thinks: "... far more important to him was the necessity to understand his situation clearly; but with these people he could not even think" (p. 4). Here his compulsion to understand first surfaces, and his vulnerability also: he cannot think with the warders present. Midway through the novel—he understands nothing more of his case, only that his position has somehow deteriorated—he continues his questioning: "And there were so many questions to put. To ask questions was surely the main thing. K. felt that he could draw up all the necessary questions himself" (p. 114). Never does he critically examine his method; being led by his executioners he maintains that "... only thing for me to go on doing is to keep my intelligence calm and analytical to the end" (p. 225). As we were told early in the novel, it is not customary for K. to learn from experience (p. 4).

It is true. There is no development in K.'s character, only deterioration. "One winter morning—snow was falling outside the window in a foggy dimness—K. was sitting in his office, already exhausted in spite of the early hours .... The thought of his case never left him now" (p. 113). Others tell him he looks bad (p. 135). His obsession with his case infiltrates the hitherto insulated reality of the bank. The degree of deterioration is evident in the following passage:

> Had he really lost his powers of judgment to that extent already? If it were possible for him to think of explicitly inviting a questionable character to the Bank in order to ask for advice about his case with only a door between him and the Assistant Manager, was it not also possible and even extremely probable that he was overlooking other dangers as well, or blindly running into them? There wasn't always someone at his side to warn him. And this was the moment, just when he intended to concentrate all his energies on the case, this was the moment for him to start doubting the alertness of his faculties! Must the difficulties he was faced with in carrying out his office work begin to affect his case as

well? At all events he simply could not understand how he could ever have thought of writing to Titorelli and inviting him to come to the Bank (p. 138).

At this late stage of the novel his case appears now more important than his job; it is his case he worries will be negatively affected by his office work. Even so, his standing at the bank remains a preoccupation; he worries over Titorelli's effect on his colleagues. But it is his admission of loss of judgment, and concomitant concern over "other dangers" that reveal the scope of his debilitation. From the (rigidly) self-possessed and indignant young banker at the novels' beginning, K. has quickly become a self-doubting, frightened, nervously exhausted man by mid-point in his trial.

While his psychological and physical condition atrophy, his intellectual method—a technical, narrowly cognitive one—remains intact. In this there is no change, no indication of self-awareness or critique. He continues to trust in his intellect (p. 225). He continues to ask for help, although he as been advised not to do so (p. 211). ["'You cast about too much for outside help,' said the priest disapprovingly."] Both this intellectual rigidity and his futile appeals to others remain in the last passage of the novel.

> His glance fell on the top story of the house adjoining the quarry. With a flicker of a light going up, the casements of a window there suddenly flew open; a human figure, faint and insubstantial at that distance and that height, leaned abruptly far forward and stretched both arms still further. Who was it? A friend? A good man? Someone who sympathized? Someone who wanted to help? Was it one person only? Or was it mankind? Was help at hand? Were there arguments in his favor that had been overlooked? Of course there must be. Logic is doubtless unshakable, but it cannot withstand a man who wants to go on living. Where was the Judge whom he had never seen? Where was the High Court, to which he had never penetrated? He raised his hands out and spread out all fingers (p. 228).

Of course there must be overlooked arguments in his case! Within seconds of his death he still permits such thoughts. He still looks for help outside himself, from someone unidentified, someone in a building in the distance who could not possibly assist him. Yet the emotional quality of this thought has altered somewhat. It is not as staccato in rhythm, not as petulant in mood. There is, in fact, a subtle tone of acceptance, in spite of the questions, indicating, as they do, continued psychological resistance.

Joseph K. is arrested intellectually, psycho-socially; he is arrested biographically. There is no movement in his life; it is a life hung upon the social structure of the bank. Where he lives he transports the reality of the bank, evident in his perfunctory treatment of Frau Grubach and the warders. He has no self-identification. He *is* a banker. He *is* his rigid personality, his abrupt manner, his anger. His relationships are atrophied fragments of a whole he has forgotten. They are instrumental; he asks for help in his case, although regularly disregarding the advice given. Only with the elderly men in the bar is there any hint of friendship, and it is anonymous. Elsa is a prostitute; he has not time and K. does not take time to develop anything resembling a relationship. K. is his career, his socio-historical identity, and thereby an arrested being. He is incapable of self-reflection, of questioning the nature of his involvements. Not once does he consider his arrest as possibly warranted, even if in some way he does not understand. Not once does he question himself, only others. He is indignant and rude, complaining that the Law, the Court, are in error, and are illegitimate. Yet his growing preoccupation with them is his complicity, is his legitimation of their jurisprudence. [He observes this very point on one occasion, to no effect upon his behavior, however. "You may object that it is not a trial at all; you are quite right, for it is only a trial if I recognize it as such" (p. 40).] The fact of his vulnerability, of his obsessive-compulsive response to his arrest suggests a man who unconsciously believes he is guilty, believes he must therefore mount an immediate and massive defense. It is, we noted, an intellectual defense of a technical-instrumental order. It is a defense of an intellect dissociated from its companion realms: the emotional, the bodily, the erotic. It is focused, outward, asking "who," "what," and "how," never probing "why." Thus uprooted the intellect lacks direction, lacks the guidance of intuition. It spins wildly, asking the wrong questions at the wrong time, making mistakes of judgment, exhausting itself and the body. It seems it is only through his wearing-down that K. is able to move. But it is precious little movement. This stasis, this arrest, is the tragedy of Joseph K.

K. is reminiscent of many of us, in some degree. K. is a prototypical being of an urbanized, industrialized, cerebral twentieth century in the West. His life history, with its emphasis upon career, on instrumentally-defined social relations, is a major constituent element of the historical present. There is some movement from this, some retreat from self-identification solely in terms of social roles, to what one might term a biographic identification, one grounded in one's life history, one's biographic present, in one's Self. Such psychic integration is what K. was without, what many of us are without in some measure, and toward which some are beginning to move. Such movement is one task of this essay to suggest, however broad the strokes, however incipient the movement. Such movement is educational experience; it is learning, as K. could not, from experience.

But it is experience first. Living in his head, in social reality, as he does, K. has little experience. He can feel his exhaustion, but with his anger he is too identified to experience. His fear is too repressed for him to know. Experience is available only through consciousness of it. As long as one resides in one's head, in one's ideas and fantasies, one's experience is attenuated. To permit experience involves a focusing of attention upon experience, upon the body, the emotions, and then on thought as it emanates from body and emotion.

I have devised a strategy the purpose of which is to permit a loosening of identification with the intellect, provides access to experience, grounding the intellect in that experience. Thus grounded, instrumental thought does not disappear; it remains available to find the misplaced keys, to design a curriculum. But what also becomes available is an order of minding that permits and assists experience, permits biographic identification and movement. By examining one's life history, even a fragment of that history, such as one's life in schools, or one's involvement in an academic discipline, one can begin to construct an etiology of one's present arrest, of one's case. This strategy is the regressive-progressive-analytic-synthetic method.

Arrest: political, psychological, metaphysical

K.'s arrest, my arrest, is multi-dimensional. It is political. One
is constrained by institutions, by the limits of acceptable social
behavior. One is conditioned to focus on the socially desirable,
to delete those parts (what Gouldner termed the "the unem-
ployed self") without social return. As a child one tends to be
told what to do and when to do it, in school and out. One's
guilt as a young person, one's nature as innocent and sinful
(however secular the contemporary expressions of these are:
one must still adapt to "reality") is assumed. One's case will be
disposed of in ways of which one remains essentially ignorant.
One may work hard but good grades and promotion in the
bureaucracy may or may not come. Both school child and K.
are oppressed by a vague, omnipresent bureaucracy which
exercises a political control as mystified as it feels complete.
The result is political withdrawal and passivity.

The arrest is psychological. The conscious self which existed
was nearly exclusively social. There was little conscious psychological life. Repressed, psychic energy escapes in gasps when
unpredicted events in the external world preoccupied the social
self sufficiently so that its "lid" on the unconscious loosens, and
energy then escapes. K. loses his self-possession with the warders, with the magistrates, and by the novel's end, he has lost it
altogether. To maintain the psychological stasis, K. extends
into the nighttime the social reality of the bank, a reality which
supports (in R. D. Laing's term) his false self-system. The conscious focus of the ego must remain outward, on his position at
the bank, on those who arrest him. To become self-reflective
invites disordering of the tenuous intra-psychic balance, as
attention tends to intensify that which it lights. Thus the power
of unconscious energy seeking expression would be increased,
and the ego threatened. It is the flow of unconscious energy or
libido outward that accounts in no small part for the vitality of
the individual. An ego congruent with unconscious forces
tends to be more able to allow more energy to pass, tends to be
less threatened by unpredicted events. The ego is incongruent
with its unconscious to the extent it is primarily social in
nature, a construction of social conditioning. It limits severely

the information it can assimilate, just as it limits what it can externalize. Such an ego is always beleaguered, always "accused" in some sense; it is arrested. Until the ego becomes more congruent with its unconscious underpinnings, it will continue to be vulnerable to events in the public as well as private world. "Acquittal" in this context means the development of a biographic perspective. One aspect of this work involves dismantling the individual's conditioned cognitive structure, his tendency to filter his experience through his intellect. This over-identification with the intellect, this hypertrophy of the intellect, accompanies psychological arrest. It is the intra-psychic corollary of political arrest, of social authoritarianism. Jung (1939) notes this correspondence: "Over-valued reason has this in common with political absolutism: under its dominion the individual is pauperized." Cultivation of a biographic point of view can have political as well as psychological consequences.

Thirdly, the arrest is metaphysical. The questions K. asks of the Court and the Law are of the order the metaphysician asks of human life. What is the nature of this case, i.e., this life? How can one intervene in one's fate? In what sense is one primordially guilty? What are the means of absolution, if any? From this view of the novel, K.'s arrest is signified by his psychological and intellectual ignorance. Angrily he demands answers to these questions, despite his contemporaries' advice. Intellectually, as we noted earlier, K. utilizes a technical-linear rationality to seek answers to questions which are neither technical nor linear.

The intellect may be used in seeking metaphysical understanding, but intellect broadly conceived, an intellect sensitive to its intuitive basis. What is necessary is an intellect that does not demand understanding on its own logical terms, but is open to deciphering information which is non-logical. In psychoanalytic terms, this is information from the unconscious. This "region" corresponds to that which is characterized as metaphysical and spiritual in other traditions. Jung (1939) notes that what the West terms the unconscious is equivalent to what in Hindu philosophy is termed the superior or universal mind. In this sense K. is estranged from God, fallen from the

Garden. Thus the correspondence between the psychological sense of his arrest and the metaphysical: to be alienated from one's psychic source, from one's unconscious, is tantamount to being estranged from the Lord. To be lost in a labyrinth of one's psychological experience is equivalent to being lost from the promised land. For the secular metaphysician, that promised land is understanding, but given *The Trial*, it is not understanding in a narrow cognitive or logical sense.

Understanding

What is K.'s significance for curriculum theory? Put simply, one's work resides, inescapably, in historical and biographic context. The issues which K. embodies are issues many contemporary scholars also embody. The historical present is a time of trial. The academy has, as has the culture, become somewhat conscious of its arrest. Now, I am not arguing that the present arrest represents a "new" phenomenon. There are, of course, degrees of arrest. For instance, as one becomes conscious of one level of arrest, and through a self-reflexive understanding of that level, one moves to a another level that will someday become experienced as static. To remain on any one level, means arrest, and arrest, as K.'s case makes clear, is death. One cannot be arrested psychologically without consequences for one's intellectual life. History stands still only for the dead.

The introduction of phenomenology to the social sciences is a significant event in twentieth century intellectual life. Phenomenology might function to melt the stasis of contemporary quantitative social science. Regrettably it might become mythologized, and if this occurs to a sufficient extent, phenomenology might function to preserve arrest. However, if this danger is exorcised, phenomenology can function to return theoreticians to "the things themselves," to what in psychoanalysis is "primary experience." If this can occur, the social sciences can avoid K.'s fate. Yet, the general question, whether the present "dark age" will continue indefinitely or give way, relatively speaking, to "an age of enlightenment" is very much an open question. What I am suggesting is that its answer is being formulated now, in the lives of those alive in the present period. The historical-cultural question concretized becomes an individual, biographic question. It is not that exclusively, of course; the culture cannot be reduced to the biographic. That notwithstanding, it is the individual where exists, at the present time, "the most room to move." Social and economic structures are sufficiently frozen as to force work in the individual realm.

We can understand Joseph K. as expressing our dilemma. He is a consequence of economic and cultural forces. It is to the extent that he can understand his case that he will escape this conditioned status. To the extent he can reclaim his lost subjectivity, and in so doing identify himself as primary and his socio-historical roles as secondary, he might become a Subject. This transformation cannot be strictly cognitive, as K.'s case demonstrates. It involves cognition, but cognition "in its place," i.e. as conveyer and interpreter of immediate experience. Thus the understanding we seek is fundamentally a mind-body relation, a mode of being. It is, in Kierkegaard's phrase, a certain "relation of the knower to the known" in which inheres the Truth. Nietzsche understood, if narrowly: an unhealthy body accompanies an unhealthy mind, and vice versa. The quality as well as the content of knowledge production is intimately associated with the quality of the theoretician's life. Thus the theoretician's examination of the biographic significance of his or her work is essential. Unless he or she attends to the character of that work, its symbolic function of his or her life and for the culture, likely it is that this work functions to maintain stasis. Unfortunately, this knowledge is available only once the initial and arduous step is taken; until then it is statement veiled from the reader. K. cannot hear those who wish him sell; he is encapsulated in his social role. He cannot be forced. Advice can be given; invitations issued. Nothing more. "More" is political oppression.

Understanding is not understanding if it is accepted as an idea in one's pre-existing conceptual system. Understanding is understanding only when it evolves in the context of an individual's life history. One comes to understand one's case as one lives it, as one goes about one's everyday business, attending carefully, unobtrusively, to what happens, and to what one thinks happens.   [Both K. and the man in the priest's tale stopped their everyday lives to demand understanding, as if it were something ahistorical and material, as if it were something that could be given.]   One brackets the "natural attitude," the perspective of everyday life.   One watches, not judgmentally but as might a court recorder, what transpires.   It is true that the watching, to the extent it is not deliberately intervening and judgmental (one watches the judgments also; one cannot suppress one's self-condemnation without regressive consequences), changes what occurs.   This changing is not manipulation.   It is movement.   Because it is not designed nor enforced, it allows one to see, more and more, the culturally conditioned dimensions of oneself.   One comes to understand how the "great issues" of the century—violence, oppression, arrest—achieve actuality not in the abstract, but in the context of one's own life.   They cease to be abstractions about which one reads, about which others lecture.   Dissociation ceases.   They become primordial, lived realities.   Thereby observed and understood, they begin to dissolve.   New realities consonant with one's historical destiny, realities increasingly those of a Subject, not of objectified social roles, evolve.

For K. such talk is insubstantial, as elusive as his case.   Given his encapsulation in a linear-rationalistic mode, he cannot see the possibility of movement and regeneration.   As does the ego when threatened by release of repressed material, K. discredits new information, discrediting in the service of maintaining the static point of view that is his present.   The beleaguered ego does not accept its own new information.   It insists on converting new experience into terms created in past experience.   This condition is arrested development.   The prognosis, as Kafka's novel suggests, is grim.

Autobiographical consciousness

Joseph K. is a being lost to himself, dissociated from his subjective experience.   He is his social role; his thoughts are thoughts of social negotiation, not fluid thoughts of free association. Estranged from primary experience, his secondary experience becomes impoverished and unimaginative. K. is unable to navigate his way. Is it possible to suggest what is missing in K.? Can subjectivity be portrayed without poetry and fiction? Clearly, subjectivity is not knowledge in any formalized, objectified sense. Subjectivity is not, as William Earle argued, a set of correct opinions, nor can it be studied through a science of universal, ahistorical laws. Earle (1972) noted:

> For if what I knew of myself were only those universal laws or principles I exemplified, then even if my thought were true, it would ignore my singularity by knowing of that singularity only that which "was predictable of many." "Knowing thyself" therefore must not be some form of knowing a universal "thyself" or any conceptual cognition at all, but rather a reflexive elucidation of the singular being that I am. Nor can any such self-knowledge be properly characterized as objective knowledge. It cannot be knowledge in the sense of knowing an object, me, since any object as such is in essence precisely that which is not-me, the subject; to know a subject as an object is to know it as what it is not. Nor can self-knowledge be objective in the scientific sense, a knowledge that depends for its truth and validity on confirmation by other subjectivities. Whatever self-knowledge may be, it cannot be an opinion about myself that can be substantiated only by public agreement (p.9).

My task is to portray singularity, subjectivity, the process of self-knowing. Yet the language available to me is that of social science, a language pretending to universality and objectivity. I am caught, with my contemporaries, in K.'s bank. Glimpses of what exists outside (a sphere many in the field of curriculum have yet to take an interest; they have not even noticed there are windows) startle me. Yet I do not know how to see or how to report what I see. How can I divest myself of this language of abstraction; how to write subjectively? Perhaps autobiography is the means. Perhaps through this mode I can capture the texture and rhythm of the subjectively-existing individual. I must leave the bank. Earle speaks to these and related points:

> And while science and certain theoretical forms of philosophy look for explanations of phenomena, "Know thyself" does not enjoin me to find explanations of myself in what lies outside myself, in what is not me. "Knowing" is necessarily explanatory, but it might be regarded as elucidation: that is, raising to explicit, reflexive consciousness that which is already implicitly grasped. It might be an effort to excavate the implicit, buried sense of existence of a singular being by that singular being—in a word, the "autobiography" of the singular being. "Know

thyself" invites me to become explicit as to who I am, what it is for me
to exist; what my singular existence has been, where it is now, and what
lies before me. "Ontological autobiography," we shall call it, with no
particular emphasis upon its "graphical" or recorded character; it is a
question of a form of consciousness rather than of literature (p. 10).

The "form of consciousness" of which Earle speaks is suggestive of intellectual and, more comprehensively, "biographic" movement. The regressive-progressive-analytic-synthetic method is not primarily to produce knowledge of oneself
and of the character of intellectual work for knowledge's sake
alone. We are not seeking to build a "body of knowledge" of
the subjective genesis and consequences of intellectual interests
as much as a method by means of which one can further one's
intellectual and biographic development. In very general
terms, this movement is from the parochial to the panoramic,
from the exclusively legalistic and technical to the poetic and
the imaginative, from the self-alienated to the self-knowing
engaged person in the world. As Earle suggests, we seek a form
of consciousness.

This form is one of self-self relationality. In classical psychoanalytic imagery, it is an ego sufficiently reflexive to take note
of its superego-id negotiations. It is an ego open to but not
overwhelmed by its id, open to but not overwhelmed by the
prohibitions of superego. It hears the infinite variations of self-
sabotage of which the superego and id are capable, but it is not
sabotaged. It notes that this is in fact the voice of superego, a
voice not to be fought, but to be recorded, not necessarily
expressed behaviorally. Preconscious material that is threatening to the ego's sense of itself and its place in its social milieu
can be permitted to surface. The ego works to open itself to
this surfacing, counteracting as it were, repression. The flow of
id is the flow of libido, and its hyper-regulation is the
diminishing of energy that can be biographic movement. This
process is akin to and overlaps with the free associative process;
it is the "raising to explicit, reflexive consciousness that which is
already implicitly grasped," of which Earle speaks.

The nature of self-self relation is foundational to and inter-
secting with self-other relations. The personality in which
superego predominates will tend to find unsettling personalities

in which this imbalance is not evident, in which, possibly, the id predominates. This is of course oversimplification, but not distortion. Similarly, the self in which the ego is more vulnerable to material surfacing from id, vulnerable in that this surfacing is regularly uncontrolled, may find academic work in the disciplines which is explicitly defined and ordered less tolerable, less satisfying, than work in a field which permits more, let us say libidinous (not meaning lewd but energetic) expression. Again, these are oversimplifications. The point is that the root of K.'s conduct is not in the Law but in the structure of his relationship to himself.

One danger in research of the order described here is reification. That is, as one examines one's relations to oneself, to one's work, to others, one situates current themes and problematics in the past. One achieves, let us say, explanation, but takes this knowledge as the work's end. What is prized is the words, the explanation; what is forgotten is the non-conceptual reality of which the words are only representations. Explanations and related understandings are significant only as they are useful, only as they contribute to release us from past patterns, as they raise hitherto buried material into explicit consciousness, thereby surrendering it. The aspiration for this work is release from the past, release from arrest, release into movement. As explanation is taken as the end-state, the structure of self to self remains unchanged. What is then required is a loosening identification with this material, and the initiation of movement. This is the mode of consciousness of which Earle speaks.

The danger, then, is that autobiographies of individual educational experience be written for their own sake without regard to their developmental consequences for the writers themselves. The potentially freeing process becomes reified as the words become taken for "the things themselves," for the phenomena themselves. The process becomes furthering as the information learned is valued for its possible liberative functions. Autobiography, we must emphasize, is important to us not as a genre of literature, but as a form of consciousness.

In a sense autobiographical work is never completed. This seems a truism on the surface, but the sense of it this morning is vivid and original. It is as if the pull of the culture, perhaps it is the pull of being human, of being a body, that presses one toward the material plane exclusively. Subtly one leaves oneself, and focuses absent-mindedly on "solid objects." One's experience of objects, of others, thins out until it seems no longer present. Continually the task is to return to the immediate experience of the object, of the text, of the lecturer. Continually, it is as if it is the middle of the night, and only with vigilance one remains awake. A few minutes without explicit consciousness of one's situation, and sleep takes one away. This remaining awake Earle terms "divestment." It is, he suggests, roughly what Descartes intended by "doubt," what Husserl termed "suspension of the natural attitude." Earle writes: "Or divestment may be taken as a 'purification' of the soul too engrossed with what it is not, too much caught up in that deceptively tempting and deceptively rewarding domain of the impurities of existence, where the poor soul futilely sought itself. ['Divestment' is a regressive shift of attention from objects or affairs back to the ego that was engrossed with them.]" (pp. 58-59).

Prologue to a method

While Cremin (1976) appears to reduce educational theory to social theory ["the theory of education is the theory of the relation of various educative interactions and institutions to one another and to society at large" (p. 183)], nonetheless he calls for studies which honor the perspective of individual lived experience ["it is as necessary to examine individual life histories as it is to examine the configurations themselves. An educational life history focuses on the experience of education from the perspective of person having and undergoing the experience" (p. 38). The point is never developed, however. Let us develop it here.

The character of educational experience as undergone by the subjectively-existing individual is illustrated in an autobiographical essay written by John Dewey. Reflecting on the history of his intellectual interests, Dewey (1960) wrote: "My deeper interests had not as yet been met, and in the absence of subject matter that would correspond to them, the only topics at my command were such as were capable of merely formal treatment" (p. 7). Although Dewey does not say so, it is unlikely that he understood this point during the time of which he speaks. Likely it is that in retrospective reflection does this situation make itself clear.

The situation is this: there would appear to be a certain agenda, an agenda that is at once intellectual, emotional, bodily, one which in a synthetical way I characterize as "biographic." This agenda becomes expressed in the socio-historical world according to a complex configuration of forces, including individual volition and choice. Erik Erikson (1975) suggested the structure of such a configuration in his discussion of psychosocial identity:

> Psychosocial identity, then, also has a psychohistorical side, and suggests the study of how life histories are inextricably interwoven with history. The study of psychosocial identity, therefore, depends on three complementarites—or are they three aspects of one complementarity? —namely, the personal coherence of the individual and role integration in his group; his guiding images and the ideologies of his time; his life history—and this historical movement (p. 20).

What is interesting, in my view, is this pre-public, pre-categorical pressing of libido that determines in varying but considerable measure, the character of the final biographic synthesis. Today a Dewey might have been drawn to phenomenology rather than to Hegelianism. Historical circumstances alter inexorably, but the biographic "need" for an absolutist perspective remains. Educational speaking, it is this biographic predisposition upon which it is useful to focus. Through certain forms of self-work the nature of one's biographical movement can be made conscious, and its expression and recreation through the forms of the academic disciplines understood and participated in more profoundly.

In the passage quoted, Dewey's deeper movement was frustrated during the time recalled, and so, symptomatic of arrest, he was absorbed in "merely formal treatment." In another passage in the same essay Dewey discussed what philosophic point of view permitted him to proceed.

There were, however, also "subjective" reasons for the appeal that Hegel's thought made to me; it supplied a demand for unification that was doubtless an intense emotional craving, and yet was a hunger that only an intellectualized subject matter could satisfy.... But the sense of divisions and separations that were, I suppose, borne upon me as a consequence of a heritage of New England culture, divisions by way of isolation of self from the world, of soul from the body, of nature from God, brought a painful oppression—or rather, they were an inward laceration .... Hegel's synthesis of subject and object, matter and spirit, the divine and the human, was, however, no mere intellectual formula; it operated as an immense release, a liberation (1960, p. 10).

Thus in a phrase is expressed the proper biographic function for intellectual work. Studies that are biographically proper might function to provoke movement and release from arrest, a phenomenon recognizable enough to hint at a dramatic word such as "liberation." It is precisely that, a release from blocked movement. So freed, one experiences intellectual ferment, as libido flows, in relative terms, uninterrupted, as it is transmutated into thought. It is not that the conceptual system (in Dewey's case Hegel's) acts merely as conduit through which energy flows. But if intellectual movement is to occur, the relations between system of thought and libido must be dialectical, as both become a sort of "ingredients" then mixed in the creative act into something new, a synthesis of primary and secondary experience (i.e. thought) which moves the thinker further through his issues, further down his "lifestream."

Because his own thought products now have their origins in a life-engaged, self-extending process, they have the potential to function similarly for others. Of course their precise conceptual content is extremely important. But so is the character of their origin, their function for the thinker himself. This issue at this point is reminiscent of Kierkegaard's description of the knower's relation to what is known: "When the question of truth is raised subjectively, reflection is directly subjectively to the nature of the individual's relationship; if only the mode of this relationship is in the truth, the individual is in the truth, even if he should happen to be thus related to what is not true" (1951, pp. 210-211). The veracity of the statement is secondary to the veracity of the relationship between statement and he or she who states.

Also in the Dewey passage is indication of the significance of life history to the shape of intellectual movement. Dewey cites his embodiment of New England culture, his "inward laceration," the intellectual equivalents of which were issues of self estranged from world, soul from body, nature from God. Of course, not any conceptual system would function to heal this fundamental but particularized self-division. Because Hegel's system wed elements which were thematically dichotomized in Dewey, Hegelianism could function in ways that for Dewey were developmentally furthering. Thus it is not only the structure of a given conceptual system—in this instance the synthesizing nature of Hegel's system—but as well the content—the particular thematic elements that were indeed wed—that permit a theoretical point of view to be meaningful for a particular student. This "fit" between life history and theoretical perspective suggests educational experience, as their articulation permits movement. If texts and teachers are not to be oppressive, or of mere technical use, then such a criterion must be employed to determine educational value.

In another passage Dewey discusses what is in effect a psychological function of intellectual interests that, if common to others, accounts in part for the adamancy if not dogmatism that seems to regularly accompany a theoretical point of view:

> Probably there is in the consciously articulated ideas of every thinker an overweighting of just those things that are contrary to his intrinsic bent, and which, therefore, he has to struggle to bring to expression, while the native bent, on the other hand, can take care of itself. Anyway, a case might be made out for the proposition that the emphasis upon the concrete, empirical, and "practical" in my later writings is partly due to considerations of this nature. It was a reaction against what was more natural, and it served as a protest and protection against something in myself, which, in the pressure of the weight of actual experiences, I knew to be a weakness (1960, p. 8).

To the extent one's articulated point of view functions as a balancing weight, one must rigidly maintain its density in order to maintain the balance with the implicit but native bent. This rigidity is dogmatism.

What may be possible, through reflection upon one's work in this way, is, over time, a conscious incorporation of those

buried elements which one's written work attempts to balance.
One's native bent can be viewed as thesis; a theoretical perspective one adopts can be viewed as antithesis. Dewey maintained
a balance by maintaining a dialectical tension between who he
was conditioned to be and what he chose to think and do. By
maintaining a tension, by his admission, his theoretical perspective emphasized the concrete, the empirical, the "practical" over
the abstract, the ideal, the speculative. It is conceivable that
through reflexive examination of this dialectic, he could have
allowed a synthesis which, embodied in his writing, would have
meant a broader, even more comprehensive and profound
point of view.

While one's achievement may not be regarded as equivalent
to Dewey's, what is structurally true for Dewey may be true for
any student. Regardless which specific themes comprise the
dialectic between native tendency and balancing intellectual
interests, regardless the profundity and social value of the
dialectic, in terms of the individual's development—intellectual,
biographic—raising to explicit consciousness this relation
between knower and known could have furthering consequences. The method is one strategy by which one might
examine the relations between self and knowledge with favorable developmental consequences.

When Dewey writes "social interests and problems from an
early period had to me the intellectual appeal and provided the
intellectual sustenance that many seem to have found primarily
in religious questions" (1960, p. 11), one expects his analysis of
social problems to be more understanding, perhaps more
shrewd, than analysis and action without this interrelationship
and this self-consciousness. Dewey's comments are retrospective, and we do not know to what extent he was self-conscious
of these dynamics earlier in his life. What is central for us is
the possibility of such self-understanding. Cultivated self-awareness can function to dissolve intellectual blocks (or arrest) and
initiate intellectual movement. That such regeneration is pro-
voked at the levels of primary experience is confirmed in
another passage from the Dewey essay. Additionally, the intellectual equivalent of psychosocial identity is indicated:

I seem to be unstable, chameleon-like, yielding one after another to many diverse and even incompatible influences; struggling to assimilate something from each and yet striving to carry it forward in a way that is logically consistent with what has been learned from its predecessors. Upon the whole, the forces that have influenced me have come from persons and from situations more than from books—not that I have not, I hope, learned a great deal from philosophical writings, but that what I have learned from them has been technical in comparison with what I have been forced to think upon and about because of some experience in which I found myself entangled (1960, p. 13).

This passage is significant in several respects. First, it does suggest the importance of primary, or in Suzanne Langer's language "actual," experience to intellectual movement. Also indicated is the role of secondary, or in Langer's scheme "virtual," experience in intellectual development. It is technical. As Dewey suggests, the technical is important, but derivatively so. Without movement at preconceptual levels, technical competence is unfinished. Intellectually arrested, the technical can be self-sabotaging; witness Joseph K. Primary experience by itself is primary experience. To become educational experience it must be employed. This reflexive process is pointed to in the last sentence when Dewey writes: "but what I have learned from them (philosophical writings) has been technical in comparison with what I have been forced to think upon and about because of some experience in which I found myself entangled." It is crucial not to have thoughts only about thoughts, but thoughts originating in and about experience. From experience one works to articulate this experience in thought and action. In such self-reflection does experience become educational.

Also in this passage is the suggestion of an intellectual equivalent of psychosocial identity. This is indicated in the first sentence. Also pointed to in this sentence is the "barebones" of the process of identification. One is receptive to others' points of view, suggested in the allusion to the chameleon. This is important. Often one observes others categorizing others according to established, rigidly maintained perspectives, closed to influence. Such "sophistication" guarantees arrest. One must be willing to hold one's own point of view in abeyance and, as Dewey knew, "yield" to another. Regularly, as he describes, one crystallizes what has been assimilated into a consistent perspective, continuous with its thematic predecessors. Intellectual identity, like psychosocial identity, is not a frozen phenomenon. There is continuity; there is transformation as well. Such movement is not linear, but diagonal as it were. One moves more deeply into repressed material, integrating what was before dissociated and unconscious, and simultaneously moves more profoundly into social space in which one's life takes form.

Also in this passage is indicated the tension between passivity and agency. Intermittent periods of instability, conscious efforts to retain something continuous and consistent throughout the flux of experience: this is a capsule description of intellectual movement as it is lived. The acknowledgement of the centrality of primary experience and the technical role that formal study plays correct the deformed view of learning common in schools of education. Such corrections become possible when an autobiographical stance is assumed, and from this perspective, one's experience described.

Carl Jung's reflection upon his life and work are also provocative of an autobiographical theory of educational experience: "My life is what I have done, my scientific work; the one inseparable from the other. The work is the expression of my inner development; for commitment to the contents of the unconscious forms the man and produces his transformations. My works can be regarded as stations along my life's way" (1963, p. 222). In a more explicitly psychological way than does Dewey, Jung is conscious of the symbolic status of intellectual work. Intellectual movement accompanies biographic movement, both of which accompany commitment to lived experience (of which unconscious content is a major "portion"). Arrest is signified by exclusive attention to the social world, denial and ignorance of the lived world.

The notion of biographic agenda, of a series of tasks and issues through which one must work, or deny or ignore, is embedded in another passage. Jung wrote: "Today I can say that I never lost touch with my initial experiences. All my works, all my creative activity, has come from those initial fantasies and dreams which began in 1912, almost fifty years ago. Everything that I accomplished later in life was already contained in them, although at first only in the form of emotions and images" (1963, p. 192). Retrospective analysis lays bare a pattern often invisible while one is immersed in it. But to K., lost to role, dissociated from what is individual in him, attentive to only what is common with others, the notion of pattern is meaningless.

To the one who attends to himself or herself, an individual path becomes discernible, a path reflected in one's intellectual work. For instance, Jung regarded his books as by-products of his own process of individuation, despite their obvious discursive links with other psychoanalytic works. He believed that authentic work is conducted in silence and may strike a chord in the minds of a very few. Autobiographical study also discloses that the individual route is detectable through cautious examination and understanding of primary experience. Such examination requires solitude and silence as well as community. This notion echoes Kierkegaard's descriptions of the significance of solitude, of remaining alone, in order to hear the voice of God, or in Jung's terms, one's own voice, the voice of the Self.

In another letter Jung underscores the priority of self work, and the possible delusion of unexamined social action: "I quite agree with you that those people in our world who have insight and good will enough, should concern themselves with their own 'souls,' more than with preaching to the masses or trying to find out the best way for them. They only do that because they don't know themselves. But alas, it is a sad truth that usually those who know nothing for themselves take to teaching others, in spite of the fact that they know the best method of education is the good example" (1963, p. 222). Of course, the self-knowing may well choose a life of social service, but it is also true that often those who take upon themselves a calling to intrude in the lives of others are precisely those who have failed to intrude in, or study, their own lives. Such people are the psychic equivalents of untrained surgeons. At the same time it must be acknowledged that for many it is work with others that is a medium through which they work with themselves. The order of meditative work with oneself characteristic of Jung's life is biographically inappropriate for many. But the fact of appropriate medium is crucial. It is a judgment properly made of one's own work. Regardless what one's work in the world is, ascertaining its biographic function is essential, not only for oneself, but for others as well.

Jung understood that self-study occurs in social context: "As nobody can become aware of his individuality unless he is closely and responsibly related to his fellow beings, he is not withdrawing to an egoistic desert when he tries to find himself. He can only discover himself when he is deeply and unconditionally related to some, and generally related to a great many, individuals with whom he has a chance to compare, and from whom he is able to discriminate himself" (Serrano, 1966, pp. 83-84). Self work occurs in social context yes, but this is not to say that the human being is finally a social creature. That is, the individual who, like the social scientist, focuses on what he or she shares with others to the exclusion of what he or she shares with no one, is bound to miss himself (herself) and others. While it is true that self work occurs in social milieux, it is not reducible to social transactions. What is important about these transactions is their biographic significance for the individual. One asks: what does this event, and my response to it, tell me about its significance, tell me about where and with what and whom I am moving? It is interesting that someone thinks that, but what is vital, from the perspective of educational experience, is the individual's use—broadly understood—of that statement. In a general way, it is appropriate to ask, with Eliot: "Why for all of us, out of all that we have heard, seen, felt, in a lifetime, do certain images recur, charged with emotion, rather than others?" (1964, p. 148).

Our studies indicate an answer. Certain images, certain texts, certain conceptual systems (such as Hegelianism) are biographically significant. They function in meaningful biographic ways, i.e., to heal an "inward laceration" through study of a conceptual system which in its structure synthesizes what is psychologically dichotomized. Biographic situations, in structure and theme, vary. But the fact of biographic situation, of biographic issues, becomes indisputable. Through their study and understanding, one moves into "new space," which then is reflected, as well as created, in intellectual interests. Newmann understood at least half the dialectic: "For myself, it was not

logic that carried me on; as well might one say that the quicksil-
ver in the barometer changes the weather. It is the concrete
being that reasons; passes a number of years, and I find myself
in a new place; how? the whole man moves, paper logic is but
the record of it" (quoted in Olney, 1972, p. 216). Cognition can
spur that movement, if pursued cautiously and with dedication.
Articulation of movement intensifies the movement, as the free
associative articulation of images, etc., during psychoanalysis
allows material to be experienced, thereby releasing the patient
from a "frozen place."

Movement recalls the image of chameleon Dewey mentioned.
Yet something—is it the chameleon itself?—remains untouched.
Discerning the continuity is discerning one's biographic and
intellectual identity. A danger remains that identification en-
genders arrest. The emphasis is properly upon the gerund.
Intellectual understanding is important as it affirms movement,
to the extent to which it enlarges and enriches experience:
"[philosophic discourse] is a comment on nature and life in the
interest of a more intense and just appreciation of the meanings present in experience" (1929, p. 407). The contemporary
emphasis on the truth-value of discourse, its verifiability, is
excessive, and distorts the multi-dimensional function of intellectual work. Relatedly, Dewey writes: "Poetic meanings, moral
meanings, a large part of the goods of life are matters of richness and freedom of meanings, rather than of truth; a large
part of our life is carried on in a realm of meanings to which
truth and falsity as such are irrelevant" (1929, p. 411).

If cognition is constituent of the biographic "place" of the
individual, then, thought that seems nonsensical may well have
truth-value for the thinker. Tolstoy understood this point: "As
my body has descended to me from God, so also has my reason
and my understanding of life, and consequently the various
stages of the development of that understanding of life cannot
be false. All that people sincerely believe in must be true; it
may be differently expressed but it cannot be a lie, and therefore if it presents itself as a lie, that only means that I have not
understood it" (1940, p. 18).

There are obvious limits to this view (the sun shines today
regardless of what you say), but they are the commonsensical

ones. The fact of similar meanings, of intelligible experience articulated in dissimilar and at times nearly indecipherable language is acknowledged in the common phrase "I know what you mean." When conceptualization reflects the pre-conceptual, the latter remains present, providing a kind of ontological background. Thus it is sometimes easier to comprehend another's point of view when the author is present, and his or her presence, and his or her words' place in that presence are visible. It is this complex process of situating thought in experience, and understanding its psychological and biographic functions that is one aspiration of the regressive-progressive-analytic-synthetic method. Jung summarized the significance of such situating when he wrote that experience, not only academic learning, leads to understanding. It is the individual, irreplicable being who, through reflection and action, comprehends this experience. Olney (1972) wrote: "it is to that taste of myself that one first awakes in the morning, not to the world. In experience as in logic, a sense of the subjective self must always be prior to a sense of the objective world" (p. 14). That is why "he [Socrates] always brought the inquirer back first of all to give an account of the conditions of his present and past life, which he examined and judged, considering any other learning subordinate to that and superfluous" (quoted in Olney, 1972, p. 14). Not only is this view acknowledgement of the ontologically prior status of primary experience, and of the profound shaping of intellectual expression biographic situation creates, but as well an understanding that what is possible is a "profound subjectivity that goes so deep that it becomes transformed into an objective vision of the human condition" (Olney, 1972, p. 87). For Jung it is a layer of collective unconscious that is the intersubjective, trans-historical experience of the species which becomes accessible. Self-understanding furthers understanding of others. With Montaigne we observe: "We seek other conditions because we do not understand the use of our own, and go outside of ourselves because we do not know what it is like inside. Yet there is no use our mounting on stilts, for on stilts we must still walk our own legs. And on the loftiest throne in the world we are still sitting only on our own rump" (quoted in Olney, 1972, pp. 87-88).

To recognize that one cannot escape oneself, and that one must confront one's own past in order to hope to grasp the present and influence the future, one engages in autobiographical work. To so work means to be in movement, and to become progressively conscious of movement, its relation to others, to the historical moment. It is what a character in Virginia Woolf's *The Years* wishes for: "There must be another life, here and now, she repeated. This is too short, too broken. We know nothing, even about ourselves. We're only just beginning, she thought, to understand, here and there. She held her hands hollowed; she felt that she wanted to enclose the present moment; to make it stay; to fill it fuller and fuller, with the past, the present and future, until it shone, whole, bright, deep with understanding" (pp. 427-428).

Method

The past hangs over the present as fog veils a highway. Because it is omnipresent, because we could not bear to live through it, it hangs as if invisible. Only through regression can one live through past pain, discern, as if it were embedded in one's very musculature, how it infiltrates the present. The past is present. To the extent one is unconscious of the past one is caught in it. One is arrested, temporally and developmentally. In schools the teacher may become increasingly identified with one's professionalized role as educator, less attentive to educating and to learning. Subtly one gives up one's own voice, and nearly exclusively relies on others, reporting this research then that, perhaps making a summary of it all which cements a psychological and intellectual nihilism, though unclaimed and unconscious. The emphasis is upon form; one judges severely the artless attempts by students to articulate in their own words issues long "resolved" by serious scholars. Death hangs in the academic air, obscured by pledges of allegiance to life and open inquiry that are in fact only slogans, as truthful as claims made in admissions brochures. The configuration is repression, unconsciousness, role-identified behavior, intellectual and psychological arrest. Like K. the response to one's case is self-sabotaging: increased number of committee meetings, longer hours in the office, more reading, less time writing and thinking. "Lived experience" becomes an enigmatic phrase associated with an obscure continental philosophy.

An initial recognition of this situation is required for work to commence and the situation to be transformed. Then, commencement, and with work that is by its nature difficult to describe. Four phases or moments: regression, progression, analysis, synthesis. It is work to uncover the genesis in one's life history of one's present biographic situation. Thematically it cannot be described. We find we can both speak of our third-grade teacher, but in our own terms. Autobiographical writing refers the writer and reader to themselves. Olney (1972) noted: "The act of autobiography and the act of poetry, both as creation and as recreation, constitute a bringing to consciousness of the nature of one's existence, transforming the mere fact of existence into a realized quality and a possible meaning" (p. 44).

The realization of this quality can come through disclosure of the past, an exorcism if you like, which shifts it outside, there, visible, apart from oneself. This can feel as literal as it is figurative. It is as if one sets on the paper or screen in front of one the past that was inside one's body. Record, beginning with earliest memories, your past in schools. It is essential to return as fully as it is possible to this past, to allow yourself to be there with your mother or father as s/he walks you to kindergarten on opening day, as the teacher greets you, with a warm welcoming smile, or perhaps a callous, automatic one. What is crucial is to bring to the present the multi-dimensional reality (visual, tactile, mental, emotional) that was. This is regression, re-entering the past. One becomes juvenile, and feels censorship, censorship that often is the present ego's attempt to maintain dissociation and denial of its archaeological layers. This censorship can spread to the method itself, can become resistance to performing self-reflective work at all. Record this resistance also, and so bracket it, release it. Record everything that happens while regressing. Recording cultivates the ego's reflexive capacity, or in Husserlian terms, a transcendental ego, a perspective that observes all, and judges nothing. Cultivation of this capacity, this point of view, permits movement. But it is slow and arduous work. It requires commitment to self. What is involved is a fundamental restructuring of one's relation to self, an opening to the contents of one's unconscious, an attunement to one's voice and to the articulation of that content and voice. But the easiness of these phrases belies the difficulty, the self-intimidating character of this work. The attempt at self-transformation initiates profound appreciation of the problematic of social and political transformation. Arrest and oppression hang like fog one has forgotten to see, as omnipresent as they are subtle.

The work is not always strenuous. The range of human emotion comes to consciousness: laughter, excitement, pleasure are relived. But the overcast is dense, dark, unsettling. In contrast to this regressive work, the progressive seems lighter, even pleasing. Meditation on what may come, on what one wishes to come, might be as determining a force as what one has been conditioned to be. Perhaps because it is not yet present, because one did not come from it, perhaps deny it, and live in its shadow, the disclosure of one's images of the future seems, in contrast to the regression, easy and pleasant.

But there is resistance throughout. There is denial of the future, fear of it, a wish to somehow escape it. Flight from the future is not unlike capture by the past. Work with the past, release from it, allows loosened identification with fear of the future, and allows heightened intuitive sense of where one may go. This recording, transposing in a sense, of what is embedded within, onto the paper or screen, allows increased freedom to choose (rather than be forced into) future possibilities. One's freedom is heightened, and one's response to unanticipated biographic and historical events are made proportionately more fluid and life-affirmative.

If articulation of past and future represents "one half" of the task from release from arrest, then understanding that is absolving and freeing is the other half. The opportunity one makes for oneself occurs during examination of what has been recorded in the regressive and progressive phases. In a sense the analytic moment is a return to the ego's perspective, and the ego's interest in the integration of "new" information. Now the task is critical reflection of what has been free-associatively recalled and lived through during the first two phases. It is imperative that the analysis not be a reduction of that primary experience articulated in the regression and progression to static conceptual categories, a restoration of the intellect to its experience-diminishing, pseudo self-aggrandizing position. Fidelity to the quality of experience accompanying the return to the past and visualization of the future must be preserved. It is the seemingly sophisticated comments of the world-weary intellect that must be bracketed. A new if knowing naiveté is one hopeful consequence of this work.

The analysis lays bare the thematic connections between present, past, and future. One comes to see themes that endure, and require honoring in ways unexpected and unprecedented. The analysis must be of an order that simultaneously distances and grounds one in experience, a making it more present and complete, and discernible and intelligible. This process occurs idiosyncratically, and general guidelines such as these can function to worry or irritate rather than to guide. If the interest and concomitant commitment to educational experience are present, then only this sketch of the method will be necessary.

The synthetical occurs throughout, as articulation of the past and release from it occurs. As one focuses upon one's imagined future, one releases material that while buried helped maintain arrest. As one analyzes material which one has uncovered while remembering the past and calling forth the future, one achieves an understanding that is at once intellectual, emotional, bodily, and perhaps a heightened reflexivity, an increased freedom to act. Nonetheless, a separate occasion, or series of them, that focuses on integration, on a reconceptualization of one's biographic situation through the lens formed by understanding past and future, can deepen the integration. This process seems to occur "below" states of consciousness and articulation, and words may be sparse. The lived sense of synthesis can be unmistakable, however.

The regressive-progressive-analytic-synthetic method is an autobiographic strategy by means of which one may understand the nature of one's life in schools, and the functions of school in one's life. It is a research strategy that produces knowledge of the character of lived experience of schools, and so contributes to our knowledge of schools and the educative process.

This knowledge is knowledge of the individual, a point of view that insists upon the primacy of such knowledge, and upon the derivative status of generalization and social categorization. The method of *currere* is a research method that is an alternative to contemporary social science, not only in procedure but in the order of knowledge thereby produced. This is knowledge that makes explicit the developmental as well as epistemological bases of its production. It is knowledge based in the concrete rather than the abstract.

The method is formulated to engender development in the researcher. It is a method self-conscious of its possible functions in the lives of researchers and the researched. It is a strategy whose aspiration is not only contribution to a "body of knowledge" but a contribution to the biographic-intellectual and thus political emancipation of those who employ it. Understood is that the character and probable functions of knowledge have very much to do with the conditions and strategies by which it was produced. Knowledge is in this sense the tip of a socio-biographic iceberg. The nature of that tip is in large measure a function of the nature of the experience of those who are its creators. This method attends explicitly to the experience of knowledge creation, from the point of view of the subjectively-existing individual. It represents movement, release from our arrest. With Virginia Woolf we might notice:

> That was the strange thing, that one did not know where one was going, or what one wanted, and followed blindly, suffering so much in secret, always unprepared and amazed and knowing nothing; but one thing led to another and by degrees something had formed itself out of nothing, and so one reached at last this calm, this certainty, and it was this process that people called living.

References

Cremin, L. (1976). *Public education*. New York: Basic Books.

Dewey, J. (1929). *Experience and nature*. New York.

Dewey, J. (1960). *On experience, nature and freedom*. R. Bernstein, ed. Indianapolis and New York: Library of Liberal Arts.

Earle, W. (1972). *The autobiographical consciousness: A philosophical inquiry into existence*. Chicago: Quadrangle Books.

Eliot, T. S. (1964). *The use of poetry and the use of criticism*. London: Faber & Faber.

Erickson, E. (1975). *Life history and historical moment*. New York: Norton & Co.

Jung, C. (1939). *The integration of personality*. New York: Farrar & Rinehart, Inc.

Jung, C. (1963). *Memories, dreams, and reflections*. New York: Pantheon.

Kafka, F. (1968). *The Trial*. New York: Schocken.

Kierkegaard, S. (1951). Concluding unscientific postscript. In R. Bretall (ed.), *A Kierkegaard Anthology*. Princeton: Princeton University Press.

Olney, J. (1972). *Metaphors of self: The meaning of autobiography*. Princeton, NJ: Princeton University Press.

Rahv, P. (1968). *Literature and the sixth sense*. Boston: Houghton, Mifflin.

Serrano, M. (1966). *C. G. Jung and Hermann Hesse: A Record of Two Friendships*. New York: Schocken.

Tolstoy, L. (1940). *A confession*. London: Oxford University Press.

Woolf, V. (1937). *The years*. London: Hogarth.

V

What is the Reconceptualization?
(1978)

I am not going to answer that question. What I intended in this short paper is to ask it seriously, which I suspect means asking another although equivalent question. Namely, can we see a collective future for ourselves in this curriculum field, and if so, what sort of future—what sort of inquiry—seems possible? I am able to see the broad outlines of one possible future, and during the course of this paper I will sketch these.

First, let me backtrack a little. The word "reconceptualization" derives from James Macdonald and his much quoted 1971 piece on research in curriculum.[1] I contributed to its popularization it by using the idea to sketch a picture of where the field had been, where it is now, and where it might be going.[2] The point to make is that it is a word I used not so much to assist us—meaning Reconceptualists—to understand the distinctions and similarities among our work, as much as to inform the mainstream of the field what might be expected from the few of us I saw working earnestly in ways that would indeed reconceptualize the field mainstream curricularists knew. The preface and other introductory comments in *Curriculum Theorizing: The Reconceptualists* (1975) were intended primarily for those who did not understand the relation of, say, Huebner's scholarship to their own. The point of these introductory pieces was to situate his and others' work in a context intelligible to the mainstream field.[3]

For a few of those whose work was published in *Curriculum Theorizing* the term has evidently always been enigmatic and unsatisfactory. I suppose that it is only from considerable conceptual distance, that provided by being a Tylerian or a Johnsonian for instance, that the work designated as the reconceptualization seems a whole.[4] This "prerequisite" for appreciating the term is illustrated by remarks overheard during the Milwaukee meeting.[5] One listener thought the word meaningless. Her companion replied: "No, it's not meaningless. While I'm unable to say precisely what it means, it does mean something. I attend American Educational Research Association [AERA] and Association for Supervision and Curriculum Development [ASCD] meetings fairly regularly, and I've attended three of these. Compare these meetings with those of AERA or ASCD and immediately it's obvious that there is something, however ill-defined, that is the reconceptualization." Such remarks I have heard several times; perhaps you have too. My point is that however vague the term seems to us who attend these meetings, it is not meaningless; it does refer to something. What I am asking today is that you and others join me in identifying exactly what this "something is."

In my view, it is not only a matter of identifying what exists now, but also a task of delineating a collective aspiration. This is a task as complex as it is ambiguous. Initially it means that we attend to the character of what we have to say to each other, to colleagues in public schools, and colleagues in other areas of education. The effort here is not to categorize others' work. It is to indicate the possibility of their interrelationships.

I propose that when we meet again next time that we report on the progress of our individual efforts, but that we also attempt to situate these efforts, not only historically in the field, but as well in the context of what others are now doing.[6] A field is not created and sustained by working in isolation, or by referring only to past figures or to work in related disciplines, although each of these is necessary. They are necessary but not sufficient. What is also required is the sketching of what one sees as the relation to his or her work to that being done contemporaneously in the field. I underline the phrase "sketching ... the relation."

Typically when one begins to examine the relation of his work to other work done contemporaneously, there can be a tendency toward criticism exclusively. This tendency to criticize only must be resisted, at least initially. First, such a response is often born in careerist ambitions, not in authentic intellectual dispute. Second, there must be a body of work extant in order for the field to proceed further. The work accumulated thus far remains incipient enough that excessive criticism at this fragile stage can stunt more than instruct and inspire.[7] Even so, of course, when genuine dispute exists, it must be acknowledged. But I am suggesting that the emphasis be, in the next three to five years, on describing the relationships among various strands of work now being done.

Perhaps we will want to think of future meetings as providing forums for exchange, for—in Freire's still useful notion—"dialogical encounter." They could be occasions to focus on the development of our individual theoretical perspectives while contributing to the formulation of a collective one. Perhaps we will want to consider smaller meetings, limiting attendance to the speakers themselves. Introducing one's work to others who do not know it, explaining it to others who question its most fundamental assumptions are useful, important orders of work. Yet a kind of dissipation occurs when one spends all one's time introducing one's work, in a sense teaching only the introductory course. I am suggesting that a field cannot seriously develop if we are unwilling, for part of our time, to take our eyes off empirically-oriented colleagues and work earnestly and intensively among ourselves, building a systematic understanding of issues which make problematic the American educational enterprise. Work of an equivalent order to "basic research" must be conducted before we achieve understanding which allows us to potently and meaningfully assist others.

Implicit in such work is the charge to construct a collective direction for the work. However vague our sense of direction is now, we must begin with this vagueness and begin to define it, else we face the diffusion and stasis of discourse typically heard at the annual meetings of ASCD and AERA. Direction isn't something one can expect to know in advance; it is created in the course of delineation. We are already in theoretic and historical context; we have a tradition. What is appropriate now is increasing acknowledgement of the relation of individ-

ual work to the tradition and to the contemporary scene. Thus
to answer the question this papers asks, we can begin to
continually sketch the relation of our individual efforts to the
tradition and to each other. Not by one theoretician but by us
all, the question will, over the years, be answered.

We must avoid the temptation to legislate the themes and
functions of the field. What can be avoided is the attempt to
stipulate, as Johnson and others have done, what the field and
what it is not.[8] These attempts, as memory will confirm, initiated little dialogue. Of course, definitions of crucial terms must
be offered, refined and when necessary, disputed. However, a
field becomes defined collectively and historically, not individually and logically. The lack of conceptual coherence in the field
at present cannot be remedied by fiat. This problem can be
addressed by conscious efforts to make explicit the relation
between one's work and others'. Coherence will develop over
time, portrayed perhaps by others not yet on the scene.

In this spirit of initiating dialogue I offer the following
response to the question "What is the Reconceptualization?"

Reconceptualization

It begins in fundamental critique of the field as it is. The order
of critique distinguishes it from most reform efforts, efforts
which accept the deep structure of educational and social life,
and focus upon "improving it." The reconceptualization aspires to critique which insists upon the transformation of extant
structures. It shares with critical theory[9] the view that criticism
must not reify that which it identifies and explains. It must
function to dissolve frozen structures. Thus implicit in such an
analysis of contemporary educational practices is their transformation.

One such analysis has been Apple's, which has demonstrated
how the schools and its curriculum function to disallow conflict.[10] Conflict is not only disallowed, it is illegitimated as a
model of social interaction. For instance, natural science is
ordinarily portrayed as if it has evolved consensually, without
rancorous debates, without non-scientific motives and aims.
Relatedly, the schools' insistence upon discipline, an important

element of its "hidden curriculum," indoctrinates our children to political and cultural, as well as intellectual, passivity. Surely the Holocaust reminds us again of the disastrous possibilities of a cultural regime trained to passivity and obedience, although the causes of that nightmare cannot be summarized so succinctly.

Many have discussed the school's overwhelming preoccupation with control, an obsession not incidental to the school's mission in a society economically and politically structured as is our own. While using terms like "learning" and "education" so constantly and ritualistically as to ensure their meaninglessness, the schools delude themselves and others as to their actual function: training. With increasing emphasis upon "career education" and "vocational education" the delusion is increasingly difficult to maintain. Schools are centers where the young are trained to perform competently the tasks their elders present to them as socially necessary and expedient. Such an analysis of school curriculum has been conducted exhaustively by Apple and others.[11]

Kliebard's work also serves to illustrate the order of critique crucial to genuine reconceptualizations of the field.[12] He has shown how the curriculum field, from its inception, has been subsumed in the ethos of "scientism," a cult of efficiency and productivity taken for granted by the business community. This unreflective emphasis upon efficiency, productivity, improvement (an "ameliorative orientation" is Kliebard's term), upon behavioral notions of psychosocial and intellectual development, molded the nation's schools into, structurally speaking, mirrors of its factories. The ideal of education evaporates; a residue of schooling, training for profitable existence in a capitalistic economic order, remains.

Teaching is reduced to instruction. As Huebner has indicated, the technical mode, a mode obsessed with control and prediction, displaces ethical and aesthetic modes of teaching and conceiving curriculum.[13] As Habermas has demonstrated, the pragmatic, a classical concern with just action in particular situations, has been replaced with the technical, even if the terms "pragmatic" and "practical" persist.[14] Examined closely, it is clear that most calls for practical assistance from our colleagues in the public shcools are in fact calls for technique, leaving unexamined the deeper structural bases of most so-called "learning problems." In an earlier piece (i.e. "Sanity, Madness, and the School") I described the processes of self-estrangement and "madness" typical school life provokes.[15] It is this scope of critique which distinguishes the reconceptualization from any recent phnomenon in American education, with the exception of revisionism in the history of education field.[16]

There is a further distinguishing characteristic. This comprehensive critique has its origins in traditions that are European, not American. They are disparate traditions—Marxism, existentialism, phenomenology, psychoanalysis—whose common bond in the context of the curriculum field is their dissimilarity to the behaviorism and empiricism charcteristic of American social science and educational research. It is from the perspective of mainstream curricularists and educational researchers that these traditions appear related. For those whose work constitutes the reconceptualization their relationships are less clear.

What is crucial for reconceptualists, I believe, is to remember that these traditions are sources for the reconceptualization. We must use their insights to create our own. We are Americans not Europeans; we are educationists not philosophers or psychoanalysts. We must avoid the temptation to uproot insights from these traditions and "apply" them to the educational issues of our time. Such work is by definition derivative and distorting, involving as it does reduction of complex issues to conceptual systems created in other times, on other soil, for other purposes. To become scholars of phenomenology or of Marxist theory first and curricularists second is to betray our historical calling. These origins are important; I do not demean them. But they are origins only, and we must create our own intellectual and practical discipline, independent of its sources, sensitive and responsible to our present.

An anecdote may help illustrate this point. During the 1977 meeting of the Philosophy of Education Society in Nashville, a philosopher of education read a paper explaining the significance of a certain phenomenological concept for educational theory. During the questioning period following his presentation, another philosopher of education, a European who had studied with a student of Merleau-Ponty in Paris, made the following comment. I reconstruct it as follows: "You have written a thorough, perhaps we can say, impeccable paper on this topic. It is clear you understand this phenomenological notion in a sophsticated way. Yet you have missed its most important point, in fact what what some would say is the point of phenomenology. Of course there are those scholars whose work it is to explicate this idea of Merleau-Ponty's and that one of Husserl's. But to take such an idea and plant it in the foreign soil that is American educational philosophy is, in an important way, to betray the fundamental charge of phenomenology. For instance, we are admonished to follow Husserl's famous little phrase, to "return to the things themselves." Don't you see that this means that we must abandon, insofar as this is possible, extant conceptual systems—not just behaviorism but phenomenology also—through employment of the eidectic reduction? We must work to make direct contact with preconceptual experience, and then articulate, not in Schutz's or in Merleau-Ponty's words, but your own, what this is you are now in contact with, what you experience directly, unmediated by conceptual blinders. You have written a careful paper on phenomenology but you have missed its point."

In his reply the speaker made it clear he continued to miss this point. He failed to see that the conceptual structure of his paper was pre-eminently logical, a linear, almost algebraic logic. If "a" (the phenomenological concept), then "b" (the logically-derived educational implication). This work is then, at base, a conceptual exercise, and bears no necessary, certainly no explicit relation, to the speaker's life world. The work of phenomenologists may contribute to the formulation of his perspective, but if he is absolutely faithful to this tradition, it must finally be his perspective, grounded in his preconceptual experience, that he must at once uncover and create, subjecting it, in later stages, to collective critical examination.

The loss of self to theory certainly occurs among some Marxists also. Rigid, automatic translation of educational issues into the language of class struggle and economic superstructure guarantees only linguistic facility. One must make use of both extant theory and preconceptual experience in the reconstruction of individual and social experience which is theoretical description and explanation. This dialectical relation between conception and perception is the structural essence of educational experience. Mere acquisition of others' languages is only training not education. It maintains a politically subordinate relationship between self and theory which both reflects and recreates the servitude of the masses.[17]

Recognizing one's complicity in the maintenance of oppressive social structures is work contiguous with discovering one's own voice, one's own language and views of others, and discovering, in phenomenological terms, the "things themselves." Such work can be as frightening as it is difficult. Yet the alternative seems to be loss of self to theory, as illustrated by the philosopher in Nashville. By performing only a logical transcription of phenomenological or Marxist concepts to educational situations, one remains ensconced in words, on the surface of things. The essential relation to reality is an estranged one.

While the traditions from which we come are immensely powerful in their shaping of our work, we must not be seduced by them, and become scholars of phenomenology, or of Marxism, or of psychoanalysis. We must take seriously our responsibility to face the educational issues of our time, both in their surface forms as well as in their deeper theoretical significance, a significance we must identify. This means being willing to speak in our own voices, with words while clearly related to established theoretical traditions, strictly speaking, belong to no one discipline. Almost as a kind of by-product we must be willing to attempt what our predecessors and contemporaries may have wished but never achieved. We must make curriculum studies into an autonomous discipline, with its own distinctive research methods and theoretical emphases. Of course, these methods and emphases will bear significant relation to the traditions from which they originated. However, they will not be identical or reducible to them.[18]

Here it is appropriate to note a confusion illustrated by the frequent use of the term "reconceptualism" rather than "reconceptualization." I suppose I contributed to this misunderstanding by subtitling the 1975 book of essays *Curriculum Theorizing:*

The Reconceptualists. Both terms—reconceptualists and reconceptualism—indicate something finished, something final, when
what is actually the case is a phenomenon just under way,
with divergent perspectives, with internal controversy over
several issues, which appears as an aggregate during these early
stages primarily when contrasted with the rest of the field. The
term "reconceptualization"—not reconceptualism—accurately
describes what is underway in the curriculum field in the 1970s.
The field is being transformed from an essentially non-theoreti-
cal, pseudo-pragmatic (i.e., narrowly technical) area into a theoretically potent, conceptually autonomous field which inquires
systematically into the multi-dimensional reality that is education and schooling, and most importantly, in ways that aspire to
transform both. Instead of being a handmaiden to the extant
technocratic order, we aspire to transform that order as we
work to transform ourselves and our work, from the static, the
oppressive, the deformed, to the fluid, freeing process that is
historical and individual movement.[19]

The issues examined will of course change. Stasis—in this
context indicated by an obsessive preoccupation with one issue
—must be dissolved. "Reconceptualism" suggests such a stasis
as it connotes a doctrine, a kind of party platform, endorsing,
say, children's rights. Children's rights may well be examined
and advocated as an historically appropriate issue, but our focus
on an issue must avoid obsessiveness. Any such issue is both
cause and effect of basic human themes, for instance,
oppression, and this essential ecological fabric must never be
obscured. Given other times and circumstances, other issues
must be addressed, always acknowledging their interrelationships, thus creating a comprehensive curriculum theory
which by its very nature alters that which it seeks to understand.[20]

What must constantly be attended to in a curriculum field
that is reconceptualized from the technical, pseudo-practical
tradition that is its past, reconceptualized from the narrowly
social scientific present that myopically continues its tradition,
to the emancipatory discipline it must become, is the historical-
biographical function of any given issue. For instance, does the
"back to basics" movement function to oppress even more

those already oppressed in the name of public education? Are there jobs for those who often must sacrifice their ethnic inheritance to acquire the language and skills of the white middle class? Does the "back to basics" movement function to enlarge the perspectives of the participants, allowing them to comprehend more complete and subtly the dynamics of social and psychological life in this bureaucratized society? The point is that any given issue must be examined according to its emancipatory-oppressive potential, as these illustrative questions suggest.

While raising such questions for colleagues and for the public we must attend as well as to the historical-biographic functions of this questioning for ourselves. We must be willing to expose our own activity to the same critical examination to which we subject others,' else risk mirroring the structure of social relations we criticize in schools and society generally.[21] We are, of course, embedded in social context as well; only through our participation in social schemata—for instance, forms of oppression—are we able to recognize them. The danger always for the theoretician and critic is deluding himself that identification of evils in others guarantees his freedom from them. Naming and critical comprehension do not always a exorcism make.

Particularly seductive, it seems to me, is examination of an issue which at first initiates transformation of the issue. However, the critic often remains with an issue after its emancipatory function has past. As Berlin notes in this regard: "The history of thought and culture is, as Hegel showed with great brilliance, a changing pattern of great liberating ideas which inevitably turn into suffocating straightjackets, and so stimulate their own destruction by new emancipating, and at the same time, enslaving conceptions."[22] The point here is that one must attend to the temporal life as well historical-biographic function of any given issue.

For instance, it is possible that the notion of "social control" will lose its usefulness and energy. At some point readers become numbed to descriptions and explanations of the myriad of ways schools control its inhabitants. With assistance from others we must determine when certain emphases have outlived their emancipatory lives, and have become incantation. It is also possible that the notion of "emancipation" itself will reach a similar cul-de-sac. We must not hesitate to drop it at that point, and speak of that which moves us and others on. As Kierkegaard understood, it is in the relation between the knower and the known where truth resides. The "truth," of course, is not a static set of beliefs, no catechism, but a vital, self-transformative state of being in which the relation between self and belief, self and artifact, self and other is, we may say, dialectical. Such a relation assures synthesis. In dialectical terms, arrest means a static tension between thesis and antithesis such that no synthetical resolution is possible. We must work to ensure, as much as this is possible, that our relationships to the Other—whether this "other" be belief, colleague, institution—be such that we both are synthesized into more historically progressive forms.

It is precisely at this point many social movements fail. Ideas become prized for their professional and political status, a necessarily static and dehumanizing order of valuing. Ideas become reified, pursued regardless of their psychologically and politically reactionary consequences. If the avant-garde falls prey to the delusion that it alone understands the character of the synthesis to come, of which it is necessarily only an antecedent element, it fails to honor its educative function. It attempts to stipulate the character of that which in principle cannot be known. In such instances an avant-garde becomes fascistic, dictating what change must come, when. Its doctrine, however humanistic its platform might sound, functions primarily to aggrandize its own professional and political position, and diminish that of others.

Those reconceptualists who have refused to acknowledge the reality and promise of the reconceptualization have done so, in part, in protest of the process of being defined by another. Such protest is healthy, but its time is now past. The reconceptualization, I am suggesting, is fundamentally a dialectical relation among knowers, knowing, and the known. Its thematic character must and will be identified and constructed through the discourse and scholarship of its participants. To imagine it a finished product, a doctrine, is to miss its point. What is essential about the reconceptualization—as the literal definition of the word denotes—is its constant redefinition. The question that serves as a title to this paper is a question that serves to invite your participation in its answering. For it is ourselves who shape our relations among each other, to colleagues in other disciplines, to the American public. The order of contribution to that public and its educational system is contingent in inescapable ways upon the quality of our self-constitution. We cannot expect to meaningfully participate in the transformation of the nation and its educational institutions if we fail to authentically participate in the constitution and transformation of ourselves and our work.

References

1. James B. Macdonald, "Curriculum Theory." In W. Pinar (ed.), *Curriculum Theorizing: The Reconceptualists* (5-13). Berkeley: McCutchan.

2. See the preface, *Curriculum Theorizing: The Reconceptualists*; also "The Reconceptualization of Curriculum Studies, *Journal of Curriculum Studies*, in press, and "Notes on the Curriculum Field 1978, *Educational Researcher*, in press.

3. W. Pinar (ed.), *Curriculum Theorizing: The Reconceptualists*. Berkeley: McCutchan, 1975.

4. Ralph W. Tyler, *Basic Principles of Curriculum and Instruction*. Chicago: University of Chicago Press, 1950. Mauritz M. Johnson, "Definitions and Models of Curriculum Theory," *Educational Theory* 17 (2), 1967, pp. 127-139.

5. Curriculum Theory Conference held on the campus of the University of Wisconsin-Milwaukee, November, 1976, chairs: Alex Molnar and John Zahorik. Proceedings (partial) published as *Curriculum Theory*. Washington, DC: ASCD, 1977.

6. At this point it is planned that *The Journal of Curriculum Theorizing* will sponsor these meetings and publish the proceedings. Those interested in submitting a paper proposal should contact a member of the editorial member of *JCT*.

7. Books include *Heightened Consciousness, Cultural Revolution, and Curriculum Theory* (McCutchan, 1974), *Curriculum Theorizing: The Reconceptualists* (McCutchan, 1975), *Schools in Search of Meaning* (ASCD, 1975), *Toward a Poor Curriculum* (Kendall/Hunt, 1976), *Curriculum Theory* (ASCD, 1977). At a 1976 conference held at the State University of New York at Geneseo, Professors Apple, Greene, Kliebard, and Huebner spoke. Each of these names has been been associated with the Reconceptualization. Proceedings were published in *Curriculum Inquiry*. Those who chaired this meeting—Professors P. DeMarte and J. Rosario—did not see the meeting in the tradition of the others.

8. Professor Johnson has hardly been alone in such attempts.

9. For an introductory discussion of critical theory, see R. J. Bernstein, *The Restructuring of Social and Political Theory*, New York: Harcourt, Brace & Jovanovich, 1976.

10. Michael W. Apple, "The Hidden Curriculum and the Nature of Conflict," in W. Pinar (ed.), *Curriculum Theorizing*, pp. 95-119.

11. See, for instance, Joel Spring, *The Sorting Machine*, New York: David McKay, Inc., 1976. Michael Young and Geoff Whitty, *Society, State, and Schooling*. London: Falmer Press, 1977.

12. See his "Persistent Curriculum Issues in Historical Perspective," and "Bureaucracy and Curriculum Theory, in Pinar (ed.), *Curriculum Theorizing*, McCutchan, 1975.

13. Dwayne E. Huebner, "Curriculum Language and Classroom Meanings," *Ibid.*, pp. 217-236.

14. Jurgen Habermas, *Knowledge and Human Interests*. Trans. J. J. Shapiro. Boston: Beacon Press, 1971.

15. In Pinar (ed.), *Curriculum Theorizing*, pp. 359-383.

16. See, for instance, the work of Karier, Katz, Spring.

17. See Paulo Freire, *Pedagogy of the Oppressed* (New York: Herder & Herder, 1971), for a discussion of the dynamics of oppression.

18. We can expect skepticism and hostility from colleagues who do not believe such a field can develop.

19. Of course the two extremes ordinarily intermingle. Nonetheless it is appropriate to state the aspiration in its extreme form.

20. This is an "ecological" view, in that if "a" is altered, the entire system is affected, including specific element "b."

21. See Alvin W. Gouldner, *The Coming Crisis of Western Sociology* (New York: Basic Books, 1970) for a discussion of this matter, which he conceives of as a sociology of sociology.

22. Isiah Berlin, "Does Political Theory Still Exist?" *Philosophy, Politics and Society* (2nd series), edited by Peter Laslett & W. G. Runciman, p. 19.

VI

Notes on the Curriculum Field
(1978)

Decker Walker concludes his recent discussion of the state of the field in this way: "I have the disquieting feeling that to justify its continued existence, research in curriculum will have to do more than increase our comprehension of curricular realities. It may also have to create new curricular possibilities, if it and public education are to survive. Comprehension is a good first step toward improvement, but it is not enough."[1]

I wish to discuss the history of Professor Walker's "disquieting feeling" by sketching briefly the recent history of the field. In so doing I will underscore the ideas "curricular possibilities" and "improvement" as these have been understood in the field, and why "comprehension" is viewed as a "first step." Finally, I will lay out in summary fashion a reconceptualization of these important ideas, referring to the work of Jurgen Habermas, especially his work on knowledge and human interests, the confusion of the technical and the practical, and the relation between theory and practice. Richard Bernstein's *The Restructuring of Social and Political Theory*[2] will be my sourcebook.

A map of the field

What is the state of the art in curriculum? It strikes me as a curious question. I can imagine its use in the present context only in order to avoid the use—or misuse our colleagues in natural science might argue—of the term "science." More than a few of our colleagues in areas like educational psychology, as well as in natural science, regard the curriculum field as in a primitive stage of scientific development. The title of this address [i.e. the 1978 AERA Division B State-of-the-Art address] acknowledges this much, but in so doing misuses the term "art." Neither the literature of this field, nor current practices of curriculum development, strike me as artful in any serious way. I conclude that this title originates only in the need to acknowledge the non-scientific character of this field. I accept that the field is not scientific; I insist it is not artful.[3] Let it be explicit that this paper attempts to answer the question I take to be behind the question printed in the program, namely: what is the state of the field?

If we are to take Professor Walker's recent study as indicative, we must answer that the state of the field is tentative. He concludes that curriculum research has increased our comprehension of curriculum but that in order for it to continue, curriculum research may have to create new curricular possibilities. The first step toward improvement has been taken, at least in part, and the second step—improvement—must follow.

Implicit in this idea is the widely-held view among what Bernstein terms "mainstream social science" that the improvement of practice involves the application of empirically-verified theory.[4] Now I do not think that Professor Walker is a strict adherent of this social scientific view, but he accepts tacitly a version of it. It is suggested in the structure of this sentence: "comprehension is a good first step toward improvement, but it is not enough." I will suggest, relying on Habermas, that such a view of theory a practice is sure not to lead to any serious improvement in the public schools.

Another widely held view is that theory is not essential to the improvement of practice; in fact, it may deter such progress. This a view associated with some traditionalists in the field. With mention of traditionalists, permit me to acknowledge the "map" of the field I am employing.[5] I discriminate among traditionalists, conceptual-empiricists, and reconceptualists. Extremely briefly and for the moment, I will describe them.

Recent history of the field

Traditionalists value service to practitioners above all else, and this service is more important than the development of an integrating theory or conducting research (as this term is used by mainstream social scientists), although some traditionalists would maintain that theoretical considerations and research findings may be employed with discretion. Ralph Tyler is the traditionalist par excellance. There are other nearly as visible traditionalists whom I will mention when I describe this category in more detail.

Conceptual-empiricists, the second group, define those terms according to mainstream social science. They tend to be trained in social science, and regard service to practitioners subsequent to years of research, although of course even one study may have "implications." Decker Walker may be regarded as a visible conceptual-empiricist. Reconceptualist is as a broad a category as the first two. These scholars tend to be prepared in the humanities, but even those whose backgrounds are social science tend to hold theoretical considerations above the conducting of quantitative research. They have not (even if some maintain they have for the time being) abandoned school practitioners, but fundamental to their view is that an intellectual distance from our constituency is required for the present, in order to develop a comprehensive critique and theoretical program that might be of assistance later. Let me develop these characterizations as I sketch a recent history of the field, a history that begins in the late nineteen fifties when the curriculum field was identified with those in 1978 I identify as traditionalists. As with all "maps," there is a continuum where the divisions suggest unconnected, discrete entities.

As the title to Professor Tyler famous book[6] indicates, traditionalists have tended to be concerned about "principles" and other considerations which are said then to guide curriculum development and implementation. The term "theory has been employed to indicate that such principles are abstractions from the actual experience of practitioners, and often at variance with actual practice. In a social scientific sense of the term, or in the sense it is used in the humanities, traditionalists have not been theoretical. In their books they have focused on school-people, and they present an overview of considerations imagined pertinent to these readers. Prototypical traditionalists include Alexander, R. Doll, Saylor, Shores, Smith-Stanley-

Shores, Stratemeyer, Taba, and in the present time McNeil, the Tanners, and Zais.[7] It is service to school practitioners that distinguishes traditionalists; service is more important than research or the development of theory. Many traditionalists tend to be former schoolpeople, and they tend to remain loyal to their former colleagues. This is understandable historically. [As you recall, the field began in the nineteen twenties as a response to a practical and administrative concern for curriculum matters, and not as a conceptual extension of extant field, as we can say of educational psychology, for instance. The first curricularists, then, were school teachers whose interest in curriculum led them out of the classroom and into administrative offices.][8]

In one sense it was the closeness of the relationship between traditionalists and schoolteachers that maintained the atheoretical and ahistorical character of the field. Working so closely with our clients, and working so continuously to speak to their questions, forbade us the intellectual distance necessary, in part, to generate adequate curriculum theory. It was the very instrumentality of traditionalists, with its constant and enslaving preoccupation with the classroom, which made likely the fact that no meaningful and systematic understanding of that classroom could develop.

Many traditionalists have been conscious—at times painfully—of this inadequacy. These individuals were not surprised, I would guess, when cognate field specialists were selected to lead the so-called curriculum reform movement of the 1960s. Curricularists were used infrequently during this time, and then primarily as consultants. This bypass was a kind of deathblow to a field whose primary justification was its expertise in an area now dominated by subject specialists. The field has yet to recover from this event.

During the curriculum reform movement the field began to undergo a fundamental transformation. The appearance of conceptual-empiricists in the field in the 1960s was part of the rise of the social sciences. The basic premise is that a scientific knowledge of human behavior (a subset of which would involve curriculum) is possible. Of course, the notion of "science" is very much allied with a natural science model for social science.

As Robert Merton observed: "Between twentieth-century physics and twentieth-century sociology stands billions of man-hours of sustained, disciplined, and cumulative research."[9] Of course, there are substantial disagreements among social scientists over several methodological and theoretical issues, but it is a shared fundamental assumption among mainstream social scientists— who accept that social science can and must be modeled in some way and in some measure upon natural science— that increasingly refined methodologies and sustained "cumulative" research will bring about a science of human behavior.[10]

It is understandable that this view, one that is so persuasive partly due to the "success" of natural scientists and those who have applied their basic research to help construct a technocratic society, would enter the curriculum field. If the traditionalists' "basic principles" were acknowledged to be of little use—at least by those who funded the 1960s curriculum reform movement—then the "problem" became one of creating knowledge of great use.[11] The "solution" lay with social science research. Enter the conceptual-empiricists, curricularists trained, increasingly nearly exclusively, in mainstream social science, and often ignorant of the field's history. This ahistorical view, not original with conceptual-empiricists, is in some degree inevitable with social science. If any knowledge worth possessing is yet to be discovered, there is little point in studying the unscientific past.

Conceptual-empiricists argue that their research functions to serve school practitioners. By creating a science of curriculum, the traditional aspiration of the field can be realized. What distinguishes conceptual-empiricists from traditionalists is the allegiance of the former to social science. Traditionalists' allegiance has been to practitioners and to "kids." Conceptual-empiricists seem to have their eyes more upon their colleagues in social science fields (upon creating nomological knowledge) than upon practitioners, who at times, given their participation in experiments, seem a means to other ends (nomological knowledge). Such a view is characteristic of mainstream social science. But it can be understood another way.

The bypass of traditionalists by the curriculum reform movement weakened the justification for traditional curricularists in colleges of education. In the 1970s, with less money for new curriculum proposals, with fewer opportunities for in-service programs and thereby fewer opportunities to demonstrate curriculum leadership in the schools, traditionalists' presence in colleges of education became increasingly dependent upon others' assessment of the intellectual quality of their writing, not its popularity with practitioners. Thus the position of traditionalists, which is to say the field of curriculum itself, deteriorated. Numerous efforts were made to put the field back to its prior status—among them several theory-building efforts such as the ASCD commission on curriculum theory.[12] While such efforts stimulated an interest in theory, the general trend continued. In 1970s Schwab would pronounce the field "moribund," a diagnosis to be repeated six years later by Dwayne Huebner.[13] The only pulse detectable was the work of conceptual-empiricists, and in the early 1970s it seemed that if a curriculum field were to survive, it would be as another colony of mainstream social science.

There appears now, however, to be another set of heirs to this field. James Macdonald in a 1971 article mapping curriculum research, described this group:

> A third group of individuals looks upon the task of theorizing as a creative intellectual task which they maintain should be neither used as a basis for prescription or an empirically testable set of principles and relationships. The purpose of these persons is to develop and criticize conceptual schema in the hope that new ways of talking about curriculum, which may in the future be far more fruitful than present orientations, will be forthcoming. At the present time, they would maintain that a much more playful, free-floating process is called for by the state of the art.[14]

Many of these individuals met at a conference in 1973 at the University of Rochester, and yearly conferences ensued.[15] Four publications emphasizing this work, including the 1975 ASCD yearbook, have appeared, and are receiving considerable attention.[16] A journal supporting theoretical scholarship is scheduled for publication in the autumn (1978).[17] These individuals I have characterized as reconceptualists, although the term is controversial.[18]

Metatheoretical context

In other places I have described these three groups and what their work indicates regarding the state of the field.[19] Today I wish to situate the three groups in a metatheoretical context, the broad outlines of which are provided by Richard J. Bernstein in his *The Restructuring of Social and Political Theory*. This study of the status of the three major metatheoretical orientations in the social sciences—empirical theory, phenomenology, and critical theory—is useful in distancing ourselves from the present state of the field. Herbert Kliebard, speaking to the professors of curriculum group in Minneapolis in 1973, discussed the distinction between the generalist and the specialist in a way which illumines the function of critical distance.

The specialist can be likened to one studying, on his knees let us say, an area of a hillside. He or she examines carefully, in detail, over time, an area of, say five square yards. He or she discovers aspects of this area which only such in-depth study can permit. The generalist, on the other hand, can be likened to one aloft with, say, a hang-glider. He is two hundred feet above the ground, and from his perspective, he can see the specialist, there over to the left, and the overall pattern of the countryside, a pattern not discernible to the specialist. While the specialist gains information not possible for the generalist to obtain, she cannot see the broader context in which this information occurs. It is the generalist who sees this, and understands the limitations of the specialists' perspective. Similarly, by leaving the corner of the field we have studied—curriculum—and situating ourselves in a broader point of view, we can comprehend more completely the relation of our area to others, illumining areas we previously could not see.

The point of view I sketch today has three aspects. Each of these is an important issue which cuts across disciplines. The first is the matter of the technical and the practical; the second is the relation between knowledge and human interests; and the third is the relation between theory and practice. Each of these is important to the work of curricularists. To discuss them, I will turn to Bernstein, and his discussion of critical theory, primarily the critical theory formulated by the German philosopher Jurgen Habermas. Habermas' work is ambitious and covers a wide area. I will confine myself to his analysis of these three issues.

The first issue Habermas regard as the fundamental problem of contemporary social and political theory. He characterizes this as the confusion of the practical and the technical. Isolating three basic principles from the work of Thomas Hobbes, Habermas lays out the nature of this confusion.

> First the claim of scientifically grounded social philosophy aims at establishing once and for all the conditions for the correct order of the state and society as such. Its assertions are to be valid independently of place, time, and circumstances, and to permit an enduring foundation for communal life, regardless of the historical situation. Second, the translation of knowledge into practice, the application, is a technical one. With a knowledge of the general conditions for a correct order of the state and of society, a practical prudent action of human beings toward each other is no longer required, but what is required instead is the correctly calculated generation of rules, relationships, and institutions. Third, human behavior is therefore to be now considered only as the material for science. The engineers of the correct order can disregard the categories of ethical social intercourse and confine themselves to the construction of conditions under which human beings, just like objects within nature, will necessarily behave in a calculable manner. This separation of politics from morality replaces instruction in leading a good and just life with making possible a life of well-being with a correctly instituted order.[20]

The practical question—how can one provide a practical orientation about what is right and just in a given situation—evaporates, and is replaced by the technical one involving increasingly subtle control of human behavior. Habermas notes that in advanced industrial societies there exists:

> ... an escalating scale of continually expanded technical control over nature, a continually refined administration of human beings and their relations to each other by means of social organization. In this system, science, technology, industry, and administration interlock in a circular process. In this process the relationship of theory to praxis can now only assert itself as the purposive-rational application of techniques assured by empirical science. The social potential of science is reduced to the powers of technical control—its potential for enlightened action is no longer considered. The empirical, analytical sciences produce technical recommendations, but they furnish no answer to practical questions.[21]

This lack of answers is a familiar lamentation in the curriculum field. Above all else, the traditional function of curriculum theory is to guide practice: curriculum development, design, and evaluation. This guidance, if we reflect momentarily, is not of a prudential sort. It is technical. The sense was that adequate curriculum theory could be applied to practical situations, transforming them from unordered potentially chaotic situations to ones of smooth and consensual procedure. I overstate here only a bit. This identification of the practical with the technical expresses, in a profound way, the state of the curriculum field. Before the reconceptualist literature, one is hard pressed to find curriculum writing which escapes this confusion. One such illustration may be Ian Westbury's 1972 essay on the Aristotelian art of rhetoric and Schwab's sense of the practical, which may be an attempt to restore a classical view of the practical.[22]

Clearly, the traditionalists attempt to write about the practical in some systematic way. Understandably these curricularists express the zeitgeist and write instead about the technical. The writing is not always sophisticated in a technical way, but its impersonality and attempt at generalization and procedure indicate its genesis in the spirit of the technical. The idiosyncrasy of actual situations, the lived quality, the ethical dimension, the aesthetic: as Huebner[23] has written, these disappear into the procedural.

The confusion of the practical and the technical is possible only in a scientific age, a time when science is the measure of what is and what is not legitimate knowledge. Habermas captures this historical development succinctly in his discussion of the "dissolution of epistemology," and its reduction to the philosophy of science. The classical and traditional interest in modalities of knowing—epistemology—has become in our time a concern for scientific knowing: "For the philosophy of science that emerged since the mid-nineteenth century as the heir of the theory of knowledge is methodology pursued with a scientistic understanding of the sciences. 'Scientism' means science's belief in itself; that is, the conviction that we can no longer understand science as one form of possible knowledge, but rather must identify knowledge with science."[24]

With this historical understanding of our present situation, we can almost regard as inevitable that conceptual-empiricists followed traditionalists. If the difficulty was that traditional framings of curriculum were insufficiently rigorous and excessively haphazard—and from a scientific perspective such a judgment is easy to make—then the "solution" lay with rigor and systematic quantitative research. Because traditionalists tended to be atheoretical they lacked any potent defense against these charges. The practical becomes even more closely identified with the technical, and the language of curriculum is reduced further to the objective language of the procedural with its atemporal, ahistorical quality. Beauchamp's *Curriculum Theory* is an example par excellance.[25]

Habermas appears to distance himself from this situation, characterized as it is by the intellectual dominance of the natural and mainstream social sciences. From this point of view he identifies three cognitive interests: these are the technical, the practical, and the emancipatory. He writes: "the approach of the empirical-analytic sciences incorporates a technical cognitive interest; that of the historical-hermeneutic sciences incorporates a practical one; and the approach of critical oriented sciences incorporates the emancipatory cognitive interest."[26] Each of these is associated with one fundamental dimension of human life. Work is associated with the technical interest; interaction with the practical interest guiding the historical-hermeneutic disciplines; and power is associated with the emancipatory interest guiding the critical disciplines, i.e. the critical social sciences. Habermas emphasizes that these interests are non-reducible, and he criticizes any attempt—whether by empiricists or by historical disciplines—to claim that one interest provides the most fundamental understanding of the world.[27]

That said, it is clear that Habermas regards the third interest —the emancipatory one—as the most basic one, although the other two cannot be reduced to it. It is the most basic in that the technical and practical interests can be pursued only to the extent that the conditions for free, open communication are present. Such conditions demand an open, self-critical community of inquirers. Habermas concludes that implicit in the technical and practical interests is a requirement for the intellectual and material conditions for emancipation, i.e., an ideal state in which free, open interactions can occur.[28]

The technical interest alone cannot maintain such a perspective; it accepts what is static and deformed in the historical present as timeless. It becomes, in its absorption with the application of "knowhow," the static and the deformed. The notion of emancipatory interest, however, provides the epistemological basis for a quite different function for the social sciences. Habermas terms these the critical social sciences, performing as they do a certain order of critique which is not static but freeing in its effect. Habermas writes:

> The systematic *sciences of social action*, that is economics, sociology, and political science, have the goal, as do the empirical-analytic sciences, of producing nomological knowledge. A critical social science, however, will not remain satisfied with this. It is concerned with going beyond this goal to determine when theoretical statements grasp invariant regularities of social action as such and when they express ideologically frozen relations of dependence that can in principle be transformed. To the extent that is the case, the *critique of ideology*, as well, moreover, as *psycho-analysis*, take into account that information about lawlike connections sets off a process of reflection in the consciousness of those whom the laws are about. Thus the level of [nonreflective] consciousness, which is one of the initial conditions of such laws, can be transformed. Of course, to this end, a critically mediated knowledge of laws cannot through reflection alone render a law itself inoperative, but can render it inapplicable.
>
> The methodological framework that determines the meaning of the validity of critical propositions of this category is established by the concept of *self-reflection*. The latter releases the subject from dependence on hypostatized powers. Self-reflection is determined by an emancipatory cognitive interest.[29]

Habermas then cites psychoanalysis as a discipline the essential method of which is systematic self-reflection. It requires, Bernstein notes, a "depth hermeneutics." Habermas: "The technique of dream interpretation goes beyond the art of hermeneutics insofar as it must grasp not only the meaning of a possibly distorted text, but the meaning of the text distortion itself, that is the transformation of a latent dream thought into the manifest dream. That is the transformation of a latent dream thought into the manifest dream. In other words, it

must reconstruct what Freud called the dreamwork."[30]   Such
work is not disinterested. The psychoanalyst is guided by his
interest in assisting the patient to move through his suffering
and be released from the debilitating symptoms from which he
suffers. This can be achieved only to the extent that the analyst
is successful in assisting the patient to become conscious of his
distinctive self-formative process. The "act of understanding to
which it leads is self-reflection."[31]

Habermas agrees with Freud that this sort of emancipatory
self-understanding cannot come through the analyst's imparting
information to the patient, or merely by applying psychoanalytic theory in a technical or strategic manner. What is necessary is a coming to consciousness by the patient, a process that
functions to dissolve resistances. Freud warns in this regard:

> The pathological factor is not his (the patient's ignorance) in itself, but
> the root of the ignorance in his inner resistances. It was they that first
> called this ignorance into being, and they still maintain it now. The
> task of the treatment lies in combating these resistances. Informing
> the patient of what he does not know because he is repressed it is only
> one of the necessary preliminaries to treatment. If knowledge about
> the unconscious were as important for the patient as people inexperi-
> enced in psychoanalysis imagine, listening to lectures or reading books
> would be enough to cure him.[32]

So it is the patient's own recollection and reconstruction of
his or her past that is the central knowledge in this procedure.
A technical manipulation of the patient by the analyst is by no
means sufficient. What is necessary is a setting off, in the
patient, of a process of depth self-reflection. Habermas comments: "First it includes two movements equally: the cognitive,
and the affective and motivational. It is critique in the sense
that the analytic power to dissolve dogmatic attitudes inheres in
analytic insight. Critique terminates in a transformation of the
affective-motivational basis, just as it begins with the need for
practical transformation. Critique would not have the power to
break up false consciousness if it were not impelled by a
passion for critique."[33]

It is psychoanalysis, then, that offers an illustrative structure
of an emancipatory discipline. Habermas is careful to note that
he regards as questionable and largely expendable those con-

ceptual categories by which psychoanalysis understands the patient's "text." It is the structure of psychoanalysis, its basis in self-reflection assisted by a pedagogue who is the analyst, that is pertinent to the formulation of critical social science.

What would an emancipatory discipline of curriculum look like? That is not clear to me, although my sense is that the movement in the field that is the reconceptualization aspires to such work. At the present time, reconceptualists generally are preoccupied with a comprehensive critique of the field as it is, a field immersed in pseudo-practical, technical modes of understanding and action.[34] The understanding is that to realize the aspiration of the field we must repudiate the dominant trends by examining their domain assumptions, such as the notion of technical interest. In a sense, the reconceptualization becomes more fully intelligible as it viewed as a surfacing in the curriculum field of the same historical moment which has surfaced in philosophy as critical theory. As a student of these matters in the social sciences, Bernstein detects "an emerging new sensibility that, while still very fragile, is leading to a restructuring of social and political theory."[35] Reconceptualists, in historical context, can be seen not as isolated, reactive curricularists, but as colleagues in a multidisciplinary transformation of fundamental issues in the human disciplines.

A danger I see in a coming stage of the reconceptualization is a flight from our responsibility to create new curriculum theory by becoming scholars of critical theory and phenomenology.[36] The temptation is powerful; such scholarship offers intellectual and psychological security, or at least the illusion of same. But critical theory and phenomenology are movements in philosophy, not in curriculum, and while explication of that work is necessary and fruitful for us, a retreat to the explication of philosophical texts represents an evasion of our professional responsibility. As curricularists we must address ourselves to the historically-established concerns of the curriculum field. We must continue to address ourselves to our contemporary in the field: to traditionalists and conceptual-empiricists. We must explicate the nature of our efforts, and at the same time, attempt to offer our work in ways which will permit others—not yet on the scene—to make syntheses of reconceptualized cur-

riculum theory and traditional and conceptual-empirical curriculum theory. The field to finally emerge will not be one
created solely from the hands of reconceptualists, but from the
hands of us all. The quality of that field yet to come, and concomitantly, the quality of that field's contribution to American
education, is very much reliant upon our capacity to move
through this complex, difficult time in the field. We must move
ahead with our theoretical program while keeping one eye to
grand syntheses, of which our own work will be but one, albeit,
important, part.

Such syntheses are some time off. The state of the field today
is fragmented and repressed. Reconceptualized notions of curriculum are not widely understood.[37] These notions aspire to
be intellectual independent of the so-called cognate field, and
aspire to produce emancipatory knowledge. One such notion,
potentially, I submit, is the theory of curriculum I have been
developing with Madeleine R. Grumet.[38] Fundamental to our
view is the sense that curriculum research must emancipate the
researcher if it is to authentically offer such a possibility to
others. We have devised a method by means of which the
researcher can examine his or her "limit situations," in Freire's
sense, his or her own participation in frozen social and psychological structures, and his or her complicity in the arrest of
intellectual development characteristic of American schooling.
Essential to our formulation is acknowledgement of the false
duality of "self" and "world." Human being is irrevocably
"being-in-the-world." The world is both cause and consequence
of the conditioned and the chosen in human life. Our aspiration is to gain increasing access to that which is conditioned,
allow it to surface, to be released or permitted to remain (in
either case in consciousness), hence open to the conscious
intentions of the individual. It is the repression of the primitive, as Jung[39] never tired of emphasizing, that has been a cost
of technocratic-industrial civilization. The primitive—including
the violent and erotic—is repressed and forgotten, but not
gone.[40] It is projected, in classic psychoanalytic fashion, onto
television and film screens, the same violence and sexual
hunger banned from the conscious arenas of daily life. They

are banned presently in unconscious subversive ways, ways which enslave us. The point for curricularists is this: the generally debilitating, arrested condition of American culture forbids profound intellectual movement and achievement. In disagreement with Freud, who tended to insist that repression is the necessary cost for intellectual achievement, it is clear in our time that intellectual movement, the fluidity of mind which we associate with the overused term creativity, the order of intellectual advance for which the movement of twentieth-century physics is one exemplar, is very much reliant upon, let us say, a certain fluidity of being. Such ontological movement, dialectically related to cultural movement, can be initiated and maintained through conscious work with oneself and others, work allowing to surface material now frozen in unconsciousness.[41] Such surfacing must be attended to cautiously, and control—of some fundamental sort that is not repressive—maintained. This subtle, complicated process occurs without psychotherapeutic structuring, without the method of *currere*. However, Grumet and I have found that discriminating, sensitive use of the method with interested students helps melt, if you will, intellectual blocks or frozen areas, and allows intellectual movement. Individual intellectual movement occurs in relation to others— those present physically as teachers and other students—and through print in books and other artifacts. This movement occurs in the context of individual life history; when it occurs it is educational experience. In this sense we research the role of curriculum in educational experience. Other modes of emancipatory curriculum research must be formulated.

The final area I wish to outline is the important issue of theory and practice. Habermas' view of their relation is helpful. In the fourth edition of *Theory and Practice* he writes:

> The mediation of theory and praxis can only be clarified if to begin with we distinguish three functions, which are measured in terms of different criteria; the formation and extension of critical theorems, which can stand up to scientific discourse; the organization of processes of enlightenment, in which such theorems are applied and can be tested in a unique manner by the initiation of processes of reflection carried on with certain groups toward which these processes have been directed; and the selection of appropriate strategies, the solution of tactical questions, and the conduct of political struggle. On the first

level, the aim is true statements, on the second authentic insights, and on the third, prudent decision.[42]

Recently, Habermas has stressed this third function of the mediation of theory and praxis, "the selection of appropriate strategies, the solution of tactical questions, and the conduct of political struggle." In attempting to answer recent criticism that he has abandoned the project of unifying theory and practice, Habermas notes that such unification is problematic, for political action does not automatically follow from a transformed consciousness. In fact, he argues that theory can never be used directly to justify political action. When it is demanded that theoretical statements provide absolute authority in determining what is to be done in the arena of social action, Habermas insists that both theory and praxis are deformed.[43] He writes:

> Stalinist praxis has furnished the fatal proof that a party organization which proceeds instrumentally and a Marxism which has degenerated into a science of apologetics complement each other only too well (TP, 36).... Theory cannot have the same function for the organization of action, of the political struggle, as it has for the organization of enlightenment. The practical consequences of self-reflection are changes in attitude which result from insight into causalities in the past, and indeed result of themselves. In contrast, strategic action oriented toward the future, which is prepared for in the internal discussion of groups, who (as the avant-garde) presuppose for themselves already successfully completed processes of enlightenment, cannot be justified in the same manner by reflective knowledge.[44]

The distinction among unconstrained, theoretical discourse, enlightenment, and strategic political action are important. In a sense, Bernstein notes, Habermas would seem to be closer to Hegel, and to Freud, than he would seem to be to Marx. This is so given that the immediate aim of critique is insight into the past. Thus it is retrospective as it aspires to initiate a process of self-reflection by which awareness of, and liberation from, the compulsion of the past are possible. As Hegel noted, the order of freedom the bondsman realizes as he becomes conscious that he has a mind of his own, is in a sense abstract and empty. It is not yet concrete freedom, and it arises in a world in which nothing has materially changed.[45]

Habermas stresses this essential point again.

The organization of action must be distinguished from this process of enlightenment. While the theory legitimizes the work of enlighten-ment, as well as providing its own refutation when communication fails, and can, in any case, be corrected, it can by no means legitimize a fortiori the risky decisions of strategic action. Decisions for the politi-cal struggle, cannot at the outset be justified theoretically and then be carried out organizationally. The sole possible justification at this level is consensus aimed at in practical discourse, among the participants, who, in the consciousness of their common interests and their knowl-edge of circumstances, of the predictable consequences and secondary consequences, are the only ones who can know the risks they are will-ing to undergo, and with what expectations. There can be no theory which at the outset can assure a world-historical mission in return for the potential sacrifices.[46]

This acknowledgement of a gap between theoretical justifica-tion and strategic action is interpreted by many as a grand "cop-out." For those who insist that unifying theory and practice means that theory tells us procedurally how to transform social reality, such a conclusion may be inevitable. Whether these interpreters by "vulgar Marxists" or "bourgeois engineers," they are attempting, in Bernstein's judgment, to reduce all strategic action to technical manipulation. The desire here is for a science and theory sufficiently secure that definitive judgments as to procedure are possible. Those Marxists who insist such a science is possible, even inevitable, follow in the tradition of the great bourgeois thinker Thomas Hobbes. They accept the central aim of his project, i.e. the achievement of a science of human beings which would provide the authoritative foundation for reconstructing society. When Marxists insist that Marxism is the true science, they fail to comprehend that they have succeeded only in making science into ideology.[47]

Habermas is attending here to an ambiguity seemingly intrinsic to the human condition. That is, as a species, as an individual, one seems never to be in a position to know abso-lutely that enlightenment has in fact occurred, that without doubt it has released one from the constraints of the past and initiated genuine self-reflection. The subtlety, persistence, and strength of the various forms of resistance and delusion; the inadequacy of intellectual understanding alone to effect complete transformation; the ever-present possibility that enlightened understanding may be, finally, another form of illusion: such considerations insist that the evaluation of the success or failure of critique must always be tentative in some degree.[48]

For some, this tentativeness brings discouragement. Such a response I regard as unwarranted. The inherent incapacity of theory to provide a definitive program of social action, in the present context for teachers, administrators, curriculum developers and evaluators, does not mean that the quality of strategy cannot be attended to. While strategy does not follow from theory in an explicit, conceptual, and predictable way, the pre-conceptual ground for strategy does have significance for the quality of strategy. An "enlightened" person, a person engaged in continual self-reflexive examination of his or her experience, will communicate that relation of self to self to others, even if material conditions force strategic action that is in some measure unacceptably modest. If the individual is preoccupied with the technical manipulation of his or her behavior to force a desired outcome, even if this outcome is claimed as humanistic, the social experience of this behavior is one of technical manipulation. The following may help clarify this slippery but important matter.

Perhaps you recall Kierkegaard's mocking of certain groups in nineteenth-century Danish society: businessmen, rushing to keep appointments; churchmen and theologians, establishing doctrines of sinless behavior while jockeying for political position within the church; and university professors, particularly Hegel of course, who vaulted themselves into god-like perspectives, divested of their individuality and location. The learning of many theologians and scholars was exceptional, yet their sensibilities were brittle, dehumanizing. What had been the function of learning for such people? Function is indicated by the character of sensibility, which is in one sense prior to the character of participation in the social world. Any use of knowledge to arrest the development of the individual, suggested by its use to aggrandize one's social position or to mystify one's political action, indicate that "the relation of the knower to the known" is an enslaving one. The quality of knowledge produced and the quality of strategic action taken when such a relation exists, are necessarily enslaving.

The production of curriculum knowledge is important to the advancement of the field. However, if this production does not originate in an emancipatory intention but in a static one—such as an essentially atheoretical accumulation of a "body of knowledge," or the application of theory (i.e. comprehension) to practice (i.e. improvement)—then no fundamental movement in the historical situation can occur. The state of the field is arrest. For movement to occur, we must shift our attention from the technical and the practical, and dwell on the notion of emancipation. Not until we are in emancipatory relation to our work will we devise theory and formulate strategic action which will, in Walker's term, "improve" the nation's schools.

Notes

1. Walker, D. F. Toward Comprehension of Curricular Realities. In Shulman, L. (Ed.), *Review of Research in Education*. Vol. 4. Itasca, IL: F. E. Peacock, 1977.

2. Bernstein, R. J. *The Restructuring of Social and Political Theory*. New York: Harcourt, Brace, Jovanovich, 1976. The first page number listed in the upcoming citations refers to the Bernstein text, the second to Habermas' texts. Bernstein argues persuasively that mainstream social science, of which educational psychology is generally an example, is not scientific in a strict naturalistic sense.

3. In my writing and in the writing of other reconceptualists, there is the attempt, clumsy as it may be at this stage, to attend to the aesthetic aspect of theoretical discourse. See, for instance, Grumet, M., "Another Voice," in Pinar, W. & Grumet, M. (976), *Toward a Poor Curriculum*. Dubuque, IA: Kendall/Hunt.

4. Bernstein, p. 6.

5. See also Pinar, W., "The Reconceptualization of Curriculum Studies." *Journal of Curriculum Studies*, in press.

6. Tyler, R. W. *Basic Principles of Curriculum and Instruction*. Chicago: University of Chicago Press, 1949.

7. Taba, H. *Curriculum Development: Theory and Practice*. New York: Harcourt, Brace, & World, 1962. Saylor, G. & Alexander, W. *Curriculum Planning for Modern Schools*. New York: Holt, Rinehart, & Winston, 1966. Tanner, D. & Tanner, L. *Curriculum Development: Theory and Practice*. New York: Macmillan, 1975. McNeil, J. D. *Curriculum: A Comprehensive Introduction*. Boston: Little, Brown, 1977. Zais, R. *Curriculum: Principles and Foundations*. New York: Thomas Crowell, 1975.

8. For a discussion of the origin of the curriculum field, see Cremin, L., "Curriculum-making in the United States," in W. Pinar (Ed.), *Curriculum Theorizing: The Reconceptualists* (pp. 19-35). Berkeley: McCutchan.

9. Bernstein, p. 8.

10. Pertinent here is Bernstein's discussion of the fallacious assumption widely held by mainstream social scientists that a field must pass through a kind of "dark age" before achieving genuine scientific status. See Bernstein, p. 99.

11. Interesting in this regard is the name of the American Educational Research Association Special Interest Group in Curriculum: Knowledge Creation and Utilization in Curriculum.

12. See Elizabeth Maccia's report of her work as consultant to this commission in her "Curriculum Theory and Policy," mimeographed, presented to AERA, Chicago, 1965. A companion commission on Instructional Theory, in contrast, produced a clean-cut "scientific" point of view. See Gordon, I. *Criteria for Theories of Instruction.* Washington, D. C.: ASCD, 1968.

13. Schwab, J. *The Practical: A Language for Curriculum.* Washington: National Education Association, 1970. Huebner, D., "The Moribund Curriculum Field: Its Wake and Our Work," Division B address, 1976 AERA meeting.

14. Macdonald, J. "Curriculum Theory," in W. Pinar (Ed.), *Curriculum Theorizing: The Reconceptualists,* 1975, p. 6.

15. Conferences have been held at the University of Rochester (1973), Xavier University of Cincinnati (1974), University of Virginia (1975), University of Wisconsin-Milwaukee (1976), Kent State University (1977), Rochester Institute of Technology (1978).

16. Books included *Heightened Consciousness, Cultural Revolution, and Curriculum Theory* (Berkeley: McCutchan, 1974), *Curriculum Theorizing: The Reconceptualists* (McCutchan, 1975), *Schools in Search of Meaning* (Washington: ASCD, 1975), *Toward a Poor Curriculum* (Dubuque, IA: Kendall/Hunt, 1976). There have been several reviews, the most recent of which is van Manen, M., "Reconceptualizing Curriculum Inquiry," *Curriculum Inquiry,* in press.

17. *The Journal of Curriculum Theorizing* managing editor is Janet Louise Miller, Center for Improved Education, Battelle Memorial Institute, Columbus, Ohio.

18. For discussion of this point see prefatory remarks in *Curriculum Theorizing: The Reconceptualists.* See also, Klohr, P., "The State of the Field," mimeographed, Xavier University Conference, 1974; Miller, J., "Duality: Perspectives in Reconceptualization," mimeographed, University of Virginia, 1975; Macdonald, J., "Curriculum Theory as Intentional Activity," mimeographed, University of Virginia conference, 1975; Macdonald, J., "Curriculum Theory and Human Interests," in Pinar (Ed.), *Curriculum Theorizing: The Reconceptualists,* and Benham, B., "Curriculum Theory in the 1970s: The Reconceptualist Movement," Kent State University conference, 1977.

19. See my "The Reconceptualization of Curriculum Studies," in the *Journal of Curriculum Studies,* in press, for one description.

20. Bernstein, p. 186 (*TP,* 43).

21. Ibid., p. 187 (*TP*, 254).

22. Westbury, I., "The Aristotelian 'art' of Rhetoric and the 'art' of Curriculum," in Raywid, M. (Ed.), *Philosophy of Education Annual Meeting Proceedings*, 1972. Edwardsville, IL: Southern Illinois University.

23. Huebner, D., "Curricular Language and Classroom Meanings," in W. Pinar (Ed.), *Curriculum Theorizing*, pp. 127-136.

24. Bernstein, p. 190, (*KI*, 4).

25. Beauchamp, G. *Curriculum Theory*. Wilmette, IL: The Kagg Press, 1964.

26. Bernstein, pp. 192-3, (*KI*, 308).

27. *Ibid.*, p. 197.

28. *Ibid.*, p. 198.

29. *Ibid.*, pp. 198-9, (*KI*, 310).

30. *Ibid.*, p. 200, (*KI*, 220-1).

31. *Ibid.*, p. 200, (*KI*, 228).

32. *Ibid.*, pp. 200-1, (*KI*, 229).

33. *Ibid.*, p. 201, (*KI*, 234).

34. See the work of Apple, Huebner, and Macdonald, for instance.

35. Bernstein, p. xiii.

36. Professor van Manen seems to be asking for just this. See his "Reconceptualizing Curriculum Inquiry," in *Curriculum Inquiry*, in press.

37. This is not only true in the field of curriculum. Witness the controversy between Greenfield and Griffiths over the nature of theory in educational administration. See *U.C.E.A. Review*, 1977, October, XIX, 1.

38. See Pinar, W. & Grumet, M. *Toward a Poor Curriculum*. Dubuque, IA: Kendall/Hunt, 1976.

39. Jung, C. *The Integration of the Personality*. New York: Farrar & Rinehart, 1939.

40. See, for instance, the work of N. O. Brown, Susan Sontag, Herbert Marcuse, Wilhelm Reich.

41. The so-called "new religions" illustrate one form of present cultural movement. See Pinar, W. (Ed.), *Heightened Consciousness, Cultural Revolution, and Curriculum Theory*. Berkeley: McCutchan, 1974.

42. Bernstein, p. 214, (*TP*, 32).

43. *Ibid.*, p. 216.

44. *Ibid.*, p. 216, (*TP*, 36, 39).

45. *Ibid.*, pp. 216-7.

46. *Ibid.*, p. 217, (*TP*, 33).

47. *Ibid.*, pp. 217-8.

48. *Ibid.*, pp. 218-9.

VII

The Abstract and the Concrete in Curriculum Theorizing (1979)

> There is a madness of those who treat the world as a dream and there is a madness of those who treat the inner life as a phantom. The second lunatic is scarcely less frightening than the former. But whereas the former gets locked up in an asylum, the other slowly acquires an ascendency amongst men who forget what it is to be a man [sic].[1]

Accompanying the stasis of the present historical period[2] is disembodied rhetoric from both the Right and the Left. The Right reaffirms the family and biblical values while attacking abortion, homosexuality, and social welfare programs. The Left reaffirms the necessity of structural transformation of society, a vision of socioeconomic and political justice, while attacking political privilege, corporate profits, and the smug self-righteousness of the bourgeoisie. Both Left and Right have enemies and loyalties. As these enemies and loyalties take exclusively abstract form, they function in antidialectical fashion. Without explicit grounding in the concrete (the abstraction "abortion" matched to a particular woman in particular circumstances), the abstraction becomes only an extension of the speaker, a sign for something of oneself that is hated or loved. In order for dialectical movement to occur, one must abandon the solipsistic world of abstraction and enter the material world of concrete individuals.

Abstractions unmatched to concrete referents signify private hatreds and loves, although the private character of the emotion is hidden in its usually strident public expression: "Ban the murder of unborn children!" Because the abstraction's referent is private, it is inaccessible. The person who so abstracts cannot see the concrete fact; that person sees only the abstraction. The fact of individual physicians performing abortions for particular women in particular circumstances for particular reasons is occluded by the abstraction "abortion."

This historical situation involves more than, in Sartre's phrase, the loss of the person into the Idea. However, it is this dimension of which critical discussion can serve two appropriate and related functions. One is illumination of the increasingly common but difficult term "liberation." The other is examination of several problems in what has been characterized as politically and economically oriented curriculum scholarship, scholarship which claims to be liberative.[3]

The somewhat loose definition of liberation with which I am beginning is this: a process of freeing—oneself and others—from political, economic, and psychological inequities. The term is, then, multi-dimensional in its meaning. As well, it is inherently temporal; that is, liberation does not suggest something finished or static. There can be no "liberated" nation, institution, or person in a final or absolute sense. There are gradations of liberation, as even a cursory consideration of the term reveals. For instance, European countries rescued from Nazi control were described as liberated, as they were. Of course, economic inequities remained that came sharply into focus after the War had receded into memory to some extent. What at one time is a liberated country at another time can be viewed as an unjust and unfree one. Another illustration may emphasize the relative and graduated character of liberation. A Soviet dissident who escapes his or her native country can find the United States a relatively free country. The gross order of restriction he or she faced in the Soviet Union is absent here. Yet for many native Americans, our country cannot be regarded as free. More subtle yet real forms of opposition are detectable. The point here is that liberation is a process and one which has gradations of realization.

The order of liberative work I have described elsewhere as the method of **currere** may seem to some a too-subtle order of work, one whose political import is invisible. To some extent this is the case. I will argue, however, that its apparent invisibility does not render it politically insignificant. I want to argue that liberative work can and must occur along several different dimensions and that the success of labor in any given dimension—say the economic—is dialectically related in important ways to work in other—say, political, psychological, sexual—dimensions. This is an "ecological" view of the human and natural world, a view in which action in one domain affects the status of the others. Work in isolation cannot occur except in a superficial sense. Work on the individual has inescapable if not necessarily predictable social and political consequences.

Relatedly, I want to focus on the problem identified at the outset of this discussion, namely the tendency toward abstraction, although I will restrict my examination to its expression in the curriculum field. Such a tendency, visible in traditional, conceptual-empirical, and certain strands of politically and economically oriented curriculum work contributes to the stasis of the field, a condition mirroring the stasis of the historical situation.[4] I seek some liberation from abstraction through the recovery of immediate individual experience, of a lived—in contrast to an exclusively conceptual—sense of the self and world. Abstractions would hardly disappear as a consequence of such work, but they would become more situated in the context of individual lives as lived. The inversion of the concrete and the abstract, succinctly captured in the phrase "loss of the person to the Idea," can be corrected, and a contribution to the field's movement made.

Traditionalists in the field have tended to focus upon "principles" of curriculum and instruction, phenomena that can somehow be studied and formulated independently of the specific individuals whose use of them gives them life. Even the concept of the individual in the traditional literature tended to portray an abstract idea only, just as curriculum that attempted to function humanistically was described as personless processes. The politically oriented scholars continue the same reduction of the concrete to the abstract, as they speak of "the distribution of cultural capital"[5] and "analyzing hegemony,"[6] phrases and accompany analyses that omit individual experience as they focus exclusively upon so-called structural relations constituent of society. Such work tends to reduce the individual to the network of structural relations which, presumably, constitute his or her context: "There are three aspects of the program that need to be articulated here: (1) the school as institution, (2) the knowledge forms, and (3) the educator him- or herself. Each of these must be situated within the larger nexus of relations of which it is a constitutive part."[7] First, the reader notes that the three aspects are not of the same conceptual order. Both numbers one and two represent complex codifications created by the third. To situate all three into a "larger nexus of relations" completes a conceptual and ontological confusion that has potentially pernicious political and well as conceptual consequences.

What is problematic about this reduction of concrete beings to an idea is the distortion of human life it sustains. The idea becomes larger than the living species who conceive it. The idea becomes more real than the concrete; it becomes a source for explanation and, worse, action. As ideas become more "real" than concrete human beings, the capacity to sacrifice the latter for sake of the former is more possible and likely. Whether the conceptual idols be the "master race" from the Right or "the people" from the Left, the fact of human sacrifice remains.

In their adherence to abstraction, in their disinterest and misunderstanding of the concretely existing individually, the politically oriented curricularists become, curiously enough, idealists, in the philosophic sense. That is, such writers reduce human experience to ideas of it and in this effort parallel the work of mainstream social scientists. The individual is present as an illustration of the general. One begins with the concrete and moves to the abstract, and as Piaget's theory of cognitive development correspondingly suggests, the greater the degree of abstraction, presumably the greater the degree of profundity and accuracy. Such assumptions—we may term this pretheoretical—often distort human experience. What is central to human experience is its particularity, in a sense even its eccentricity. Scientific laws and abstractions cannot capture the singularity of individual experience.

William Earle develops this point, arguing that what is essential to human life is not what is common to individual, although knowledge of what is common is often interesting and useful. However, such knowledge cannot escape the status of the superficial. What is profound about human life can be found only in the realm of the singular. Mounier discusses the matter this way: "He is a Frenchman, a bourgeois, a socialist, a catholic, and so on. But he is not a Bernard Chartier, he is Bernard Chartier. The thousand ways in which I can distinguish him, as an example of a class may help me to understand him, and above all to make use of him; they show me how practically to behave toward him. But these are merely sections taken, in each case, through one aspect of this existence. A thousand photographs put together will not amount to a man who walks, thinks, and wills."[8]

The point is not to acknowledge "individual differences." Such a phrase is possible only from a perspective that retains the superiority of the common, the general, over the unique and irreplicable. What is necessary in order to portray human activity and experience more accurately is descriptions of particular individuals, on particular days, in particular circumstances. Economic and political elements achieve actuality—and escape idealism—as they configure in the concretely existing individual. Put another way, in the singularity that is an individual alive on a certain day during a certain moment is a complex configuration of political, economic, and cultural forces. This certain moment, which can be likened to a crystal with its many facets, all present and interrelated but significant only as they are just facets of a single unique crystal, can be revealed in part through the report of the individual himself. Earle notes in this regard: "What I am for myself has an absolute priority over what I am for another.... And though at the same time I may be indirectly apprehended as an object by someone else, my possible objectification to another can have no effect on my own first-person subjectivity. My subjectivity therefore underlies any derived objectification and remains logically and ontologically prior to any of its derived appearances or modes."[9]

Earle speaks in absolute terms. In relative, everyday terms, another's objectification of oneself often does take precedence over one's "first-person subjectivity." In an outer-directed culture, children are socialized from early on to care very much

about others' objectifications. While the content of objectifications may vary according to class, the fact of vulnerability to
others' characterizations does not. Perhaps those who objectify
me are not traditional authorities (such as parents and teachers); perhaps they are peers. The fact of outer-directedness
remains the case. What is described in the above passage is a
developmental possibility. Those who can free themselves from
the power of others' objectifications without trading their outer-
directedness for a form of autism can achieve a degree of independence that is political as much as it is social and psychological.

Of course, there is no attempt here to deny that the individual is a cultural, political, economic being or that these dimensions cannot be investigated fruitfully. These dimensions are
extremely important, and calling attention to them in itself has
been an important contribution of the politically oriented curricularists. However, what is clearly ignored in the work of this
group is the fundamental fact that these dimensions are rooted
in the lives of concrete individuals, and it is this biographic context that must take logical, as well as political, precedence. To
insist that the individual is primarily an economic category, a
social animal, primarily the person created through conditioning, through the accumulated objectifications of others, is
finally to make an autobiographical statement. What many
Marxists—I suppose "vulgar" is an appropriate although curiously bourgeois, even aesthete term—are telling us when they
insist upon the primacy of economic and political determinants
of human life is that they themselves are so conditioned. They
have lost touch with "first-person subjectivity," with the self
behind the persona, behind the social mask created through a
myriad of complex social interactions. Having lost contact,
they have become social animals, vulnerable through their
outer-directedness to social winds. Structurally they are no
different from their counterparts on the Right. Both confess
their vulnerability to the social by their preoccupation with it.
Human beings are what they are in public, and the rest of
human life is reduced to the public or dismissed as "private life"
or "subjectivism." This inversion of what is the case character-

izes, to some extent, politically and economically oriented curriculum scholarship.

There is a further tendency in this work to judge all other work according to the degree it acknowledges economic and political factors. There is a tendency to insist on a kind of recitation of structural analysis. By such insistence, this work produces its own form of hegemony. To the extent that it insists upon the superiority of its own view—rather than viewing itself as a constituent element in a larger dialectic, the synthesis of which will be formulated in years to come and perhaps by individuals not yet on the scene—this work functions in antidialectical, politically reactionary ways. It aggrandizes itself into a kind of litany to be murmured endlessly by the faithful.

Rather than adherence to seemingly apolitical, seemingly theoretical principles of curriculum and instruction, we are now asked to submit to an equally abstract and ideological perspective. No longer can we feel the naive hopefulness of the traditional ameliorative orientation (let's roll up our sleeves and improve these schools!). Nor can we believe the bourgeois abstraction "the individual," whose claimed independence was in effect a disguise for self-aggrandizement at the cost of community and economic justice. From the false safety of "principles" and amelioration and pseudo-individualism, we are now offered another set of abstractions—"mechanisms of cultural and economic preservation and distribution"[10]—equally divorced from the realities of everyday life. While political and economic analyses of curriculum have clearly advanced the field from the naive views of traditionalism and conceptual-empiricism, they have reached their own liberative limits as they establish themselves as "the final word." It is in this appraisal of all work according to its own theoretical emphases that it becomes doctrinaire.

The power of the political focus is not in dispute here, only its excesses. The concrete is lost to the abstract; the relationship between consciousness and matter deformed. Mounier states this relation succinctly: "One cannot speak of any object, still less of a world, except in relation to a consciousness that perceives it. It is therefore useless to seek to reduce matter to a network of relations.... The dialectical relation between matter and consciousness is as irreducible as is the existence of the one and the other."[11] In order to honor the dialectical relation between consciousness and matter, the latter must be explicitly linked to the former. Such linkage has been aspiration of auto-biographical work. "*Currere*: A Case Study"[12] was an early attempt to portray curriculum—in this instance one particular text—in dialectical relation to consciousness—in this instance the consciousness of a particular student. Descriptions of his response, a response that included both dialogue with the text and with himself, concretized abstractions such as "conscious-ness" and phrases like "the response of the reader." Similarly, the descriptions of that reader's conflict over political, spiritual, and social issues also portray these very issues in the context of a concretely existing individual in the midst of his life, facing certain biographic issues. I submit that it is in such a context that concepts like "network of social relations" have reality or do not.

By focusing upon the individual, it is possible to reclaim the abstractions and begin to extricate oneself from capture by ide-ology. One's voice becomes discernible. By working regres-sively, progressively, analytically, synthetically,[13] one begins to reclaim oneself from intellectual and cultural conditioning. It is work to initiate a dialectical (rather than passive) relation to scholarly work, to oneself, to the world. Such work is hardly political withdrawal or psychological narcissism. On the con-trary, the method of *currere* is one way to work to liberate one from the web of political, cultural, and economic influences that are perhaps buried from conscious view but nonetheless comprise the living web that is a person's biographic situation. The complex configuration of political, economic, and cultural life converges on this "site," the lives of concretely existing individuals. It is individuals' unconscious perpetuation of static structural relations that in part constitute the present historical period. Of course, collective political action is necessary. Cul-tural action is necessary as well. Unless "the people" are pre-pared, psychologically and intellectually, for the equality of a just political and economic order, they retain the same passivity to authority, their same status as functionaries of the state, as the case of the Soviet Union certainly appears to document.

While the stated message of some politically oriented curriculum scholars differs from their counterparts on the Right, their "hidden curriculum" is not so easily distinguishable. We observe the same loss of self to abstraction. We observe the same interest in social control. We observe the same biographic function of scholarship, that is, as a tool of professional aggrandizement. Theory ungrounded in the individual life of the theoretician easily functions for the theoretician as does the expertise of any professional in a capitalistic order—as trade to be bartered. Thus while a social message is intended, a capitalistic one is received. From the speaker's jokes we infer that he views his "radical" scholarship finally as the academic equivalent of stock, which he has invested carefully, the final significance of which is its "return," that is visibility and professional acclaim.

Self-reflexive examination of the biographic functions of one's intellectual work makes its unconscious use less likely. When its use is relatively unconscious, it is more likely that it will perpetuate dominant cultural themes, such as the commodification of scholarship. Further, one begins to glimpse how autobiographical work of this nature, as it transforms the individual, must transform the material structures of society. While the linkage between the individual's work and social transformation cannot be explicit or simple, we know—given the inseparable and dialectical relation between consciousness and matter—that self has its material consequences. What is perhaps easier to comprehend is that individual work necessary contributes, microscopically although not negligibly, to the transformation of the culture.

The unquestionable success of politically oriented curriculum scholarship has now becomes its limits. It rightly pointed to the political character of curriculum, to its status as a kind of cultural codification and means of social reproduction. It rightly pointed to the delusion of individuality that is the bourgeois individual, who lacks psychological or intellectual agency and yet uses his monadic status to deny the web of social and economic relationality in order to further his own position in that web. And it underscored the importance of theorists' and practitioners' commitment to social and economic justice. These represented major successes.

For some of us who came of age with such views and commitments during the 1960s, the limits of this general view had already been reached. This recognition hardly makes illegitimate the political-economic emphasis. Nor does it suggest political withdrawal. Conventional political action as well as continuing commitment to socioeconomic justice remain prerequisites to responsible professional life. Yet there are orders of understanding not yet achieved. Now that we know the significance of economic structure for cultural and intellectual life, what next? Of course, there must be political action. But what else?

Clearly one next step in the dialectic that is the abstract and the concrete is reclamation of the individual, not as an apology for bourgeois self-aggrandizement but as a concrete, irreducible expression and determiner of economic and political structure. Individuals can be producers as well as products of the culture that permeates them. We understand, in large due to the work of Marxist scholars, the order of structural transformation necessary to seriously honor commitments to human rights. We understand to a considerable extent what order of collective political action is necessary to support such transformation. While this collective work continues today, there is a companion effort that to date, politically oriented curricularists have refused to appreciate. This is individual work.

In one sense I am speaking of Freire's *conscientizao* or learning to perceive social, political, and economic considerations and to take action against oppressive elements of reality. As Freire's pedagogy demonstrates, praxis can occur only as these contradictions are understood in the context of immediate individual and social life. Freire alludes, for instance, to analyses of peasants' afternoon drinking. What is necessary is that these students analytically grasp the political meaning of this drinking; that is that it is born in frustration that has not been politically expressed or materially remediated. The necessity of matching abstractions such as "oppression" to concrete incidents (such as compulsive drinking or incidents of "horizontal violence") is clear. This work is, in some measure, autobiographical. It aspires to assist the student to return from submersion in reality to a distanced, self-reflexive comprehension of his life and its relation to cultural and economic life. Such work may initially occur by didactic instruction but only initially. In didactic instruction the students remain passive. In Freire's term, the procedure is "banking education."[14] It is, in the extreme, indoctrination. Extrication from reality, from unconscious, conditioned participation in oppressive political reality to self-reflexive, active movement in order to alter that reality is an important function of the autobiographic work that is the method of *currere*.

Liberative activity very quickly—especially when espoused by educators caught in a scientistic understanding of the relation of theory to practice—becomes something they do to others. When it is only that, when it is reduced to a mode of social interaction, even when it is characterized by "dialogical encounter" in which both self and other are transformed by the encounter, an important order of liberative work is lost. This order of work involves the relation of self to self, of self to work, of self to others, relations which can be progressively uncovered and progressively transformed by careful autobiographical work with oneself. This order of investigation is necessary given the individual's and the group's seeming infinite capacity to delude itself as to the function of its activity. Humanistic rhetoric can easily function in politically and intellectually reactionary ways. The content of any statement or position is secondary to its function for its maker. The function of work for the worker requires self-reflective examination to uncover.

Apple[15] misunderstands my focus on the individual for two reasons. One is that the individual, as treated historically in the field, has been without conceptual content or ontological fact; it becomes finally only a slogan. The second reason is perhaps more germane to the present discussion. He misunderstands "Currere: A Case Study," relegating it to aesthetic significance only, because the individual is an abstraction in his work. In this one regard his work differs little from the work of traditionalists and conceptual-empiricists. Despite allusion to "consciousness of people in a precise historical or sociohistorical situation"[16] and "day to day practices"[17] neither phrase achieves concrete actuality in his writing. His concern is theoretical explanation in the tradition of mainstream social science, a tradition that, like academic philosophy, "apes the natural and mathematical sciences."[18] This is a tradition concerned preeminently with discovering nomological knowledge of human behavior and action, knowledge that will enable us to comprehend action in reliable enough ways to permit its prediction. In this respect, politically oriented scholarship does not reconceptualize the field. In this respect, such scholarship tends to function in politically and intellectually reactionary ways, as it continues the reduction of concreting existing individuals to evidence for theoretical explanation. Such a focus maintains subservience of individuals to theory, subservience of individuals to vertically positioned "superiors" generally. It is little gain if the working classes shift their passive allegiance from the bourgeoisie to economic and political theory, which not incidentally is by and large promulgated by members of the bourgeoisie. The capacity for passive allegiance—the structure of oppression—is left undisturbed.

Almost needless to say, politically oriented scholarship does not function only in reactionary ways. Insofar as it forces awareness of economic and political determinants of curriculum and of curriculum theorizing, and insofar as it represents a fundamental shift in focus and method of theorizing, it does indeed contribute to a reconceptualization of the field. However, to the extent that it insists upon the omission of the individual and refuses to situate its grand abstractions in the lives of those concrete individuals they are presumably in the service of, to the extent that it insists that all other curriculum scholarship conform to its thematic contours, then politically oriented scholarship will function in reactionary ways. Liberation must not be permitted to be reduced to a slogan, another meaningless abstraction, acting as a Maypole around which curriculum writers dance in service of the careers. For liberation to escape such a fate, it must be examined carefully as to its function in professional lives and projects as well as grasped analytically. Without question, the concept implies economic, political, and social justice. It implies as well individual justice, working to extricate the individual from the psychological and intellectual inequities of childrearing and schooling, working to release the individual from characterological limitations. The two orders of liberative work—collective and individual, matter and consciousness—are correlative. They are companion efforts that ought not to be at war with each other.

Notes

1. E. Mounier, "Be Not Afraid," quoted in T. Roszak, "The Third Tradition: The Individual, the Collective, the Personal," *New American Review* (Fall, 1977).

2. I am referring to a rather short lapse of time, the past three to five years.

3. A phrase Michael Apple has used to describe his works. I use it to refer to all curriculum scholarship that emphasizes the political.

4. Situation here refers to past three to five years and a continuing sense of stasis. The world economic situation continues to deteriorate slowly, as does the political situation in Africa and the Middle East. A persuasive sense of "viscosity," of an inability to move through present issues, is discernible.

5. J. Rosario, "Aesthetics and the Curriculum: Persistency, Traditional Modes, and a Different Perspective," *The Journal of Curriculum Theorizing*, 1:1, in press.

6. M. Apple, "On Analyzing Hegemony," *The Journal of Curriculum Theorizing* 1:1, in press.

7. Ibid.

8. E. Mounier, *Personalism* (London: Routledge & Kegan Paul, 1952), p. ix.

9. W. Earle, *Autobiographical Consciousness* (Chicago: Quadrangle, 1972), p. 55.

10. Apple, "On Analyzing Hegemony."

11. Mounier, *Personalism*.

12. G. Willis (Ed.), *Qualitative Evaluation* (Berkeley: McCutchan, 1978), pp. 316-42.

13. W. Pinar & M. Grumet, *Toward a Poor Curriculum* (Dubuque, IA: Kendall/Hunt, 1976).

14. P. Freire, *Pedagogy of the Oppressed* (New York: Seabury Press, 1973).

15. M. Apple, "Ideology and Form in Curriculum Evaluation," in G. Willis (Ed.), *Qualitative Evaluation*, pp. 492-521.

16. Apple, "On Analyzing Hegemony."

17. *Ibid.*

18. Earle, *Autobiographical Consciousness*, p. 33.

VIII

The Voyage Out: Curriculum as the Relation Between the Knower and the Known (1979)

> Without going out of my door
> I know the universe.
>
> In the child is the adult;
> in the seed, the tree;
> and in the raindrop, the ocean.
>
> —Lao Tze

One task of the curriculum theorist is a continual, careful, insistent pressing the limits of our thinking. Part of this effort must be critical and historical. In this respect, it is no accident that the Reconceptualization began in criticism. It cannot, however, remain there. There must accompany critical and historical work, post-critical work, a phase of theorizing in which the theorist turns his or her attention away from what exists, and toward what does not. As the tradition is discredited, anew one must be created. And in twenty years time perhaps (although the life-span of an intellectual tradition can hardly be predicted), it will be subjected to the same critical scrutiny that gave it its birth. The concept of the dialectic, while used nearly ad nauseam, remains to my mind the most succinct and powerful statement of how development occurs, collectively and individually. Opposing ideas or forces or individuals meet each other in ways which allow each to give itself up for the sake of the transformation of both, and attainment of a hopefully more comprehensive, less parochial point of view. In only slightly different terms really, Dewey's concept of experimentalism expresses the same possibility: new information is integrated into old, allowing the knower to comprehend himself or herself, his or her environment, and their inter-relation, in more subtle, intelligent and instrumental ways.

This last understanding, that true theoretic advancement carries with it increasing pragmatic sophistication, has been nearly completely forgotten in recent time. Part of Habermas' significance for us is his reconstruction of this fact. Pragmatic action cannot be frozen into principles and concepts composed before such action, and assumed to be legitimated logically and empirically. Pragmatic action is born only in the arena of action, and to the extent one enters this arena with static principles of how to behave, one deforms the situation. Necessarily one has shaped, let us say, the pedagogic situation, and selected out many possibilities. Depending upon the extent and rigidity of one's "conceptual grid," one has precluded dialectical interaction and movement. One is, if rigid or mindless of the importance of offering oneself up to social experience, automatically freezing the Other into his or her position as well. What usually occurs, then, unless the Other is passive or for instrumental reasons pretending to be passive, is conflict. Of course this word describes classrooms across this country. Increasingly this conflict is open and explicit, but even in calm, repressed classrooms, conflict occurs.

Thus the importance of the dialectic pervades many domains: a teacher's relationship to his or her students, the theorist's relationship to his or her own theorizing, his or her relationship to his or her field, and that field's relationship to its constituents (in our case school personnel). What I wish to suggest is that one task of the curriculum theorist is the demonstration of dialectical movement in one's own theoretical work, his or her social-intellectual relations with colleagues and students, and with his field, a category obviously not distinct from former ones. One must act as antithesis to certain prevailing theses or tendencies, but as well one must aspire to contain within one's own self-work and self-self relation a thetic-antithetic tension.

In order to initiate and maintain such an intellectual state, the theorist must continually be willing to give oneself up, including one's point of view. Of course, a point of view exhibits development. It begins immature, and its intellectual lineage is more visible than the idea itself. As it matures, its linkages to extant ideas and traditions become submerged in its own uniqueness. Mature, it is a clear idea in itself, with linkages to other formed ideas. However, it exhibits a kind of intellectual autonomy. It is at this stage that the theorist is often seduced, particularly if the ideas have gained a wide audience, and students have begun to sketch in detail its implications. One is invited to lecture; one has a reputation. If I am seduced, I write only variations on the basic theme. I may well spend the remainder of my career writing such variations. Such a career is hardly reprehensible. The point is that this person has become intellectually arrested, however useful to oneself and to others this arrested state is. In curriculum, a field concerned in part with the relation between the knower and the known, it is especially important for the theorist to demonstrate continued development.

How can one work with oneself in order to initiate and sustain such development? This question was one of those which resulted in the formulation of the method of *currere*. This method, as its most basic, represents a call for the cultivation of an internal dialectic. It is a call to examine one's response to a text, a response to an idea, response to a colleague, in ways which invite depth understanding and transformation of that response. One version of the academic sensibility exhibits the notion that one develops a position which must be firm and unyielding. Then one makes cases for it, arguing it endlessly, hoping, presumably, to persuade others to adopt it. I cannot avoid thinking of Jonathan Edwards and his "Sinners in the Hands of an Angry God" at this point. The content of sermons has certainly changed; the fact of preachers has not. A few scholars and theorists lay claim to timeless truths, and having completed the task of their own salvation—intellectual not spiritual in this secular age—they then devote themselves to the conversion of others. To change to a political image, this view is tantamount to a kind of intellectual imperialism, with its interest in colonizing the uncivilized regions of one's field.

Part of what attracted me to the study of education, and especially to curriculum, was acknowledgement that one's point of view—if one were intellectually alive—is in constant transition; and it is this view of not only of one's intellectual life but of life itself as some profound experiment which brings me to the present work. In our field this has meant that we have tolerated even encouraged, I suppose, dissertations and other forms of scholarly work of varying conceptual sophistication. Our colleagues in the arts and sciences have tended to view much of this work disdainfully, considering it primitive. This judgment is often accurate. And it is understandable, given our colleagues' preoccupation with the quality of scholarly products. What is mistaken in their judgments involves the ignorance of the nature of the study of education that it discloses. We are interested in the process of intellectual and psychosocial development, not just its expression in consensually determined forms. We are hardly disinterested in the forms such development takes, witness our vulnerability to attacks on the quality of our students' work. Yet we must answer firmly that quality is not our complete preoccupation, and if it is becomes, our field has lost part of what has made it distinctive: an interest in the process of education.

In one sense we can liken this interest to a psychoanalytic focus upon the unconscious, what lies below the proverbial tip of the iceberg. We are interested not only in the brilliant monograph, but its history as well, its origin in the life of the scholar, its relationship to issues in his life. Why such a focus? By examining the history of ideas in the life of individuals who formulate them we can begin to understand—and not in the fragmented way which mainstream social science offers—the nature of intellectual development, the process by which the individual learns, the process by which one becomes less parochial, more understanding, more humane. Of course, academic study hardly ensures the development of such a person, but it is not controversial to note that such development is the traditional ideal of our training. At least in the humanities we have spoken of the cultivation of sensibility, the training of a

gentleman, by which was meant a certain point of view of experience that is subtle, yielding, capable of transmutation. True,
this notion of a gentlemen was frozen, and identified with
socio-economic status and the capacity to affect gestures and
conversation that were au courant.

You see something of the tradition from which I am working.
It is nearly a lost one, as I am hardly the first or only to
acknowledge. With specialization—now a cliché, yet like most
clichés still true, only blurred from overuse—we view our task as
the training of professionals. Skills are what we impart, not a
more generalized attitude toward experience. You know this
story too well. You also know that there are important currents
of twentieth-century intellectual life which did not succumb:
existentialism, psychoanalysis, and critical theory. I hope the
current project will be viewed as one, however modest, expression of resistance. For historical and present reasons, curriculum is a field in which this neglected educational idea can be
established and perpetuated. I say historically because curriculum professors have always tended to demonstrate more interest in concrete issues and concrete individuals than in abstractions and the development of a conceptually coherent field.
[That this interest finally worked against us as the field is a
phenomenon I have discussed elsewhere.] We have the precedent, as yet not maturely developed theoretically, which allows
investigations not possible in other fields of education. The
present reasons have to do with the crisis in the curriculum
field, in a word, that we are field that is nearly extinguished.
The name "curriculum" has been dropped from the departmen-
tal designations at several institutions, recently at Ohio State.
The symbolic significance of this fact is that time is running out
on us to develop any field at all. Given the paralysis of will and
intellect which seems to pervade the field, in discouraged
moments one wonders if any effort can succeed. It is remembrance of our tradition, particular those curriculum scholars
with whom one has studied, and the possibility of establishing
an extraordinary field, which persuades one to make what may
be a final effort. I think we have ten years left, at most. There
may remain departments called "curriculum and teaching" after
that date, but they will be empty of any genuine disciplinary

meaning unless by that time it is clear to us who are committed to this field, and to those in other fields who observe us, that we are working in a vital area, with important consequences not only for the advancement of the general field of education, but for the transformation of the nation's educational institutions as well.

What is our task in the coming decade? The superficial answer involves scholarly production. Less superficial are considerations of motive. We cannot produce curriculum scholarship for the sake of producing curriculum scholarship. There is no point is rescuing a field merely for the sake of rescuing af field. That should be obvious. Why do this work? The Jonathan Edwards among us answer that it is for the sake of the salvation of the ignorant and reactionary. There is little or no loyalty to a field here. The field is only another medium through which the ideological struggle is waged. Another answer is less concise, partly because I do not fully understand it myself. But the sense that it is an answer is unmistakable, and persuades me to write about that which I am only vague. This answer has to do with giving up the safety of the rigid point of view, whether it be critical theory or experimentalism or empiricism. It involves allowing one's point of view to be transformed in dialectical process, with oneself and others. The possibility is staggering. What is possible is a genuinely experimental field, a field which sees itself as deliberately abandoning present understandings, unearthing material of which we have been unconscious, which may have seemed outside our domain of study.

How can such a spirit be cultivated? I think it involves focusing upon the quality of our relationship with our work, how it functions for us, and giving up the obsession with the judgment of others. The judgments of others can be left to others. We must take our eyes off our colleagues in the other fields of education, and if necessary off our colleagues in curriculum—if their gaze functions to make one intellectually timid—and examine closely our experience. This may mean social and economic analyses; it may mean class analyses. Certainly it may not mean autobiographic study (and those who read this exposition as a thinly disguised argument for the necessity of autobiographical work have missed its point completely). We cannot know what it will mean. This is the meaning of experimentation in its most profound sense. We give ourselves up to where our experience leads us. We attend as closely and faithfully as we currently can to our immediate experience of educational institutions—we are experts, most of us have never left them since age six—and we describe and attempt to understand this experience as honestly as we can. Of course such work forces us to make use of work in related disciplines. To read this as a call for intellectual myopia or isolationism is also a total misreading. It is a call for authentic investigation of experience, in which our theoretical expositions are dialectically linked with that experience. We curricularists are conservative people. Regardless however experimental, our studies will not be chaotic. They will not be idiosyncratic. Our built-in-conservatism will guarantee that if we err, it will be on the side of safety and conservation of what exists already. Finally, what a field means is that we tell each other what we think of each other's investigations, and this social and intellectual process also functions in service of caution. We will, on occasion, take unproductive lines of work; there will be culs-de-sac. But we will make important discoveries as well, if we are brave.

Design

The autobiographical study which follows is, in one sense, an attack on the concept of curriculum design. Some will say it is already a dead concept, or if alive, one not worthy of attack. I agree it is dead for many students of curriculum. If one peruses universities catalogues, however, one observes that there remain many courses entitled curriculum design. It is an idea, I think, many in our field still take seriously, and that, to my mind, gives it a kind of social if not intellectual currency. After Kuhn, one must acknowledge that the basic idea or paradigm of a field is that which is agreed upon by that field's practitioners, and this process of agreement (and the process of agreement breaking down, as has been the case in our field during this decade) is not altogether a purely rational one. Thus will many who regard themselves in the forefront of the field cannot take seriously the notion of curriculum design, I argue we must, given our colleagues' continuing acceptance of it.

There is much wrong with the idea. What I will argue is that one cannot, in many meaningful sense, design an educational experience. I will not only argue this point, I shall work to demonstrate it. The obvious yet evidently generally unknown fact is that one cannot predict human response, except in trivial matters and in artificially circumscribed circumstances, as necessary for experiments. Classrooms, while certainly limited artificially, are not sufficiently limited for the teacher to know with much certainty the response his or her lesson will receive. Conventional educational researchers typically bemoan this fact, i.e., the classroom is said to contain too many variables to permit a true experiment, given the state of methodological science. Thus the information educational experiments now yields is too tentative and circumstantial to permit one to design an experience.

All of this strikes this writer, and probably many of my readers, as tediously obvious. Yet the courses remain; at ASCD and AERA meetings the concept of "curriculum design" is still discussed as if it were meaningful. Of course, curriculum must be planned, described in brochures, but it can hardly be a matter of serious scholarly and theoretical attention. It is work for competent journalists and publicity personnel in the case of catalogues, and work for teachers in planning their courses. But it is hubris to imagine one can design and predict experience. What must be retained in teachers' plans is their individuality. To force them to follow some "scientific" course plan, forcing them to write behavioral objectives, only impersonalizes their classrooms, helps turn teachers into bureaucrats, alienated from their teaching, their subject matter, and their students. This is, of course, a kernel portrait of our public schools in the late 1970s, and so-called scientific models of curriculum and teaching can claim credit, albeit modest credit as they are more expressions than causes, for this dismal state of affairs. While ridding ourselves of the concept of design is hardly a primal move in the transformation of curriculum of our schools, it is another small step that must be taken. In fact, there is little evidence that, at the present time and in the foreseeable future, anything but small will be possible. Often critics are unwilling to fool with such order of issue, arguing that such work is only tinkering. My current view is that tinkering is our only option, and while not losing sight of fudamental issues, the broad view, it is quite appropriate to aim one's reform effort at a somewhat modest target: curriculum design.

What are my objections to the idea? One, as mentioned, is that one cannot predict with much certainty the response of one's listeners. One's utterances, I am thinking of teachers here, are not heard exclusively in the context in which they are spoken (although this sometimes occurs), but as well in the context in which they are heard. This latter context is that of the individual lives of those listening. They are vastly, though not completely, different from that of the teacher. Even momentary reflection reveals this fact. It is the fact of individuality. Even if those the teacher addressed were roughly the same age—and more likely to be facing similar developmental issues—his or her words are heard through the "filter" of individual interests and preoccupations. For elementary and secondary school teachers there is as well the matter of age which insists upon greater psychological and intellectual distance between them. Their biographic issues are different—as junior-high teachers often lament and all will recognize. This is nearly platitudinal; yet many in the curriculum field treat the notion of design—which these observations undercut—as if it were an issue that could be resolve by principles or procedures. Impossible. Of course teachers ought to attend to their daily lessons, to the sequences of lessons, and certain persons—such as the department chair—ought to keep a look over the entire program. But this is work to be done almost casually, through deliberation as Walker and Reid have both (after Schwab) argued for, and through individual teachers keeping journals of their interests and those of particular students. This matter of planning and design ought to be kept as informal and personal, i.e. individual, as possible, to allow and encourage each teacher and each department to shape its offerings according to its preferences. After all, that is the gift (hopefully it is a gift) of working with a teacher—and not a computer or televised lecturer—at all, to share in her or his presence, to observe the

gestures and the mind-state behind the talk, to help participate
in the formation of the classroom experience.

This last phrase takes me to the second objection. Of course,
there are more than two, but these settle the matter for me, and
it is difficult, I confess, to imagine the reader for whom they do
not. What is special, what is unrepeatable, potentially interesting and on occasion revelatory, is the moment by moment
experience of particular individuals in particular room at particular times. There are always issues to be addressed, often
not conscious for either students or teachers, which the aware
teacher can help identify, and make use of in order to ground
whatever the planned lesson is in the actual and immediate
experience of everyone in the room. Much misbehavior, from
one point of view, is related (although not caused in a simple-
minded linear way) to the teacher refusing, because she or he
has become an automaton teaching a standardized curriculum,
simply trying to get through her or his day, to address the specific individuals in front of her or him, to acknowledge in any
explicit way what is occurring at any specific time. Or if it is
acknowledged—usually when there is misbehavior—it is to mold
it into his or her plan. I do not want to follow this link of thinking further, as it begins to sound like "blame the teacher," easy
enough to do, not entirely inappropriate, but useless in this
context. However a teacher drones on, and there are many
individual as well as bureaucratic and cultural resons for it, we
curriculum specialists can be accused of having contributed to it
to the extent we have supported standardized curriculum and
teaching procedures. To the extent we have standardized is the
extent we have disallowed idiosyncratic behavior, which is the
extent to which alienation must be said to characterize social
relations in the classroom. Information may be processed and
acquired in such settings—it is unlikely except for the most pro-
grammed, usually suburban students—but education—dialogical
encounter in which social and intellectual sitaution is dialectically transformed—does not and cannot occur.

If we delete "curriculum design" as a central concept in the
conceptual structure of the field, have we not weakened that
structure? If design is not worthy of serious study, what is?
Much is, but here I will limit myself to one area: the relation

between student and curriculum. More abstractly, I am focusing upon the relation between the knower and the known, as Madeleine Grumet has described the subject matter of the curriculum theorist. With such a conception of our work, we immediately leave the ethically questionable and intellectually vacuous area of design. More interesting as well than manipulating the "educational environment" in order to secure predetermined "outcomes," a view which claims all agency for itself, ensuring passivity for the Other, is examination of what the response is. Response is not the most apt word, as it subtly continues an active/passive dichotomy, and can lead to a simplistic "information processing" view. What I intend by the word is not just the text's influence upon a particular student or teacher, but the reader's influence upon the reading of the text as well.

In order to reveal the detail of this relationship between knower and known, to ground this abstraction in concrete experience, I will describe one student's reading of one text, Virginia Woolf's *The Voyage Out*. To show detail of this interaction between individual and text, I will attempt to construct a "blow-up" of this process, much as a photographer might do. To so construct, the reading will be portrayed in discrete units, although it must be remembered that each unit is part of an experiential continuum which occurs as a whole, and in an instant and series of instants. These units, which also constitute steps of the method, are as follows. First, as the student reads he notes passages (words, sentences, paragraphs) which interest him in any way. Perhaps the language is felicitous, perhaps it is the thought which is provocative. Perhaps he has no conscious idea why he marks a particular passage. What is important during this first phrase is to attend closely to reading and to make note of what in the text strikes him. At this stage he does not interpret; he gives himself to the text. What he records, i.e., the passages which interest him, represent the surface content of his reading.

Next, the novel has been read now, we go over the passage noted, and study them. What, if any, themes are evident? While his selection may seem fortuitous (he had no predetermined criteria by which to select except his interest), examining

the passage shows that he was drawn to certain themes in the
novel. These present themselves, and under each thematic
heading—for instance, "relationship"—he lists the page numbers
on which pertinent passages can be found. After this second
step is completed, he sets the material aside for some time.
When he returns to it, he studies each theme and the identified
passages which express it. Now he writes—loosely in the tradition of literary tradition—short pieces about each of these
themes based on the passages cited. This writing is still focused
upon the text. Of course, it is not strictly speaking the novel's
view, given that he writes from passages according to his interest rather than according to their significance for the novel. In
fact, the text has been employed as a kind of Rorschach test in
which what the viewer reports he sees indicates as much about
his inner experience as it indicates about the text. This description of themes distorts the reading process as it occurs ordinarily in schools. But it is a necessary distortion, much like that
involved in the magnification of a photograph. In both instances we now see detail that before we could not. However,
in order to understand the detail we see we need yet another
sketch, this time of something quite different from the text.
We want a sketch of what we will call the the reader's biographic situation, a deliberately nebulous term which allows him to
describe his life at the time of the reading. The shape he gives
to his life through its description is signficant in the same way
his choice of passage signified his reading of the text. As with
the reading of the text, we ask him to focus upon the "object,"
and describe as concretely as possible—it is not yet time for
interpretation—the elements which comprise his biographic
present. After this description is completed (and completion in
this stage, as in the others, is somewhat arbitrary; in the rain-
drop the ocean), we place both pictures side by side, and see
what, if any, corespondence exists. In a certain sense we have a
blow-up on the text and one of the reader; now we attempt to
trace the relationship between the two. In so doing, we glimpse
the relationship between knowner and known.

As interesting and instructive as this glmpse may prove to be,
as important as understanding, however incipiently, the relationship between knower and known is, we remain dissatisfied.

With Habermas we must ask what human interest does this knowledge satisfy? It is not a technical interest; nor it is a practical one. It is, we hope, a liberative one. That is, we seek in this work not only to present information which permits us to understand the relation between knower and known, we seek transformation of both. By attending loosely to individual experience of the text, and by reflexive description and analysis of that experience, we alter that experience.

Politics

> I dream of the intellectual who destroys evidence and generalities, the one who, in the inertias and constraints of the present time locates and marks the weak points, the openings, the lines of force, who is incessantly on the move... who, wherever he moves, contributes to posing the question of knowing whether the revolution is worth the trouble, and what kind (I mean what revolution and what trouble), it being understood that the question can be answered only by those who are willing to risk their lives to bring it about. —Foucault

The focus upon the singular, upon the concrete, has been attacked in the curriculum literature. This attack suggests the excesses of contemporary Marxian theory in the curriculum field. Taken a whole, this work is probably the most vital body of serious scholarship in the field at this time. However, as I noted in "The Abstract and the Concrete in Curriculum Theorizing," it is incomplete. In its appropriate attack on bouregois individualism it has tended to delete the individual in any form, except as a passive figure in the reproduction of the status quo. As Sartre argued twenty years ago and the so-called new philosophers argue today, neglect of the concrete individual in concrete circumstances invites only another form oppression. The abuse of the masses by self-aggrandizing individualists must not be traded for the abuse of individuals for the sake of "the people."

In the obsession with abstractions, such as "cultural reproduction," the individual evaporates into a conceptual field of raging forces and currents (classes, structural determinants, historical inevitability). While any form of theorizing requires abstraction, such abstraction must retain its explicit links to concrete, material reality. This loss of the concrete represents an excess of contemporary Marxian theory in the field today.

Pointing to this excess must not be interpreted as another, albeit disguised, attack from the right. It must not be misinterpreted as insisting that the conceptual tools of dialectical analysis are inherently distorting. What must be appreciated is that for many of us a companion order of analysis and program of action must be developed. Accompanying the critique of socio-economic functions of curricula must be critique of the biographic functions of such curricula. Autobiography has embedded within it political, economic, sexual, and intellectual dimensions of lived experience. In fact, each of these dimensions achieves actuality in the material everyday life of the individual. An antithesis to the philosophical idealism evident in some Marxian critiques must come autobiographic description and analysis which functions to establish, theoretically and concretely, the perspective of the individual. Curriculum scholarship generally lacks such a perspective, despite traditional calls for attention to "individual needs." In the literature, and often in practice, this call has rarely left the status of abstraction and slogan, and Marxists have rightly criticized this as "the cult of the abstract individual" as finally phony, a construct only, and in the service of, at worst a dehumanizing capitalism, and at best, a progressive reform of same. This political function becomes evident in these traditional writers' irascible refusal to acknowlege the political function of the school. Thus the focus upon the abstract individual in the traditional literature does function to discourage class solidarity, and the location of oppression in structural relations such as economic and ideological forces.

Autobiography offers the curriculum field a point of view it simply has not had. In the literature we have no concrete descriptions of an individual's experience of texts, teachers, students. It is now past time for such description and analysis. But it must be acknowledged that such work provides us more than information and a point of view of experience we have not had before. Autobiography has a political function as well.

One basic expression of the historical situation is alienation, among groups and individuals, and fundamentally, the individual from himself. As Marcuse, and from other traditions, Laing and Cooper have suggested, we are hidden from ourselves. Our needs are often false, as often are our personae. Coming of age is a process of losing oneself to role, to a complex configuration of interpersonal, economic and political influences. The fact of what Laing (1969) termed a false self-system and an oppressive economic system are meaningfully related. Combating oppression must occur in both "domains." What is necessary is analysis of the socio-economic system, of hegemony, and the location of same in the self-system. But the examination of the individual life must not be limited to these concepts and interests. It must be more free-floating, because part of mystification of self and culture is blindness by abstraction. Part of this work must involve recovery of the body, of feeling, of a primitive self which the abstract individual has suppressed but not escaped. Individual strength, born and kept alive in self-knowing, in reflexive analysis of experience, is a necessary although an insufficient condition for liberative movement. The same is so of collective solidarity. The fact of fascism in the Soviet Union indicates that public ownership and class solidarity gaurantee only the perpetuation of the State. Individuals whose consciences cannot be sacrificed for achievement of a collective object are safeguards, albeit tentative and vulnerable, of a genuinely progressive culture.

But individual lives are sometimes messy, often boring. This former comment I have heard several times during these seven years I have studied autobiography as a mode of curriculum research. With repetition the comment has become more interesting, its latent meaning clearer. Such a comment can come from one whose life is avoided. Reading another life, which can be boring to the extent its representation has missed its singularity and captured itself stereotypically, refers the reader, as Doris Lessing has noted, to oneself. It offers not escape into a world of logical forms and elaborate conceptual scaffolding. It offers a kind of mirror to oneself, and to the extent it reflects itself clearly, without reducing itself to preconceived ideas, is the extent to which the reader is invited to challenge his own taken-for-granted explanations of his life.

In the excerpt of the study to follow the individual's representation of his reading and his situation is of course incomplete. A careful reading indicates he is captured by several
"domain assumptions" which allow him to glimpse only certain
features of his situation. But the point of this study is not
achievement of some objectivist-inspired self-explanation. It is
to illustrate the order of reflexive examination of experience, in
this case reading, which might point to the recovery of the individual from abstraction.

Due to considerations of space, much of the study is deleted,
although its illustrative function is not, I think, lost. The listing
of passages from the text—step one—is deleted. Assembling
them according to themes is also deleted. We begin with the
third step, i.e. brief sketches of these themes, using the passages
identified earlier. Three of the several sketches are printed
here. Next will be a description of the reader's situation.
Finally, we read his commentary on that situation and its relation to his relation. He gains a glimpse of the relationship
between the knower and the known.

Step 3: Themes in Virginia Woolf's *The Voyage Out*

June 5, 1974. Happiness. The references to happiness are
sparse. *The Voyage Out* is not a happy story. The mood is varied throughout, as is the rhythm of the prose. A certain som-
berness, sobriety, and slowness change quickly to intensity,
rapidity, and a movement that is rushed. This becomes light-
ness, as in many of the social scenes at the hotel, as well as
quickness, but then can disappear to become depth, fear, and
far below the surface, desperation. There is a sort of happiness
in the book; most of the visitors at the hotel are happy, if only
in a superficial social way. More precisely, they are cheerful.
They make jokes, and make conversation which then makes for
smoothness and ease of meeting, but only their surfaces are
engaged. One senses troubled people underneath those surfaces.

The few explicit references to happiness indicate that it
comes, what little of it comes, after youth, if at all. Mrs. Dalloway tells Rachel how "crammed" the world is with "delightful

things." Her happiness is a sort of fascination with objects. One easily imagines Mrs. Dalloway endlessly going to parties, to theater, to restaurants, an unceasing round of diversions. There is a rapidity to her movement and conversation that hints at "running," and one has no difficulty imaging "rough spots" (as she would no doubt call them) in her life. These probably come from inside, and one's impression is that Mrs. Dalloway, if ever as a youth looked to her center, firmly decided against it. The strength of her absorption with the "pleasures" of life, solid objects, implies flight from an unpleasant internal state.

Rachel is not happy, although in the first section of the novel she appears to be in some middle state, neither this nor that. As she is uninitiated in love, so she is in emotion. It lies dormant inside, built up over years, waiting for expression. This imbalance, i.e. repression, is indicated in the quickness with which she is ready to disclose herself. Soon after they begin talking, she tells Mrs. Dalloway: "I am lonely" (p. 58). We are told that she is "overcome by an intense desire to tell Mrs. Dalloway things she had never told anyone" (p. 58). Her loneliness and need for expression require a confidante.

Mrs. Dalloway also reflects the importance of the Other for happiness. She tells Rachel: "no one understood before Richard. He gave me all that I wanted." His importance for her is also consonant with general "outward" orientation. The implication of her statement is: before I met him I was alone, misunderstood or at least no understood. Since we can see Mrs. Dalloway is not so unusual and idiosyncratic as to make likely this state of affairs, we can read her statement as code for "I didn't understand myself." Clarity about herself remained absent until Richard came and apparently told her who she was. Self- understanding and meaning, for her, came from another.

We see further evidence of Mrs. Dalloway's confusion and unhappiness as a youth when she remarks to Rachel: "I think young people make such a mistake about that—not letting themselves be happy." Such a generalized statement, that is, one without a specific referent, tends to be projective in nature, and one can infer that she speaks autobiographically. Yet she talks as if unhappiness were somehow willful, somehow a function of ignorance—young people "make such a mistake." If Mrs. Dalloway's life is a model of happiness, then the mistakes consist of isolation and being too much with oneself. Her husband agrees children are not happy and says: "I never suffered as much as when I was a child" (p. 68).

So it would seem that happiness, if it comes and to the extent it comes, comes with age and with the end of isolation, the finding of another, and active absorption with diversions. Fairly clearly this version of happiness is a mixed one. Mrs. Dalloway is happy, as far as we and she can tell (although, as I have speculated, it is possible to detect some deep, repressed unhappiness), but it is at the expense of something. Is it depth; is it autonomy (that she would do without Richard); is it intelligence, that kind which comes from one's depths, from standing apart from convention? Mrs. Dalloway stays on the surface fluttering from object to object, person to person, amazed, happy. However, a subtle hysteria resides not far underneath this congenial surface, for there is no place to rest for long. Except Richard.

There is another sort of happiness hinted at in the novel, and that is one more rooted in oneself, and less in another. Of Evelyn, after one of her outbursts, it is said: "Her voice mounted too, in a mild ecstasy of satisfaction with her life and her own nature" (p. 261). Despite her later uncertainty (after Rachel's death) and her own slightly ridiculous character, this statement stands. It implies that acceptance and satisfaction with oneself, not dependent on the conduct of tea, or upon one's husband, is possible. If fact, Evelyn is not married, and while her independence is not precisely used, she accepts who she is, and we see one can take satisfaction, and one surmises, feel happiness, in being who it is one is. This happiness would seem the more desirable, at least ideally, although we cannot deny both characters are not entirely admirable. However, we must grant them their happiness.

June 13, 1974. Spirit. " 'Does it ever seem to you, Terrence, that the world is composed entirely of vast blocks of matter, and that we're nothing but patches of light?'—she looked at the soft spots of sun wavering over the carpet and up the wall—'like that' " (pp. 292-293). We are "soft spots of sun" on the material world. We are transparent; one looks at sunlight on the wall and one sees the wall. If the light is subtle enough one might easily miss the light and see only the wall, although of course one could see nothing without the light. Light, given our current developmental status, can be perceived only as it lies on a material surface: "consciousness is always consciousness of something" writes Sartre; it is always of something else. I am conscious of the ink being left on the page as I write, of the cat grooming herself near me on the bed where I work, and it is those objects of which I am conscious, but what, who is this "I"? It is my hand which writes, but it is "my" hand, it belongs to me. I am my body; I feel it from my toes to my head, but it is not what I am. It is as I were inside a bottle; I fell myself pressed against its wall, my skin, but inside, where I am, I can move. I can be in my head (where I am most of the time), but as well in my feet, in my stomach, or with my cat still on the bed, or with Virginia Woolf's photograph hanging on the wall opposite. But I am none of that; I am here, moving, watching. I am aware of my unconscious, which I experience as a weight, a burden. It lies below me, sedimentations of memories, emotions, fantasies, primarily pain, and so, frightened, I cling to the surface and to what is outside of me. I cultivate a calm because I know I must go down, but I must do so manageably, as undisruptingly, as possible. I digress; what I wish to say is: my unconscious, while I am "it" also, it does not constitute me. I am no thing; I am consciousness; I am light:

> The morning was hot, and the exercise of reading left her mind contracting and expanding like the mainspring of a clock. The sounds in the garden outside joined with the clock, and the small noises of midday, which one can ascribe to no definite cause, in a regular rhythm. It was all very real, very big, very impersonal, and after a moment or two she began to raise her first finger and to let it fall on the arm of her chair so as to bring back to herself some consciousness of her own existence. She was next overcome by the unspeakable queerness of the fact that she should be sitting in an armchair, in the morning, in the middle of the world. Who were the people moving in the house—moving things from one place to another? And life, what was that? It was only a light passing over the surface and vanishing, as in time she would vanish, though the furniture in the room would remain. Her dissolution became so complete that she could not raise her finger anymore, and sat perfectly still, listening and looking always at the same spot. It

became stranger and stranger and stranger. She was overcome with
awe that things should exist at all .... She forgot that she had any fin-
gers to raise .... The things that existed were so immense and so desolate .... She continued to be conscious of these vast masses of substance
for a long stretch of time, the clock still ticking in the midst of the
universal silence (pp. 124-125).

I go over these words very slowly, taking one by one, phrase
by phrase, allowing their meaning to melt, looking up from the
page and the pen, to the walls of my room, my bed, the plants
and the windows over them, and the gray light of a cloudy mid-
day lighting it all. It is my room I repeat, I live here, work here,
but all of it does seem odd at times. Why I am here rather than
there, why with these people rather than those? Looking over
the passage again, I feel unstuck from the physical, the interpersonal, even internally ajar.

If we are light, then our dwelling apart from each other,
encapsulated in our bodies and social habits, is not inevitable.
This possibility is indicated in *The Voyage Out*: "The dreams
were not confined to her indeed, but went from one brain to
another. They all dreamt of each other that night, as was natural, considering how thin the partitions were between them,
and how strangely they had been lifted off the earth to sit next
to each other in mid-ocean, and see the very detail of each
others' faces, and hear whatever chance prompted them to say"
(p. 52). The partitions are thin, and the word has its social and
psychological senses as well as its physical ones. At night one
leaves the publicly constructed world, and one lingers, descend-
ing we might say, into the upper layers of the unconscious. In
such a state, one's distance from another would be less concrete, less final.

The characters' cultural hold is loosened in that its familiar
physical and geographical settings are removed. They create a
facsimile of England in the hotel, but the land and the people
around them are different. So the visitors are less inclined to
accept the take-for-granted, more inclined to see their modes of
relation as constructed and contingent. Rachel, in this unfamiliar setting, comes out of herself, emotionally, intellectually, sexually, and she dies. Just before the voyage ends, she visits

Evelyn, whose visit to the new land has also loosened her hold on the familiar:

> Suddenly the keen feeling of someone's personality, which things they have owned or handled sometimes preserves, overcame her; she felt Rachel in the room with her; it was as if she were on a ship at sea, and the life of the day was as unreal as the land in the distance. But by degrees the feeling of Rachel's presence passed away, and she could no longer realize her, for she had scarcely known her. Bu this momentary sensation left her depressed and fatigued. What had she done with her life? What future was there for her? What was make-believe, and what was real? Were these proposals and intimacies and adventures real, or was the contentment she had seen on the faces of Susan and Rachel more real than anything she had ever felt (p. 264).

What is real, and what make-believe? "Soft spots of sun wavering over the carpet and up the wall."

June 17, 1974. Relationship. "On the following day they met—but as leaves in the air" (p. 70). Thus are the possibilities of relationship in *The Voyage Out.* Cut from our source and our home, we drop toward death, buffeted by the wind, sunned on, rained on, and by chance (it would seem) we meet one another, he on his descent, she on hers, together only for the time and in the way the currents permit, then separate again, always falling.

Such a view of relationship (and of life) implies isolation and frustration. Different characters speak to these conditions. Richard Dalloway complains to Rachel: "This reticence—this isolation—that's what's the matter with modern life!" (p. 75). Earlier he had said to her: "D'you know, Miss Vinrace, you've made me think? How little, after all, one can tell anybody about one's life! Here I sit; there you sit; both, I doubt not, chock-full of the most interesting experiences, ideas, emotions; yet how to communicate?" (p. 68). The social forms in the novel are inadequate to the message they must carry. Consequently, there is a split between public and private; what is significant lies within, usually inaccessible to the other (and thus the importance of the "stream-of-consciousness" technique). So come withdrawal and isolation. Of Mr. Ambrose it is said: "Unfortunately, as age puts one barrier between human beings, and learning another, and sex a third, Mr. Ambrose in his study was some thousand miles distant from the nearest human being, who in this household was inevitably a woman" (p. 70).

Such distance brings frustration. Richard Dalloway and Rachel are unable to reach to each other except erratically and confusedly. Terrence and Rachel are similarly estranged at first; Rachel even does not know herself the extent of her involvement. For his part, Terrence is ambivalent and uncertain. And when some sort of emotional exchange begins, when relationship between the two becomes established, Rachel dies. Frustration of relationship dominates the book. Helen remarks, and not with inordinate cynicism: "The lives of these people ... the aimlessness, the way they live. One goes from one to another, and it's all the same. One never get what one wants out of any of them" (p. 263).

Like leaves in the wind, human lives scatter, this way then that, and what one wants from others? It may well be what one wants from others cannot be gotten, at least not without a crushing cost. It may be what we want is the stability of attachment, the living of the semi-conscious memory of floating safely in the womb. That order of stability may not be achievable interpersonally.

Autobiographic situation

June 23, 1974. Willa, John, and I went to Mendon Park today, and walked and walked. I'm tired now, but I don't want to sleep. Thinking about this work, and how to proceed. What I'm considering is writing a journal, with the idea that my situation will present itself more honestly, more artlessly, if I write about what occurs day to day than if I begin right away to summarize and analyze. I would need to do that at some point, making explicit any connections between reading *The Voyage Out* and my situation.

Stephen Spender's photograph appeared on the front page of today's *New York Times Book Review*. The lines, creases, the flesh sagging, and his eyes, slightly dull, vacant, looking past the photographer. I recall Virginia Woolf's remark that the lines on the faces of the middle-aged make the young think that they see something horrible the young can't yet see. My own face and body will age like that; already it begins. When I've had a lot to drink—like last night—I can see the lines coming, the face aging. It awes me, and I suppose, frightens me. Always wanted to age slowly, as if I were getting away with something, as if I had avoided some of the harsher effects of living. Although one incontestable thing I've managed to learn these past couple of years is that life must not be avoided, that the pain of trying to avoid the pain—flight and its accompanying isolation—is, as Kafka noted, the only pain that one might have avoided.

Joseph just here. Thursday night after Jim's I told him I responded to him with anger. Today he asked me why; I told him. It feels as if he doesn't take me seriously. I'm sure it's complicated and interesting why he doesn't—cross transference. etc.—but I don't care enough to unravel it with him. Nor does he.

A cabin on Lake Keuka. With Paul Klohr. A relief to be away from Brighton Street; maybe now I can write about it. such a relief that I remind myself to be cautious, don't ride this wave too far, prepare now for its conclusion, being washed ashore. Thoughts of moving out as soon as I return, of working in the office. This work has been stalled; I've been stalled.

July 3, 1974. Brighton Street. No one there is an intellectual, although each is bright. When she chooses, Willa discusses astutely capitalism and psychosocial development. People who know her any length of time cannot help but see the brilliance she evidently works to keep hidden. As John's reticence dissolves, a perceptive and analytic mind is disclosed. Johanna is practical if not shrewd, reads more than any of us, and even takes an interest in what I'm trying to do. So it is not that my companions are dull; is that their primary mode d'etre is not mental. Their basic method of functioning is not cognitive, but, I would say, intuitive. I tend to be more mental. For instance, I continue to be astonished how necessary it appears to be for me to articulate at relatively abstract levels what I experience. Otherwise my experience does not appear to surface.

At Brighton Street we speak to each other less often than I am accustomed to. Willa speaks the least, then I, then John.

Johanna speaks, it seems, the most, in fact constantly. Our talks tend to refer to matters associated with the house, and often they refer to internal states at the time. There is comparatively little talk about people who are not present. There is little talk of the "new," or of books just published, or of our individual futures. The focus tends to be the present and ourselves. I see this as somewhat consciously chosen, a consequence of our belief that continual self-reference heightens our awareness of immediate experience, and awareness which permits us more understanding of the present biographic situation, what is at stake, and what or paths must be.

I fear I sketch a group of egoists. We are in a certain sense— we have not forgotten ourselves and work not to—but we do spend considerable time in de-centered listening to each other, attempting to help the other explicate his condition, offering observations and suggestions when possible. During these times the self slips into the background; I am focused on John who describes his dream of the night before. I listen carefully to his choice of words; I watch his gestures, the tone of his voice and his apparent emotional state, in order to attempt to see underneath his words to what they (and the dream they describe) refer to. Then, if possible and solicited, I offer my analysis.

Mornings. Usually I awaken some time between seven and nine. Sip coffee, propped up in bed or in the backyard, warming myself in the morning sun. Then yoga postures, then zazen. Then, if possible, I work. I have met with difficulty recently. Always, I suppose, I meet with difficulty, but now with school over and the summer set aside for writing, I face it more. Often, after an hour of being blocked, I accompany Willa to the park, or walk in the neighborhood, visit friends in the afternoon, or take a nap, practice the piano and the saxophone, and then it is six o'clock: Willa who has been waitressing, John who has been doing carpentry, and Johanna temporarily a receptionist, all come home. Dinner, drinking, and long walks as night falls.

Walking. Looking at houses, expressing preferences occasionally, mostly observing. The summer nights have been cool or just right, the air comfortably flows around the face, the legs, the arms. Traffic on major streets sounds dully in the distance. Trees accentuate the sense of stability the old houses give the area. Imagining it in 1770, woods and Iroquois. How contingent social life is. How isolated we are now, how fearful (bright street lights newly installed, everything lit harshly like a freeway). Ugly stained hard streets, metal boxes and their fumes, danger, to Molly dog "hoa!" at each corner. A few on their porches, watching as we pass, sometimes a gesture, a visible acknowledgement of each others' presence. Walking, walking, fast at first, then block after block a little slower, something inside ground down, a tension made dull, like a knife worn dull by use. I in my head, my body gliding underneath, each picture slightly different, moving past this tree, approaching that house, a car, memories, associations, patterns I'm tired of, a tiny effort to return to the walking, the houses, the night, this night. The presence of John next to me, walking rhythmically, a word, then nothing, then "ready to go back?" Number 22 Brighton Street, Rochester, New York, comes closer, on the porch the people who live upstairs, guitar, voices, beer bottles, the moon overhead, my body, my head still now, tired, enough has passed to be done with the day.

* * *

Birds. Sitting in the cottage, writing this. The leaves, like muffled applause, crescendo, then subsiding, chirping here, answered over there. An insistent sound, like a windhammer only it's a bird, soft, lifeful. Now a motor from the lake. Fisherman. My head dull, everything odd, everyone asleep as dawn begins. The wind louder, louder; rain falls.

Johanna and I are friends. She is fond of me, and I of her. As she puts it, she leans on me, tests her ideas on me, and complains to me, even about Willa and John. I am sympathetic, mostly. She is talented; she sings, plays the trumpet, acts. She is flamboyant, exuberant, loud, sometimes stubborn. Sexually she is frank, and discusses her sexual interests and acts in detail. Regards herself as bisexual, although her explicit sexual interest in women seems small, and her experience with them limited.   Her boyfriend is a heroin addict and lives in New York; he drops in from time to time.

Willa and I are friends, but the fit is less snug than it feels with Johanna. We listen to each other, discuss our dilemmas, get advice; we're there for each other. But we don't lean too heavily upon each other; she continually refers me to myself, often unsympathetic to my unhappiness or frustration. She comes to me more to hear herself, to get what is blocked, then to seek advance and sympathy. This is her way, but it is also correct in terms of our relationship. Finally we are at cross purposes; we speak past each other, never quite hit the mark. Our gift to each other may be mutual respect.

I admit I am fascinated with her. She is spirit in body; sometimes I almost expect her to step out of her. Whenever I look at her she is artful. It is only partly conscious. She appears to glide, though inside I know she's working hard nearly all the time. She is earnest about living. She breaks down of course, regresses, becomes petty, aggressive, self-indulgent. Sometimes she is a shrew, but the odd thing is that finally it makes no difference.   Her anger, which all three of us try to avoid, is obscured by her grace, her intelligence, in a word, her presence.

"John is wonderful." Each of us talks about him that way. On the surface he is steady and I feel steady when around him. Underneath he feels angry, and this is blocked on the whole. In fact, he is generally repressed, and knows it. He has worked hard to make contact with his repressed material, and his movement is discernible. It is astonishing actually, and often I am delighted by an observation he has made. We take long walks together, discuss our dreams, emotions, ideas; we like and respect each other. Sometimes he frustrates me; I imagine he talks to me because I am the only other male in the house. Yet, a friendship not quite that impersonal has developed, however much in the shadow of Willa it is. He and Willa are splitting up, however. Already a week has passed since they slept together, although he still comes over and considers her his lover. Willa told me the day I left she considers him just a friend. I hope he can make the adjustment it appears he'll have to make with relative ease.

What am I doing? On Brighton Street, living with people so different from how I am. It is temporary; I sense that. I'm to learn from them; learn to live with diversity, to see my interests, particularly my intellectual interests, in a broader context, to diminish my egocentricity, to speak out from my heart, to live on another basis and put the intellect in its place. All these reasons yes, but it's so instrumental. I want a family, a home, a place to rest from work, not yet another place to work. Is that self-indulgent?

I am backed down, unable to work. I know enough not to force it, but what if it never comes of itself. This week I am rewarded. In this cottage by Keuka Lake I am able to write. But when I return? And what is this I am writing?

I am blocked, uncertain, isolated, unhappy. A Zen master says the twenties are the most difficult. I am twenty-six.

* * *

July 30, 1974. Blackwater Falls, West Virginia. In a cabin, in the middle of woods, with Mark, birds in the background, sun and shadows. Again it takes absence for me to write. After the week on Lake Keuka, a week in Columbus, back to Rochester and the move.

I had decided, rather realized, while at the lake that I must move, that what I was doing at Brighton Street was over. A mild fear of living alone dissuaded me, but away I saw how little work I was doing, how dissatisfied I was emotionally, in a word, how I must leave.

When I returned from the lake (a Saturday morning, everyone still asleep, my room used and unrepaired, a plant dead from no water, another overturned and unattended), I began looking for a place, saying nothing to anyone for a couple of days.

As it turned out, Willa had taken a place too, around the block. Johanna took to bed, feeling abandoned. She acted hurt, then angry, then cold. As usual, I withdrew. I moved quickly, feeling guilty a little, angry a little. Disappointed that the three of us (Willa and I had had a silly fight which angered me disproportionately) were unable to separate more calmly.

Initially I blamed the two of them (John remained constant throughout: uninvolved, aloof, but friendly). Willa had started the fight; Johanna was overdramatizing her practical difficulties (no roommates to help with the rent) and her emotions. Now I know I participated in the general tension. I recall being angry and withdrawn and attempting to mask this state with a rather frozen friendliness.

So I left Brighton Street. To East Avenue. The George Eastman house sits on East Avenue, a boulevard lined with huge old places. The house I moved into, I am told, Mr. Eastman built for his mistress; another says it was for his physician. Whoever it was built for lived in a remarkable place. One room has a wall that is nearly all glass. Outside the window is an ancient lilac bush, smaller trees and bushes and a hedge which forms a back curtain. The windows face west, and the soft late afternoon sun is filtered into leaf-like patterns on the walls and floors by the plants outside. The other room is long. At one end is a marble fireplace, its mantle, polished and darkgrained, with lion's heads carved at each end. Leaded windows. The two long walls are old, polished, worn wood. The ceiling is stone and carved to form lines of flowers extending from side to side.

In contrast to Brighton Street, this apartment is order and stability. One room is light, nearly outside, the other dark, somber yet not depressed. Quiet, and now that I am its only inhabitant, reflective of my mood.

Commentary

June 9, 1976. Sitting in my office on campus, sweating in the summer heat. It occurs to me to take each theme I identified in *The Voyage Out* and use it as a sieve through which to pour biographic situation. Correspondences, if any, should become discernible.

First, I read the piece on happiness in the novel. I thought of the reference to a Zen master somewhere in the biographic description; he says the twenties are difficult. In the novel happiness comes, if at all, after youth. It is clear to me I focused on this aspect in the novel—on happiness and when in characters' lives they felt it—because it is something of an issue for me in 1974. As I remember this time now, I see I was fairly unhappy. I wonder if this is evident in the biographic description, and if I acknowledge it there. I'll reread this section now.

There is a conscious fear of aging near the beginning of the June 23rd entry. Soon after a mention of pain, of the pain created by trying to avoid pain. In the cabin by the lake: "it's a relief to be away from Brighton Street. I've been stalled." Conscious of my readers when I write: "I fear I sketch a group of egoists." It makes me think that some of the fear I sense in this section comes from anticipated criticism. I do not know how to extricate this fear from fear of my housemates or fear of my future. All I can say is that some of it was focused here, some there: what is fundamental is the fact of fear. I carry it with me, and pour it onto different "objects."

Just before the section beginning "walking." I describe my day briefly, and succinct as the description is—well, that's the point isn't it. It *is* succinct, bordering on terse; the lack of emotion is indicative of the defense, repression in this instance. The quality of my lived experience of those days was sufficiently painful to have to exclude it. I'm now more able to allow myself to feel more my pain.

The "walking" section: "how isolated people are ... how fearful. Ugly stained hard streets. Walking, fast at first, then block after block a little slower, something ground down, a tension made dull." This passage corresponds with Richard Dalloway's remarks to Rachel on the isolation and tension of modern life.

Speaking of Brighton Street: "I want a family, a house, a place to rest from work, not yet another place to work. Is that indulgence?" There is pain here. Today I see the importance of the work I did then. It has to do with relationships, with the emotional life in general, and today I don't want to escape from it as I wanted then. I don't expect escape. There are times of rest, but it is clearer now than it was then that a major portion of life's work involves relationships, involves the intimacy and emotional disturbance often attending them. This sense of relationships is reflected in my reading of the novel.

The tension involved in this writing. Fear. Yes, there it is, just before the July 30th entry: "I am blocked, uncertain, isolated, unhappy. A Zen master in Japan says the twenties are the most difficult." The hope at end of the description.

I was not conscious of how unhappy I was during that period in 1974. It is easy to see why I chose happiness as one theme of the text. [In the same vein, it is easy to see why I chose *The Voyage Out* itself.] There is little of it in the novel. Rachel is repressed; her life in the novel is a kind of emotional coming out. The parallel is my own repression. I begin the description with everyone but myself, and only after I've worked through the others I find myself, and it is a constricted and unhappy self. That's what Rachel finds as well. For her, however, the pain is physical, the result of the illness she contracts. There is divergence at the end: in the novel Rachel dies and in the description there is hope.

June 11, 1976. Describing Brighton Street, just after the paragraph on the university: "our talks tends to refer to matters ... in the present." Such an agenda is in reaction to trivial talk, talk no more significant than baseball statistics. The commitment is to speak about what occurs within, refusing to become like those Rachel imagined in churches: "innumerable men and women, not seeing clearly, who finally gave up the effort to see, and relapsed into praise and acquiescence, half-shutting their eyes and pursing their lips." Anything but half-shut eyes, pursed lips, lives not lived.

June 12, 1976. Spirit. Having read the piece on spirit in the novel, I have nothing to say. To the description. Early in the June 23rd entry. Stephen Spenders' photograph and aging. I think of Rachel musing on how the furniture remains after one disappears. The aging of the body fascinated me then. The spirit inside changes, moves, expands, but the body: it slowly creases and sags. In contrast to Rachel's observation, it seems as if it is the spirit which has duration, and material objects, like the body, which seem to deteriorate before our eyes.

At Brighton Street we were committed to what we called development, to what many friends called spiritual work. At that stage we worked to focus on the present, on the biographic meanings of events, and our responses to them. This is a different sense of "spirit" than occurs in the novel, but the fact of an interest in the spiritual in my life, and the interest in it in the text, is not fortuitous.

About Willa I write: "she is spirit in body; sometimes I almost expect her to step out of it." I think of Rachel's question: "'does it ever seem to you, Terrence, that world is composed entirely of vast blocks of matter, that we're nothing but patches of light'—she looked at the soft spots of sun wavering over the carpet and up the wall—'like that?'" Willa is sunlight in the flesh.

My questions near the end of the description mirror Evelyn's at the end of the novel. She asks: "what had she done with her life? What future was there for her?" From the biographic description: "what am I doing on Brighton Street, living with people so different from how I am?" A sense of unreality, of things not grounded, of light on solid objects but unattached, roving here then there. Solid objects have stability; light does not. My life was light: unattached, meandering, unstable.

June 13, 1976. The description of my housemates reminds me of many relationships in *The Voyage Out*, relationships characterized by a certain formality and lack of consciousness. One plays a role for another; one makes use of the other. She complains; I listen. Two people present to each other, mutually negotiating that presence: such a relationship seems absent in the text (except for Terrence and Rachel) and absent at Brighton Street (except for the relationship between Willa and me, which, while attenuated, was nonetheless present). Reading the description of Willa I notice I haven't portrayed the relationships among us. There is little mention of her relationship to John (except that it is ending) or to Johanna. There is discussion of my response to the three, but I am struck now how little discussion of relationship generally there is in this biographic situation.

Regarding Willa's relationship with me: "frustrated because no man she has met is so developed ... she tends to express her frustration, anger, and disappointment in her analysis of the other. Thus her knife cuts deeper and with coarser movements that such a delicate operation properly permits, and some injury and bleeding occurs." Remembering this I feel anger, anger at Willa, anger at relationships generally. Always after something not found in oneself. I think of Helen's observation in the novel: "the lives of these people ... the aimlessness, the way they live. One goes from one to another, and it's all the same. One never gets what one wants out of any of them." This morning I see why I chose *The Voyage Out*, why it came to me that spring. Its relationships mirrored mine at Brighton Street.

Conclusion

In this brief exercise we hint at the reciprocal relation between knower and what is known. The student of the text creates the text as it creates the student. Issues "in the text," it becomes clear, are also issues "in the reader." His issues shape the character of his reading, and the reading shapes his understanding of his biographic situation. If the work is done investigatively, that is without attempting to force a reciprocal relation, it can have developmental effects. These are brought by heightened awareness of what is at work in his situation, a situation, we note, which changes as he works. Reading the novel functioned to invite awareness of my situation, and this awareness invited its transformation. That is a fundamental psychoanalytic premise we find operative in this autobiographical work.

In this specific text-situation relationship we note a basic structural relationship between intellectual work in general and, if you will, the intellectual worker. One's intellectual interests are formed by the character of one's biographic issues, whether conscious of these or not, and these issues are in turned shaped by the content of one's intellectual issues. Employing this version of the method of *currere* one invites first heightened awareness of both interests and situation, in what Habermas terms the relation between knowledge and human interest (although here in kernel—individual—form), and such awareness thus invites transformation of both interest and situation. In a certain sense the method is one device by means of which the curriculum theorist may work to cultivate his or her own intellectual development. If one feels himself arrested intellectually, probably one is arrested biographically. If one wishes to focus upon his interests, one cannot do so without attention to the situation these interests are both cause and consequence of.

Awareness and transformation are never absolute, final acts, and while material circumstances may change, the fundamental biographic issues—of, say, relationship or happiness—may remain. The notion of figure/ground is useful in describing the relative prominence of any given issue in any given period of one's life. While one is hardly finished with issues of relationship, one may work through these issues sufficiently so that another, until now latent, issue presents itself as central to the composition of the biographical present. There is, we have found, a definite sense of development to the identification and examination of these issues and their symbolic expression in intellectual interests. It is not a matter of a static "this issue then that one." "That one" depends upon resolution of a prior one, and one experiences them as sequential. While such a concept is quickly too linear to comprehensively describe the experience of development, it is partially expressive. Success in this work is felt as movement, as awareness of issues and the biographic function of intellectual work that were before veiled, and transformation of both issues and work. One experiences intellectual and biographic movement.

In a certain sense this work often feels like a voyage out, from the habitual, the customary, the taken-for-granted, toward the unfamiliar, the more spontaneous, the questionable. The experimental posture in its most profound meaning suggests this openness to what is not known, a willingness to attempt action the consequences of which cannot be predicted fully. Such a capacity to risk—intellectually, biographically—can be cultivated through the work described here. It is a capacity those of us interested in education are obligated to develop.

References

Apple, M. (1978). Ideology and form in curriculum evaluation. In G. Willis (ed.), *Qualitative Evaluation* (495-521). Berkeley: McCutchan.

Foucault, M. (1978, Summer). Interview in *Telos*.

Levy, B-H. (1979). *Barbarism with a human face*. Trans. G. Holoch. New York: Harper & Row.

Reid, W. A. (1978). *Thinking about the curriculum*. London: Routledge & Kegan Paul.

Sartre, J-P (1963). *Search for a method*. New York: Knopf.

Walker, D. F. & W. A. Reid (1975) (ed.). *Case studies in curriculum change*. London: Routledge & Kegan Paul.

Woolf, V. (1920). *The voyage out*. New York: Harcourt, Brace, & Co. Copyright by the George H. Doran Co.

IX

Understanding Curriculum as Gender Text: Notes on Reproduction, Resistance, and Male-Male Relations
(1981)

Introduction: the reproduction of father

Reproduction theory, that is, the explanation of the context, structure and experience of the curriculum by pointing to its reproductive function for the socio-politico-economic status quo, has now been surpassed. Its mechanicalness, its reduction of the Subject to passivity, its obfuscation of structural contra-dictions and of resistance, have been condemned in several recent essays[1] and conferences.[2] With few exceptions, curricu-lum theorists on the Left now call for examination of resis-tance, not only as an empirical reality to be documented and understood, but as well as a call for political action.

I wish to situate reproduction and resistance theory oedipally. I do so not to reduce them to their oedipal status and functions. I offer this sketch in order to illumine feminist and gender issues which in their current stages of formulation, reproduction and resistance theory only tips its hat in acknowledgement of. While such courtesy is appreciated, it is insufficient. It denies the seriousness and scope of gender issues as it co-opts the anger and actions of those who live them. Further, I believe the broad political project of which resistance is a historical, theoretical moment, is finally sabotaged by reducing feminist and gender issues to their political and economic concomitants.

What is the oedipal status of reproduction theory, and of its offspring, resistance theory? In a word, I see them as the analyses of the heterosexual son as he observes how the authority of the Father is reproduced and can be resisted. The oedipal function of such theory is parallel to the action of the heterosexual son: the replacement, someday, of Father. Heterosexual sons become Fathers, and fathers require sons, daughters, and wives, all metaphors for underclasses. Father is reproduced, regardless the rhetoric of horizontal social relations, i.e. brotherhood and sisterhood. Educationally, resistance theory, *née* reproduction theory, appears confined to altering the content of curriculum but not its political consequences. The conversation of Father may change but not his position at the dinner table. Schooling in this sense is the story of the son's and daughters' initiation into the Father's ways, and their consignment of the Mother, sometimes with her complicity, to the status of unpaid or underpaid laborer and sexual slave. The family drama is the cultural-historical drama writ small and concretely.

Understanding curriculum and curriculum theory oedipally is not fortuitous. The feminist and gay movements[3] have brought to attention issues of gender origin, identity, and prejudice. In curriculum studies, rapid theoretical movement is evident.[4] For instance, in a recent paper, Madeleine R. Grumet traces the gender history of pedagogy in American common schools during the nineteenth and early twentieth centuries. She concludes that the growing number of female teachers, i.e. "the feminization of teaching," functioned to ensure "pedagogy for patriarchy."[5]

Grumet argues that male administrators enlisted the assistance of female teachers to induct the children into their ways, ways which conditioned the boys to become docile, efficient workers, and the girls to become willing and grateful housewives and full-time mothers. Feminist analysis attacks this complicity and passivity, and in so doing has helped initiate and name the struggle beyond them. In curriculum theory this struggle and its naming have just begun.[6] It is a struggle that will be sabotaged by men who refuse to examine their role in its origin and necessity. Feminist literature has examined this role from points of view that are Hers; I wish to sketch it from His.

Specifically I am interested in how male-male relations are implicated in male-female oppression. My focus will be primarily, but not exclusively, male pre-oedipal, oedipal and post-oedipal experience. While this focus may make this essay of minimal use to feminist struggle and theory, I hope it will be viewed as politically allied with them. However, men's analysis cannot be expected to coincide with women's, even if they originate with them.

I suspect that men cannot usefully appropriate feminist understanding and substitute it for their own. We cannot become "feminist men" for long or very deeply without denying our gender-specific life histories. As feminists have discovered for themselves, we must distance ourselves from those we learned to need and love and—as feminists have documented—violate. Such psychological distance from women is in the service of understanding our relations with them, not only from their point of view and certainly not from our taken-for-granted view. While feminist understanding provokes an analogous process of our own, that process is undergone by ourselves. Further, I agree with some feminist separatists that women cannot fully support us without denying their oppression. If aware of that oppression, women have little good will to extend to us, at this historical juncture. Having relied upon women, traditionally, for succor, we face a difficult, potentially dangerous task without them. We men do exhibit "stunted relational potential."[7] Intimacy with women threatens us, but less so than intimacy with other men. I am suggesting that in order to understand our oppression of women, we must work to understand our oppression of each other. This work has begun in the culture at large, with men's groups of various but often superficial sorts. Our work with ourselves is well behind the work women have done with themselves. This analysis, I hope, can contribute to an acceleration of this necessary study of male-male relations.

Pre-oedipal relations and post-oedipal distortions

To begin to understand male gender history, we can focus upon two items which influence that history. One is the nature of the pre-oedipal relationship with the mother; the other is the inferential character of paternity. Both are described by Nancy Chodorow in her *The Reproduction of Mothering: Psychoanalysis and the Sociology of Gender.*[8] This is a carefully argued work which delineates the constellation of elements associated with the fact that it is women who mother. Chodorow outlines the implications of that seemingly natural fact for ego and gender differentiation. The book focuses upon the experience of women appropriately enough, and tends to only hint at the experience of men. I will attempt to take that hint and suggest what male experience tends to be.

Let us begin with the second item, namely that paternity is necessarily inferred. The male seed is nameless and not easily identified. Even the physical appearance of the child cannot be relied upon to verify the identity of the father. Jokes about the "milkman" illustrate the commonness of male concern arising from the ultimate ambiguity of paternity. Chodorow suggests that this fact stimulates an anxiety which males attempt to mask and control by specifying rather precisely kinship patterns. He becomes excessively interested in the lines of reproduction, and in most cultures insists upon the use of his name to identify "ownership" of "his" children. The compensation appears to succeed. Fatherhood tends not to be the vague, inferred status that it is. Instead, it is the father who is the "cause" of children; the woman is said to only "carry" "his" baby. The woman becomes a kind of cocoon in which the father's creation incubates until ready for "delivery," surely not a woman's word for childbirth.[9]

Ambiguity of paternity is intolerable for men possibly because ambiguity of ego was renounced, an outcome of the oedipal crisis, and the second item of male gender history we will notice. Ambiguity of ego refers to the relative sharpness of ego differentiation. Chodorow argues that during the early phases of the pre-oedipal period, both mother-daughter and mother-son relationships are undifferentiated. During pregnancy the infant was literally a part of his or her mother, and during the early months the infant is totally reliant upon her. During this period the infant has no defenses and internalizes without much modification the emotions, and in the case of breastfeeding, the milk of the mother. The infant identifies with her mother; he *is* his mother. Only slowly, during moments of absence, does it begin to dawn on the infant that he or she is a separate being. Chodorow locates the beginning of individual ego differentiation during these moments. As soon as the process of ego differentiation begins, it begins to differ for boys and girls. The mother-daughter relationship remains less differentiated than the mother-son relationship. The mother knows that this daughter will also know pregnancy, parturition, possibly breastfeeding. Because they are the same sex, and because it tends to be women who mother and men who do not, the mother projects "sameness" onto her daughter, permitting the elongation of their ego merging and intertwining.

The son elicits a different response. He will not know pregnancy; probably he will not share the same experience of feeding and caring for "his" infant. The son is different than she, and she projects "otherness," sometimes eroticized, onto him. As a result, the process of ego differentiation proceeds more quickly for him than for his sister. By the time he confronts and is confronted by his father over each other's relationship to the mother/wife, and over their relationship to each other, the boychild is separate enough to experience his mother as separate and as an "object" of desire. The "otherness" projected onto him by the mother makes more facile his compliance with his father's demand that he move further away from her and from "women's things," that he see as strange and not-male the domestic, female world, more credible the stigma of "sissy," and finally more complete his repression of his initial identification with Her.

Chodorow underlines the matri-sexual nature of the infant's experience. She concludes that this mother-infant relationship leaves the daughter in a homoerotic position vis-a-vis her mother, a position she must abandon during the oedipal crisis. The boy is in a heterosexual position, a position reinforced by his later identification with his father. This analysis is incomplete, however, as it ignores the primal layer of social experience which occurs before the process of ego differentiation has advanced sufficiently to permit the mother to be an "other" to be desired. The initial relationship to the mother, a relatively undifferentiated and undefended one from the infant's position, suggests that underneath the desire for the mother is incorporation, in the case of the heterosexual mother, of that mother's desire for the father. If this is so, and the relatively undifferentiated mother-infant relationship would suggest so, then the primal layer of sedimented memory is heterosexual (again in the case of heterosexual mothers) for the girl-child and homosexual for the boy-child. Only as both separate and distinguish themselves from her, do they experience desire for her.

From this view the male child's earliest pre-oedipal experience, the oedipal admonishment to put away childish things, i.e. mother and female-associated items and feelings, is also a call to suppress his desire for the father. Thus the oedipal resolution for the son involves not only heterosexual sublimation, i.e. postponement and redirection of his desire for the mother, but it involves homosexual repression as well, i.e. the denial of desire for his father. This repression is reinforced during subsequent social experience as males "police" themselves, ensuring that no action interpretable as homoerotic is expressed. Further, young boys tend to seize upon the discovery of a feminized boy as an opportunity to locate, or more precisely, to dislocate and displace, their own repressed homosexuality. Heterosexual male relations, then, are complicated by homosexual repression; they become fragile, easily sabotaged and conflictual. The result of contemporary male heterosexuality, because it requires repudiation of the initial identification with the mother, is misogyny, and because it involves repression of the internalized desire for the father, heterosexual warfare, literal and symbolic. With this observation, however, we have jumped ahead of our story.

We may surmise that the pre-oedipal period, with its vulnerability and increasing awareness of dependency, has terrifying moments for the infant. For the daughter this terror is complemented by her submersion in the mother. For the daughter the oedipal crisis permits further differentiation from the Other, but it is a struggle for ego identity that often lasts long into adulthood, so powerful is the mother-daughter symbiosis.

Ego identity and differentiation, according to many psychotherapists, is a common if not the most common presenting symptom in women seeking psychotherapy. [10]

As noted, the symbiosis of the mother-son relation is briefer as the mother projects "otherness" onto him, creating a distance from her which makes the construction of a male identity possible. It is an identity that must be acquired through repressing his earliest identification with the mother, and through observation of his father's ways. Because the father's relative absence from the home makes him an idealized, nearly imaginary figure for both boys and girls, the son relies upon the father's words as well for his picture of what it is that men do and do not do. As he becomes more male (i.e. aggressive, assertive, competitive), more identified with his father, he comes to feel His desire for his wife overlaying his nascent desire for his mother. We have reached the moments of oedipal conflict as the son's desire for the father has now been repressed, and sublimated into identification with him; he becomes now a rival for His wife. The father now moves to remove his son to a non-competitive position with him, transferring that competition onto his peers, symbolized into social activities of various kinds, such as school and sports. The father achieves this "removal" by logic and by force. Although not communicated succinctly or even verbally at all, he persuades the son that the son will be compensated for a) completing the repression of the now attenuated identification with the mother, and b) for abandoning his desire for her. In return for his repudiation of the female in him, he can possess a female—a wife, a lover—later. In return for disowning the mother in him the son as adult will obtain a "wife," i.e. a woman reified and externalized, whose actions and presence in his life he can regulate according to custom and law. Such regulation is psychologically necessary for the male as her spontaneous movement would threaten evocation of Her inside; yet her presence in regulated ways satisfies his need for the woman he has denied internally.

If the son fails to accept the logic of latency, the father resorts to force. The careful father attempts to restrain the use of force as it inhibits the recently-acquired and developing personality characteristics associated with being a man, i.e. competitiveness, etc. Still, some force, some struggle, is necessary as it strengthens and hardens this imprinting. Excessive force may produce a defeated son, one who sees no point in resisting the father, or in identifying with him, in the latter case feeling betrayed by the father's oedipal treatment of him. The successfully endured oedipal crisis produces a son who delays his desire for the female and intensifies his identification with the male. Because both consequences involve mechanisms of denial and repression, the son produced is one with an overly-determined ego, an ego with less access to emotion and to sedimented memory, i.e. unconscious process and content, than does the typical ego of the daughter. This overly-determined ego results in "stunted relational potential." Feelings of separateness and individuality can rather easily become feelings of loneliness and dissociation. To "stand up on one's own and be a man" comes at the cost of debilitating repressions. Post-oedipal intimacy, especially as an adult, with a woman, tends to stimulate his repressed pre-oedipal, undifferentiated intimacy and identification with the mother. Adult intimacy with another man threatens to renew his repressed desire for the father from the early pre-oedipal period and/or his less-repressed rage from "losing" the oedipal competition for the mother. Condemned then to an over-determined self, isolated from its own unconscious processes and content and capable of only attenuated forms of intimacy with others, the adult male in our time, in our culture, can tend to seek refuge and escape from his condition in work (careerism and the problem of the "workaholic") and pleasure (hedonism, including sexual promiscuity and drugs, including alcohol).

Seduction, not resistance

The over-determination of the male ego makes the ambiguity of paternity intolerable. He compensates for its inferential character by claiming "first cause," the origin of creation. He further compensates with an excessive interest in kinship patterns, i.e. the lines of reproduction. In this sense the recent interest on the Left in reproductive theories of curriculum are patriarchal in nature, although given the political status of the Left in the United States it is the nascent patriarchy of the aspiring Son, not the mature and established patriarchy of the Father. As the son, leftist curriculum theorists search for room for resistance, which at one conference was characterized as "non-reproductive" education.[11]   It is oedipally significant that the inspiration for this move "beyond passive analysis" seems to have originated in Paul Willis' account of "the lads." It is the resistance of adolescent boys, of "boys being boys," a resistance the Father understands as more-or-less normal, no final threat to His authority.

The position of the reproduction theorist, and his most recent transmutation, the resistance theorist, can be likened to that of the son who observes the ways in which the Father (the embodiment of power and ideology) reproduces his status. Young and powerless, the pre-pubescent son is awed if angered at the power of the Father, a power which seems to reproduce itself lawfully. Older, he sees the relative contingency of the Father's position, and the possibility, indeed the duty, of resistance. Through "mobilization" and "struggle on all fronts" he can resist Him. We need only examine the subsequent history of the son to observe the outcome of this struggle: the son rarely wins this battle; he ordinarily replaces the Father by outliving Him. The point is that the son does replace Him; he occupies his position. Is it possible that resistance reproduces patriarchy?

I want to suggest an oedipal strategy which differs from the traditional one, in fact a strategy whose aim is dissolution of the oedipal complex, of the familial, social, and economic structures which accompany it. This strategy shares the interest in "non-reproduction." It is a male who loses interest in his political status as "first cause," as the locus and impetus of generation. He becomes a degenerate. He no longer wishes to resist Him and thereby replace Him. Now the son seeks to sleep with Him. Such desire does not begin in love. Given the historical moment, it begins in the same fury as does resistance. But now the son turns on his father in a way the father is unprepared to co-opt. The son refuses circumcision, that index of the oedipal wound signifying male repudiation of the female and the father's consequent promise of the world for the son's complicity. Instead, the son stares at the father, saying: "I refuse your ritual of manhood and its denial of the woman in me and of the woman who gave life to me. My mother, the source of my life, from whose body I came, in whose care I have lived, my companion and lover, but through whose complicity with you is also my traitor, as she turned me over to you, I stand by her, remain a part of her, and refuse your contract. I refuse to exchange her for you, her world (the private, expressive, intimate, relational world) for yours (the public, abstract, codified, hierarchical world). I refuse your lie (that I can have her again when I'm big like you, in the form of a wife, trading my mother for sexual object and unpaid laborer), and your repudiation of me (now that I have relinquished her, now that I am your "little man," you dispense your affection, such as it is, in units designed to manipulate me to achieve the dreams you failed to realize), and I refuse to displace the pain from her loss and the fury at your deception onto all others female and male. I reject the whole oedipal contract, and in so doing retain my longing for you, a longing now laced with hatred. It is not your power I want now. It is you."

Phallocentrism is the embodied ideology of oedipally-produced male sexuality. Screwing and getting screwed are what homosexual men do literally, and what heterosexual men do to each other symbolically; one form of sexuality is the shadow of the other. In their contemporary expressions, both tend to be socially distorted as they are dissociated fragments of a forgotten human whole. We men are at war with each other, on battlefields, in corporate meeting rooms, in lecture halls, all symbolizations and abstractions from the father wound and the mother repudiation. Homosexuality becomes the site of the politics of the concrete, of the body, the potential politics of authentic solidarity and mutual understanding. Let us confront each other, we the circumcised wounded ones, not on the battlefield as abstracted social roles and political pawns of the Father, but in bed, as embodied, sexualized beings fighting to feel what we have forgotten, the longing underneath the hatred.

Heterosexuality as political institution

Hocquenghem reminds us that the concept "homosexual" did not exist prior to the nineteenth century. The capacity and desire to sleep with same-sexed persons was presumed to exist to lesser or greater extent in everyone, hence the scope and intensity of efforts to prohibit the expression of such desire. During the latter part of the nineteenth century, a medicalization of the socially deviant began to occur. That is, medical terms became employed to describe the culturally marginal and the socially deviant. This medicalization of the social terrain served the political and economic interests of cultural homogeneity, which accompanied industrialization and bureaucratization. By assigning such labels as "homosexual" which indicated illness, the medical and legal communities could identify, prosecute, and punish, under the guise of providing "helping services," those whose lives were viewed as intolerably outside the mainstream. Those who were observed (voyeurism, as Hocquenghem notes, accompanies Law and Medicine, themselves bureaucratic systematizations of desire) to sleep with same-sexed persons more often than not, and/or those who exhibited personality characteristics sufficiently incongruent with prototypical feminine and masculine ideals, could be classified as pathological. Hocquenghem traces this story of increasing medicalization, including the appearance of "homosexuals," during the twentieth century, and documents that, contrary to popular belief, homosexuality is being increasingly suppressed, if more subtly.[12]

The lie is that there is homosexual desire. Following Deleuze and Guattari,[13] Hocqueghem insists that there is only desire. The polymorphous perversity, as Freud would have it, of infancy, becomes codified into genital sexuality. The story of oedipus is in this regard the story of the production of "heterosexuals," and the eradication, however unsuccessful, of homosexuals. Adrienne Rich describes heterosexuality as "compulsory," and as such "needs to be recognized and studied as a political institution."[14] Politically, it reinforces the position of the Father and guarantees its reproduction. Contemporary forms of heterosexuality tend to be phallocentric. For the male the phallus is the sign of his power as a man. Successfully socialized heterosexual women experience "penis envy" and desire its incorporation. While the phallus is the occasion for a man's pride or shame, he does not sexualize it. It is as if that which a woman desires is unworthy to be desired by him. He scorns the homosexual's interest in fellatio and in anal intercourse. In a phallocentric culture few homosexuals escape the fascination with the phallus; they concretize the heterosexual's fascination with its abstraction: power. Both groups reify their existence; both fail to see how the existence of each relies upon the existence of the other.

Men's (and many women's) fascination with the traditional masculine ideal, i.e. the macho man, is not without some merit. This ideal is comprised of several character traits which are admirable, such as courage and strength. However, we must acknowledge that these qualities are the socially fortunate outcomes of oedipus; often as not the macho man utilizes his strength and courage to rob, rape, and kill. In both prototypes these characteristics are not chosen but conditioned; they result from repressing the pre-oedipal identification with the mother and resisting semi-successfully the authority of the father. His "manliness," that discernible way of being in his body, tends to come at the expense of being in his mind and heart. His maternal repression—the more macho he is the more complete the repression is—makes him clumsy interpersonally, primitive intellectually, and a Neanderthal emotionally.

For his more civilized variations, the physical is abstracted onto the social and intellectual. Boots and jeans are traded for three-piece suits (at least during the day), and his manliness is determined not by his muscle and phallus size, but by the size of his bank account, stock portfolio and corporate position. He trades physical strength for acumen and shrewdness, and the macho man's narcissistic experience of himself as a body is now mediated through the bodies of the women with whom he sleeps. These characterological prototypes are crude but common. Perhaps less common and less crude are academic variations, including one version we might call, not entirely for mischief's sake, the macho Marxist. His body and probably his bank account have been exchanged for a long list of publications, physical strength and corporate shrewdness for tough logic, witty asides, and a virtuoso knowledge of Marx, Gramsci, and Bourdieu. He vanquishes his oedipal foe not with his fists or by outpositioning him corporately, but via skillful argumentation, and cogent denunciations of revisionist and obscurantist tendencies in his opponents' positions. The macho Marxist substitutes dialectical materialism for the crass kind, the terminal smile of the young executive "on the make" for the suffering frown and angry scorn of the wounded but resisting activist. The content of the personality and of the social relations which express and sustain it differs for each version of man. However, the structure of the personality and its social relations (competitiveness, aggressiveness, exhibitionism) does not. Each is interested in the phallus, his own and/or others; rather, each is interested in its abstracted social form: power. Each aggrandizes his own while diminishing his opponents; after the battle all tend to return to the nurse and lover for solace or celebration.

To attack patriarchy and fascism in their graduated and symbolic forms requires attacking one's own internalizations of them, however subtle their expression. We men are our fathers' sons; he resides within us, and his relation to his wife and to his children resides there as well. It is not only the Father we must resist, but our internalized relationship to Him. To be sure, working with one's relation to Her is useful and important. One can strive to become a feminist man. At some point, however, it is our repression of Her and identification with Him, with one's "compulsory heterosexuality," that must be unearthed and confronted. Political attitudes and actions are informed characterologically as well as systemically. In addition to a politics of the state, there is a politics of the individual, a hierarchy of internal object relations. If we are male and straight likely it is we have repudiated the woman in us for the fabricated male we were and He pretended to be. In our renunciation of Her and identification with Him we are committed to become Father ourselves, regardless of the political content of our rhetoric. And in becoming Father we will require wives and children, and the hierarchization of power will be reproduced, however consciously denied or resisted. We might cease our longing to become the Father, and instead long for Him, seducing Him, bringing Him down to us, in bed, on the floor, no longer son-father, now lovers. In the act of love we might become brothers, and as brothers we might help Her to become our sister. De-oedipalization is pro-feminist, and during the present historical moment, homosexual. It represents the decodification of desire, the dehierarchization of power. It is the de-territorialization of the libido, the de-possession of persons. In the discovery and expression of homosexual desire, we crack the dam of repression, psychological and political. What is leaked stains the social fabric, altering its composition even if it is reincorporated.

Dirty work

Hocquenghem observes that "the law is clearly a system of desire, in which provocation and voyeurism have their own place."[15] Systems of knowledge production and distribution, such as school curricula, are likewise systems, or in the present context, codifications of desire. The knowledge we choose for presentation to the young is in one sense like the parts of our bodies we allow them to see. Both the physical body and the body of knowledge are cathected objects, and decisions and policies regarding them follow from our own organization and repression of desire. This is not to ignore the so-called internal logic of the curriculum, i.e. those technical considerations which accompany its formulation and presentation. Nor is it to ignore its political, economic, and social functions. However, the present view does aspire to situate, although not reduce, these considerations and functions oedipally. Doing so reveals how curriculum reproduces compulsory heterosexuality and homosexual repression: the overdetermination of desire. Curriculum is the dictum of the Fathers, their conversation, rather pronouncements, to their children which seduce them to his reign, his power (phallus) at the center. And through the use of female teachers, as with mother's complicity in circumcision, the sons and daughters are delivered to Him. For sons, it is the circumcision ceremony in which they complete their repudiations of Her, and accept the wound—the scarred penis, the over-determined ego—which demarcates their initiation into the tribe of heterosexual men.[16]

For most the pre-oedipal experience is forgotten. It remains as "sedimentation," a primal memory of the nature of the world. One aspect of this memory is how the world is known. As Grumet has shown, the relatively undifferentiated relationship between mother and infant is inscribed epistemologically as subject-object reciprocity and mutual determinancy. The mother or the infant is the "other" or "object," but object boundaries are blurred. If the infant son could speak, his words might be: "She and I, we are one. My crying brings her comforting of me, sometimes her irritation with me, and my laughter brings her smile, her own laughter. No barrier insulates me from her love, sometimes from her anger, her joy, her impatience and fatigue. I taste these in her milk as I inhale them in the air, exuded as they are from her organs and her skin." The primal experience of the world is Mother, then gradually it moves to the bed on which he rests, the walls of the room, and so on, a slowly expanding world experienced through Her, changed through Her and through the infant. During the oedipal crisis, the groundwork for which has been laid by the mother's projection of "otherness" onto the son as well as the son's experience of her absences, the son dissociates himself from this viscous intermingling of self and other, subject and object. He denies mother so that she becomes the "other," not me, as opposite. Father, the absent abstract one, identification with whom involves far less co-mingling than imitation of what I the infant observe, and remembrance of what He tells me to be, becomes the knowable "other." I am to become like the "other," depersonalized, desubjectivized, objectified. Father and I are separate, discrete, and it is possible to know what is He and that which is I. Rather than my subjectivity intermingled with objectivity in moments of continuous mutual constitution, subjectivity and objectivity are now divorced. My subjectivity becomes an intrusion upon my clear perception of what He is and what He tells me There Is. I understand that my emotions, fantasies, etc., are "smudges on the mirror," to be kept cleaned off if I am to replicate without distorting the world "out there." In the oedipal experience is the gender foundation for a series of epistemological assumptions associated with twentieth-century mainstream social science. These assumptions include claims of value and political neutrality, and the objective to discover, through increasingly refined methods of observation, quantification and analysis, the nature of human reality. Oedipally it is the heterosexual son attempting to comprehend his father, a world that is removed yet discoverable, as it is the world into which father disappears each morning, and from which he returns, with stories, each night. It is this primal oedipal experience of father as a discrete "other" to be known, and of the world as alien but discoverable and knowable, that has become elaborately symbolized in modern mainstream social science, and in the school curriculum.

The daughter's experience, as we have seen, is different. She retains a more-or-less undifferentiated relation to the mother; her sense of the world thereby remains more fluid than her brother's. Intuitively she understands that experience is flux, some of it beyond our words, much of it beyond our numbers. She understands that influencing one aspect of a situation alters all aspects, and that quantification tends to freeze situation as it stops flux, and fixes aspects of experience to one level of conceptualization. During the oedipal period she complies with her father's desire for her, creating the distance from her mother necessary to feel her desire for her. Unlike her brother who must suppress identification with the mother, she maintains both that identification and desire for both parents. Thus a triangular relational configuration saturates her primal experience of the world. There is the relatively rigid, the demanding, the powerful and seductive: the father, world, objectivity. There is the relatively bending, the compliant, the intuitive: mother, self, subjectivity. Each influences the other; each contributes to the other's transformations, processes which she observes and perhaps reformulates. In this pre-oedipal and oedipal experience is the basis for a constructivist epistemology.[17]

For the son a more linear view of events, their causes and effects, is compelling. In repudiating his early mother identification, he commits himself to contradicting his initial experience of Her and the world as relatively undifferentiated and mutually constitutive. This commitment expresses itself in his efforts to contradict the inferential character of paternity. Recall that in order to deny the ambiguity of his causal status in semination, he posits himself as the cause, and the woman as the intervening variable, in the effect which is parturition. His compensation for his inferred status as father and for the loss of the feminine in his conscious ego knows few bounds as it extends into systems of kinship (his name replacing hers in marriage and becoming the children's is the familiar instance which hints at his general obsession with lines of reproduction), sexual slavery (including compulsory heterosexuality and homosexual repression), and epistemology.

In this latter domain he makes supreme systems of knowledge production in which knowledge of the objective world (a bifurcated, false concept in itself) is sought and systematized, and knowledge of subjective worlds, and their inter-relationships, is avoided or grudgingly accepted. We speak of "hard" research and "soft." Such gender values are expressed not only in the intellectual hierarchy within disciplines, but in the power structure of universities across disciplines. The highest salaries tend to go to scientists, the lowest to arts. The apex of patriarchy is the age of science. Even the arts and humanities are masculinized as evidenced by the use of computer programs in historical research (which of course can be helpful but which become ideological as they become de rigueur) and formalistic prose in literary and aesthetic criticism.

Where are we historically in the process of masculinization? Its abstracted forms will lag behind—given their relative autonomy—the specifically gender formation, and these indicate contradictory tendencies. For males a subtle yet discernible demasculinization can be observed.[18] Its sign is an evidently increasingly male interest in the appearance of masculinity, implying its loss of substance. Specifically, traditional masculinity was unaware of its appearance. Beauty, and working to make oneself beautiful, were professions of the "lady," although this sex-role expectation varied across class and according to ethnicity. Men who were especially handsome, and certainly those men who spent time attempting to be, were somehow less masculine than those "rough and ready" types who knew women would love them for their prowess, for just being men, not for their moustaches, tight jeans, or clear skin. I believe that the interest in the signs of masculinity, including not only dress but cosmetics, small-bed trucks with over-sized wheels, the renewed interest in "working-out" and in athletics generally signal the loss of a more traditional masculinity, a loss we can loosely attribute to changing market conditions (i.e., the increasing importance of "appearance" and "style" in successful corporate life), and to the feminist movement (including some women's explicit eroticization of the male body, for instance in publications like *Playgirl*). The emphasis upon masculinity at the time of this writing (December, 1981) represents a reactionary response to the feminist movement, as it attempts to reaffirm masculinity. But in its absorption in signs not substance men disclose their defeat. The delicate and changing balance between the oppose sexes is now clearly upset.

While there is de-masculinization, men have yet to recognize it. The reactionary response to feminism will probably pass, although not easily or quickly. The deep structural changes men must undergo to achieve equity with women come very slowly, partly because some women fear to press too heard, and mostly because most men are unwilling or unable to initiate or sustain such changes. Instead, they make surface alterations. Those middle-class men who apparently comply with their wives' and lovers' requests and demands for shared housework, parenting, and decision-making are only complying, on the whole. The deep structure of sexism, the socially-induced, oedipally-produced desire to become the patriarch, is not changed. Resentment accrues in unknowing men and in possibly unsuspecting women. We can expect violent crimes against women to continue to escalate in the short-term. We can expect abstracted masculine forms such as conceptual formalism to solidify and proliferate as compensatory developments to the disappearance of conventional masculinity.

Reinforcing this tendency is pressure upon women who enter the work force (typically at unequal pay for equal work) to conform to male expectation and standards of conduct. Those few who have managed to enter the academic work force, for instance, are pressed to acquiesce to dominant research paradigms. Being a woman and an autobiographer or a phenomenologist is having two strikes against you in most curriculum departments. This conformity expectation often intersects with the developmental project of many women to extend and sharpen their ego differentiation from the mother. To achieve this distance, to contradict this symbiotic object relation, many women embrace the stark logic and conceptual neatness of mainstream academic work in most disciplines. It may be we men (men who refuse to participate in the reproduction of patriarchy, or at least attempt to refuse), joining with certain feminists (those who celebrate not contradict their matrisexuality) who might rediscover and reformulate hermeneutic research methods, methods which portray more fully, if more messily at first, the flux and mutli-dimensionality of experience. Such an effort toward Reconceptualization cannot occur intellectually only. It involves a de-oedipalization of the person, and with it, a de-oedipalization of the intellect. This intellect of he or she who remains in a relatively undifferentiated relation to the Mother is not the masculinized, calculating, instrumental intellect, caricatured in modern literature by Joseph K. in Kafka's *The Trial*.[19] Instead it is the intellect which portrays the simultaneity of thought, feeling, and action, not of atomized individuals (those with overdetermined egos, characteristic of the modern professional male) but those still connected, co-mingling, capable of community. It is the intellect of Virginia Woolf.[20]

Similarly in schools we cannot rely upon all women to sabotage—even if conditions were favorable for attempting so—bureaucratization, standardization, and the bogus "individualization" of many classrooms. Grumet notes:

> So the male educators invited women into the schools expecting to reclaim their mothers, and the women accepted the invitation and came so that they may identify with their fathers. Accordingly, female teachers complied with the rationalization and bureaucratization that pervaded the common schools as the industrial culture saturated the urban areas. Rather than emulate the continuous and extended relation of a mother and a maturing child that develops over time, they

acquiesced to the graded schools, to working with one age group for one year at a time. Rather than demanding the extended relation that would bind them over time to individual children, they agreed to large group instruction where the power of the peer collective was at least as powerful as the mother bond.[21]

Grumet locates this complicity with the father's agenda at the "crossroads" of male and female efforts to contradict their internalized object relations. The male attempts to recover the repressed "other" in him by arranging her presence about him, a presence he regulates as he controls—as administrator, schoolboard member, and textbook author and publisher—the curriculum. His political control intersects with her project to escape the symbiotic relation to the mother by gaining access to the public domain of the father. As Grumet concludes, pedagogy for patriarchy was achieved through the feminization of teaching.

The culture of the classroom is a patriarchal one as it is drained of the personal, the intimate, the psychological, as it is drenched in competitiveness, task-orientedness, and achievement. The overdetermined ego of the male (with gradations of the macho personality as a result) is celebrated in literature as it is required to adopt to the demands of those who serve it, those who do its dirty work—female teachers. She speaks in his absence, by his authority, and the tales of human life she tells the children ensure that the culture of the classroom is reproduced. Yes, there is resistance, as Willis as shown, autobiographers have always known and reproduction theorists have recently discovered. But it is the resistance of the oedipally-produced son, a resistance that is tolerated because it can be coopted. The son must not be squashed, only repressed. He must complete the estrangement from the feminine by amplifying the aggressive and angry. Of course, he must not "get out of hand." As black radicals have known, the gender of the enemy is male; it is "the man." Resisting pleases the Father as it assures Him the son wants what He has: power, position. His son's lust for the Father has now been abstracted from the physical onto its political derivative. It is lust that will ultimately assure the complicity of the son in his Father's regime, and his Mother's domesticity and relative slavery.

Father's authority is communicated by his pretentious seriousness, his virility, his cold capacity to oppose and suppress the Other when he judges it necessary, to compete for scarce commodities (and to keep them scarce), by sons who serve as his policemen, his military, his bureaucrats, his rebels (who underline his importance as they keep him mobilized), and by women who praise his achievements, attend to his wounds, and do his dirty work.[22]   This authority of the Father is corroded primarily by the son who refuses to obey or defy him, to be his cheerful clone or his frowning—with clenched fist—opponent. It is corroded by the woman who returns his lust with indifference. Authority is defiled by the son who stares at him with a partly secret smile, and winks. The Father's authority is demystified as it is returned from its abstracted form to its concrete presence, from the the body politic to the body. The son's eyes only momentarily meet his Father's, but move quickly below them, wandering about his hips. The son who has not disclaimed his mother knows how she is humbled by His objectification of her, and now he uses this knowledge against him. The Father is no longer Authority; he is a piece of ass. The mother's gaze may solidify her husband's cockiness, his fascination with his power over her, his sense of himself as the Fuhrer. But the son's lascivious stare, which has embedded with it the rage of the oedipal struggle as well as the not-forgotten love of the wounded and wanting, this stare mocks Him as it transforms Him into an object of desire, a plaything, and dissolves his seriousness into panic. If the son fellates him, acting out concretely what the complicit straight son performs symbolically, the father's power flows from his body into the son's. The blood-swollen phallus becomes limp in its orgasm, and the son knows what heterosexual women have always known: the father's power is transient; it can be consumed; in a moment it is gone. Now is limpness, weakness, sleep. If the father penetrates the son, the same dissolution of power occurs. However love is made, love is made. Father becomes lover. Even Freud knew that "the behavior towards men in general of a man who sees in other men potential love-objects must be different that that of a man who looks upon other men in the first instance as rivals in regard to women." [23]

"From behind we are all women"

Patriarchy is in one sense phallocentrism. The location of power in the male, and its hierarchical arrangement among them, requires the distillation of libido into the phallus: "The body gathers around the phallus like society around the chief."[24] The phallus symbolizes power, power which is organized vertically. This organization is a system of "jealously and competition," Hocquenghem writes. Of the phallus he writes: "It is the detached, complete object which plays the same role in our society's sexuality as money does in the capitalist economic: the fetish, the true universal reference point for all activity. It is responsible for the allocation of both absence and presence: the little girl's penis-envy, the little boy's castration anxiety." [25]

The phallus is a public organ. In locker rooms men compare its size. In parks they expose it, an act of exhibition, the aim of which is to frighten the female, and in so doing, reassure himself. It reminds the little girl of Daddy's power. Rape is her ultimate reminder, this forced entry into her private body and psyche. The phallus symbolizes power, and like power it is aggressive. It seek use. It seeks victims.

Whereas the phallus is social, the anus is private. It is hidden from public view by the buttocks, just as it is hidden from psychological view by its repression by the ego. This repression is necessary to the production of oedipalized individuals in competition with each other: "If phallic transcendence and the organization of society around the great signifier are to be possible, the anus must be privatized in individualized and oedipalized persons."[26] Phallocentrism is inversely related to anal eroticism.

Freud associated the anal stage of sexual development with the formation of identity. While Freud's theory is not a simple linear, maturational one, there is the suggestion that the anal stage must be lived through in order to achieve genital sexuality. Anal eroticism must be sublimated, or repressed, in order to reach phallocentrism. The "desiring function" of the anus is replaced by exclusively excremental one.[27] The relegation of the anus to an exclusively excremental function bifurcates the private from the public, the subjective from the objective.

These bogus divisions accompany the formation of bifurcated persons whose internal lives are kept discreet from their public lives.   Private psychological material is excreted at home in order that it not interfere with efficacious public performance. Hocquenghem notes:

> Every man possesses a phallus which guarantees him a social role; every man has an anus which is truly his own, in the most secret depths of his own person. The anus does not exist in a social relation, since it forms precisely the individual and therefore enables the division between society and the individual to be made.... Lavatories are the only places where one is alone behind locked doors.... The anus is overinvested individually because its investment is withdrawn socially.[28]

One's private life is especially charged emotionally because it is withdrawn socially, because it is regarded as private. This withdrawal, the distillation of energy to the phallus, i.e. of conscious energy to the public domain, accompanies the particular vertical organizations of power characteristic of centralized states and corporate economies. The myth of the private individual keeps him or her politically weak and economically manipulable. Freud: "The entire Oedipus complex is anal."[29]

Surplus capital accumulation is made characterologically possible through anal repression; the joke "he's a tight ass" is suggestive. In fact, the character structure of the capitalist is such that the anus, in effect, disappears. The private self, and the capacity to empathize and suspend ego boundaries, are repressed, buried under the mask, the persona, produced by social conditioning. In the present historical circumstances, the anus becomes more than itself; it symbolizes the body as well. Anal eroticism draws libido from its overinvestment in the phallus and diversifies it throughout the rest of the body, de-territorializing not only sexuality but power as well. The anus does not lend itself to comparison and competition, and from the anal point of view, what criteria could be employed to judge them? Sexuality is equalized as it is diversified, not only within the male sex, but between sexes. After all, as Hocquenghem notes, "from behind we are all women."[30]

The overregulation of the anus accompanies the overdetermination of the male ego. The blocking of *élan vital* bodily mirrors the blocking of psychological life in the rigid male personality formation.   Denying its undifferentiated relation to others, the individual male ego deludes itself into believing "what is mine is mine." Hocquenghem: "Control of the anus is the precondition for taking responsibility for property. The ability to 'hold back' or to evacuate the faeces is the moment of the constitution of the self.   'To forget oneself' is the most ridiculous and distressing kind of social accident there is, the ultimate outrage to the human person."[31]

So it is when someone lets something "personal" slip during public conversation.   Others are embarrassed or irritated that he has "forgotten himself." He has excreted the private in public. The reduction of the anus to self-regulation and excretion accompanies the commodification of self.[32]   Subjectivity becomes repressed, and its explication publicly thereby becomes one form of cultural sabotage. Autobiographical description, to the extent it escapes the commonsensical, becomes free associative and genuinely confessional, invites deregulation of others: "To reinvest the anus collectively and libidinally would involve a proportional weakening of the great phallic signifier, which dominates unconsciously both the small-scale hierarchies of the family and in the great social hierarchies. The least acceptable desiring operation (precisely because it is the most desublimating one) is that which is directed at the anus."[33]

To refuse to maintain the schizoid distinction between public and private, and to excrete in public what commodification requires we save for our wives, lovers, or psychiatrists, soils the social fabric. The seriousness of the Father at the dinner table, the taken-for-granted naturalization of social life, cannot be maintained by the jokes, wails, and confessions of the subjectivity-existing person.   Subjectivity is suppressed intellectually across the academic disciplines as anal eroticism is repressed and organized around the male public organ. Father maintains his position by pretending phallic superiority, at least by persuading us that that is the name of the power game. He maintains his position by sitting "on his duff," hiding his private self from the scrutiny of others and perhaps from himself. He eradicates homosexuality because it threatens to bring his ass into public view. His reign depends upon its absence.

Anal repression accompanies a certain order of character structure indicated by constant and relatively high tension as the organism is under (unconscious) surveillance and regulation. The erotization of the anus threatens this construction, and no doubt this knowledges makes anal intercourse one of the most dreaded punishments one man can inflict upon other. The particular series of personality formations associated with macho men depends upon the overdetermination of the ego as it has successfully suppressed the feminine in itself. Suppressed is not equivalent to gone, and the male regulates himself carefully in order to prevent its unwelcome surfacing. The masculine identity, based as it is upon repression of the preoedipal identification with the mother and the construction of identification with a relatively absent father, is in fact fragile and easily threatened. The intensity and pervasiveness of homophobia among men suggest this constant need to "remember oneself." Homosexuality in this context becomes a call for a return to pre-commodified forms of experience and identity: "Homosexual desire is related in particular to the prepersonal state of desire. To this is linked the fear of loss of identity, as it is state of desire.... The direct manifestation of homosexual desire stands in contrast to the relations of identity, the necessary roles imposed by the Oedipus complex in order to ensure the reproduction of society."[34]

The codification of desire according to Oedipus is the identification of individual self and social location. The biological interest in reproduction becomes culturally intertwined in the socio-political interest in reproducing His status. The resistance of the heterosexual son initially angers but eventually pleases the Father as it assures Him of the son's interest in the power the Father claims. The resistance of the heterosexual son may result in the deposing of a particular father, but not in the deposing of the archetype—Father. The victorious son discovers that it is the Father in himself he has resisted as he has resisted his father. Fathers are not deposed through resistance, only replaced. Vertical social relations continue. Fathers require children and wives as capitalists require workers. Brotherhood and sisterhood, concepts depicting horizontal social relationships, are not opposite-sexed relationships.

Conclusion: schooling as circumcision, curriculum as the codification of desire

From the viewpoint sketched here, schooling is a gender cere-mony in which, as Grumet has suggested, female teachers trans-fer their children, particularly their sons, to the Father, to patri-archal conceptions of economic, social, and intellectual life. Circumcision demarcates manhood, the point after which the son is regarded as a member of the tribe of Patriarchs. The wounded phallus and the scar that remains are a cattle brand indicating ownership and gender identity.

The culture of the classroom is patriarchal. Circumcision occurs symbolically. The wound is psychic, political, and eco-nomic. The elements of the first category include hypertrophy of the fantasy life, loss of self to others, and internalization of the oppressor: the development of a false self-system.[35] Politi-cally the sons are domesticated, conditioned to accept and par-ticipate in the "jealously-competition" system which sorts them according to class membership. As a gender ceremony of man-hood, contemporary schooling compels heterosexuality as well, implicating it in the complex configuration which is suffering in the West. Homosexuality as it now exists is implicated as well. Many homosexuals, like most oppressed groups in initial stages of political rights work, tend to believe what their enemies say about them. Thus many homosexuals tend to believe in some measure that they are indeed a "third sex," unique, "queer." They tend to believe in a substantive category called "homo-sexual," not seeing that it is in the service of their oppression, and in the "heterosexual's" self-delusion regarding his own gender composition. Homosexuals are often embarrassed over the relative prominence of sadomasochistic sexuality in gay life, not realizing that they only act out concretely and privately what "straight" men do to each other abstractly in the public domain. In schools, as in homes and offices, men get women to do their dirty work.

Curriculum like the oedipal complex is a codification of desire, a symbolization of libido into codes which are patriar-chal in nature and function as they contribute to bifurcated personality formations, suppressing what subjectivity remains from the preoedipal experience. Curriculum theorists and social theorists of education have correctly identified curriculum as the conversation of the Father. Curriculum contributes to the reproduction of "civilization," but so does, finally, resistance to it. Resistance as a concept and as a call for political action is no doubt "beyond passive analysis." But it too is only a moment in dialectical understanding and action. Exposing its oedipal ties and functions suggests another moment coming, one in which we sons and fathers work to become brothers and lovers. It is a struggle fought not only on the streets and in classrooms, but in bed. On that "site," curriculum might become the de-hierarchicalization of power and, indeed, the celebration of desire.

Notes

1. See, for instance, Henry A. Giroux, "Hegemony, Resistance, and the Paradox of Educational Reform," *Interchange*, vol. 12, nos. 2-3, 1981, pp. 3-26, and Michael W. Apple, "Reproduction, Contestation, and Curriculum: An Essay in Self-Criticism, *Ibid.*, pp. 27-46.

2. Philip Wexler, "Body and Soul," *Journal of Curriculum Theorizing*, vol. 4, no. 2, 1982, pp. 166-180. The papers cited in note no. 1 were read at a conference entitled "Beyond Passive Analysis," held at the Ontario Institute for Studies in Education, in Toronto, November 11-13, 1980. "Beyond Passive Analysis." Indeed.

3. Guy Hocquenghem (1978) suggests it is no accident that the two movements have been co-extensive: "Experience in Europe and the U.S.A. has shown that the women's movement and the gay movement have coincided. It is as if society could not bear to see in man what it demands to see in women, as if to dominate women and to repress homosexuality were one and the same thing" (p. 126). *Homosexual Desire*. London: Allison & Busby. Misogyny and homosexual repression are of course related.

4. I review this progress in "Gender, Sexuality, and Curriculum Studies: The Beginning of the Debate," *McGill Journal of Education*, vol. 16, no. 3, 1981, pp. 305-316.

5. Madeleine R. Grumet, "Pedagogy for Patriarchy: The Feminization of Teaching," *Interchange*, vol. 12, nos. 2-3, pp. 165-184.

6. The initial interest in sexism expressed itself in textual analyses, i.e. examination of textbooks, especially textbooks used in elementary schools, for sex stereotyping. In the past five years feminism has had a more theoretical impact upon the field. See, for instance, Madeleine R. Grumet, "Conception, Contradiction, and Curriculum," *Journal of Curriculum Theorizing*, 3:1, pp. 287-298. See also Janet L. Miller, "Feminism and Curriculum Theory: The Breaking of Attachments," *Journal of Curriculum Theorizing*, 4:2, pp. 181-186.

7. This is a conclusion of a rather elaborate argument concerning the consequences of women being primary caretakers of infants by Nancy Chodorow in *The Reproduction of Mothering*. Berkeley: University of California Press, 1978.

8. In this section I amend Chodorow's thesis to suggest that the initial preoedipal identification with the (heterosexual) mother places the son in a homosexual position.

9. Grumet, "Conception, Contradiction, and Curriculum."

10. See William F. Pinar and Lee Johnson, "Aspects of Gender Analysis in Recent Feminist Psychological Thought and Their Implications for Curriculum," *Journal of Education,* vol. 162, no. 4 (Fall 1980), pp. 113-126.

11. Jean Anyon, "Elementary Schooling: Distinctions of Social Class," *Interchange,* pp. 118-132.

12. Hocquenghem, p. 48 ff.

13. Gilles Deleuze and Feliz Guattari, *Anti-Oedipus: Capitalism and Schizophrenia.* New York: Viking, 1977.

14. Adrienne Rich, "Compulsory Heterosexuality," *Signs,* vol. 5, no. 4 (Summer 1980), p. 637.

15. Hocquenghem, p. 52.

16. Phyllis Chesler takes seriously the idea of the father wound, and at one point suggests that male heterosexual promiscuity may not represent a search for the mother, but rather for the father, a search, given the homosexual taboo, that is bound to fail. Misogyny is in this sense is related to the man's anger that she is not the man: "Why can't a woman be more like a man?"

17. In this section I have relied heavily upon the argument Grumet develops in her essay "Conception, Contradiction, and Curriculum."

18. A companion way to think about this process is the following. One consequence of the feminist movement has been a greater candor from heterosexual women regarding their sexual preferences and their appreciation of the male form, cf. *Playgirl* magazine. Many men, especially middle class men, have become correspondingly more sensitive to their appearance, and groom themselves in order to amplify their sexual attractiveness to women. It is a short step to groom and appreciate one's body as it is attractive to women to appreciating one's body period. And it is a larger yet negotiable step to take from appreciating one's own body as an erotic object to appreciating other men's bodies as erotic objects. It would be an ironic outcome of that aspect of the feminist movement which has functioned to bring women's sexual preferences and voyeurism "out of the closet" if it initiated a process of male sexual appreciation for the male. In this scenario, feminism may produce male homosexuality on a scale not seen in the West since pre-Christian Greece and Rome.

19. Joseph K.'s rationality is an instrumental one. The questions he poses
in attempting to comprehend his case begin "how, "who," and "what."
"Who could these men be? What were they talking about? What authority could they represent?" (p. 4). He asks such questions throughout the trial. Midway through the novel—he understands nothing more
of his case, despite his questions, only that his position has somehow
deteriorated—he continues his questioning: "And there were so many
questions to put. To ask questions was surely the main thing. K. felt
that he could draw up all the necessary questions himself" (p. 114). K.
never critically examines this method, this mode of cognition; being led
by his executioners he maintains that "the only thing for me to go on
doing is to keep my intelligence calm and analytical to the end" (p.
225). Kafka, Franz (1968). *The Trial.* New York: Schocken.

20. A characteristic passage of Woolf's which portrays the mutli-dimensionality and simultaneity of experience is the following:

"Yes, of course, if it's fine tomorrow," said Mrs. Ramsay. "But you'll
have to be up with the lark," she added.

To her son these words conveyed an extraordinary joy, as if it were
settled, the expedition were bound to take place, and the wonder to
which he had looked forward, for years and years it seemed, was, after a
night's darkness and a day's sail, within touch. Since he belonged, even
at the age of six, to that great clan which cannot keep this feeling separate from that, but must let future prospects, with their joys and
sorrows, cloud what is actually at hand, since to such people even in
earliest childhood any turn in the wheel of sensation has the power to
crystallise and transfix the moment upon which its gloom or radiance
rests, James Ramsay, sitting on the floor cutting out pictures from the
illlustrated catalogue of the Army and Navy Stores, endowed the picture of a refrigerator, as his mother spoke, with heavenly bliss. It was
fringed with joy. The wheelbarrow, the lawnmover, the sound of
poplar trees, leaves whitening before rain, rooks cawing, brooms knock-
ing, dresses rustling—all these were so coloured and distinguished in his
mind that he had already his private code, his secret language, though
he appeared the image of stark and uncomprising severity, with his
high forehead and his fierce blue eyes, impeccably candid and pure,
frowning slightly at the sight of human frailty, so that his mother,
watching him guide his scissors neatly round the refrigerator, imagined
him all red and ermine on the bench or directing a stern and momen-
tous enterprise in some crisis of public affairs.

"But," said his father, stopping in front of the drawing-room window, "it won't be fine."

Had there been an axe handy, or a poker, any weapon that would
have gashed a hole in his father's breast and killed him, there and then,
James would have seized it.

Virginia Woolf's literary accomplishment is, of course, beyond comment here. For curriculum theorists her fiction holds considerable
methodological as well as aesthetic interest, as it captures convincingly

the immediacy and complexity of experience. Additionally, Woolf was an astute observer of gender politics, as this passage illustrates. *To the Lighthouse*. New York: Harcourt, Brace & Co, 1955, pp. 9-10.

21. Grumet, Madeleine, "Pedagogy for Patriarchy: The Feminization of Teaching."

22. Of course, this is hardly all that women do. Nor does this analysis disclose the ways in which women have used men's reliance upon them to control them (men). In her chapter on "romantic love" in *The Second Sex*, Simone de Beauvoir details how the man's "for itself-ness," or the tendency toward isolation and independence, is the source for the women's interest in man and becomes what she attempts to control. If successful, the man loses that quality which drew her to him in the first place. Thus the woman is caught between being enslaved and being enslaving, with no exit.

23. Sigmund Freud, "Some Neurotic Mechanisms in Jealously, Paranoia, and Homosexuality," in *The Complete Psychological Words of Sigmund Freud*, vol. 18, p. 232.

24. Hocquenghem, p. 82.

25. *Ibid.*, p. 81.

26. *Ibid.*, p. 82.

27. *Ibid.*

28. *Ibid.*, p. 83.

29. Freud, "On Narcissism: An Introduction, in *op. cit*, vol. 14, p. 101.

30. Hocquenghem, p. 87.

31. *Ibid.*, p. 85.

32. Philip Wexler, "Commodification, Self, and Social Psychology," in *Psychology and Social Theory*, vol. 1, no. 2, provides an important explication of the process of the commodification of self.

33. Hocquenghem, p. 89.

34. *Ibid.*, p. 92.

35. William F. Pinar, "Sanity, Madness, and the School," in W. Pinar (ed.), *Curriculum Theorizing: The Reconceptualists* (359-383). Berkeley: McCutchan.

X

The Corporate Production of Feminism and the Case of Boy George
(1983)

First I want to acknowledge the mischief in this title, implying that the complex and significant social and political movement called feminism in some way has been fabricated by corporate interests. Also in a prefatory way, let us name the considerable and not unquestionable assumption that social movements can be traced to economic origins. Mischief and assumption acknowledged, let us see if that combination can take us anywhere interesting.

Two broad historical developments during the past one hundred years or so need to be named in order to situate the present state of gender, politics, and work. These are a profound change in the nature of the workplace, and a profound change in the nature of the family.

For economy's sake let us start briefly in the late feudal and early capitalist West, when work for the masses was overwhelmingly physical in nature. Agriculture and elementary forms of technology production characterized the medieval feudal period, although the growth of the cities, accompanied by the development of commerce and capitalism, signaled the three-century exodus from the field to the factory. In the U.S. this transition from the hard, long days of physical labor in the fields to the hard, long days of physical labor in the factories occurred especially during the later half of the nineteenth century.

Until industrialization emptied the fields and filled the factories that Dickens and Dreiser, for instance, so vividly portray, the economic unit of production tended to be the family. Not the family you and I probably knew, rather an extended family which would have included not only, say, your parents, but one or more of theirs: aunts, uncles, their children, your cousins, and so on. The land which this extended family tilled probably was not their own, at least not in Europe, but the organization of work and economic production occurred within the extended family and with others, rather than away from the family, as during the industrial and current corporate periods.

Industrialization accelerated the formation of the middle classes, and in the middle classes, management and service (meaning accounting, clerking, and the whole range of service industries that arise in organizing a business corporation) work began to replace the physical labor of the assembly line. As the middle class standard of living increased, the extended family decreased. More and more families lived in separate dwellings, and the so-called nuclear family—one father, one mother and several children—became common by the twentieth century.

Jobs became careers, and instead of working when food and shelter were scarce, the ethos of working every day, whether one need money that day or not, spread throughout the middle and working classes. Especially in the middle classes women tended to work on jobs less, and men became "breadwinners." Historians of the family such as Christopher Lasch and social theorists of gender such as Nancy Chodorow detail what these essentially economic developments meant for the family and for gender identity.

Motherhood became an almost sacred task, not something woven into a day of work but a psychological calling which required ever-increasing levels of subtlety and sophistication in order to fulfil oneself as a mother and to raise a healthy child. The mother-infant, mother-child bond became a more intensified relationship than in earlier periods when a sizable number of persons enjoyed everyday contact with the child. By the twentieth century, the pre-school child often had contact mostly with her or his mother and any siblings that might still be at home. The father became, as Chodorow terms it, an "imaginary figure," someone whose intermittent presence and ascribed status as the one who makes the home possible, inflated and distorted his significance in the family, a significance that became increasingly imaginary.

What were the consequences of these developments for gender identity? It is easy, in imagining the young mother, relatively isolated in an apartment complex (in the middle class instance) in a large city where her husband has been transferred, to see how the personality of the mother became increasingly influential in the development of her infant's personality. For the daughter what is feminine becomes more "specialized," more a psychological, stylized, even professional calling. [In one 1920s curriculum development project for the then all-women Stephens College in Columbia, Missouri, over 700 activities associated with the outstanding "wife" and "mother" were identified—mostly by men!—as necessary components of the modern all-women's college curriculum.] For the son what is masculine is precisely what is not everyday, not feminine, and his conceptions of what it means to be a man come from his conversations with his father (who tells his son what is "manly" and what is not), and what he imagines the world of work, the world of men, to be. Masculine sexual identity becomes more imaginary, more tentative, while feminine sexual identity becomes more real, more everyday, if more confined to the home.

Let us quickly review what is a very broad sweep of economic and family history by noticing what is common today. Many fewer jobs in the agricultural and manufacturing sectors are available now. During the Reagan administration we have witnessed the disappearance of tens of thousands of manufacturing jobs. This means that now relatively fewer (as a percentage of the total) jobs remain which require physical strength. What do jobs require today?

First, many require sophisticated technical training, as we are perhaps overaware. In fact, no doubt more than a few of our students are discovering that sophisticated preparation in the university hardly guarantees a sophisticated job upon graduation, but that is another story. Most jobs now require less specialized training than students are likely to have undergone by the time they are finished with undergraduate work, but note that the vast majority of jobs are associated with bureaucracies: corporations, private and public institutions of educational and research sorts, governments jobs, and so on. Many of these are clerical or gradations above clerical jobs, but all require a minimal literacy and mental ability of some degree.

As well, most jobs in a bureaucratic and corporate society require social skills. Whether in sales, management, or research and development, it is increasingly necessary not only to "get along" with one's peers, subordinates and superiors. As well, one must be able to participate in a variety of group processes, committees, research teams, sales teams, and so on, in ways that are sensitive to the feelings, perceptions, and even to semi- and unconscious motives of others.

Further, it is acknowledged even in the newspaper advice columns as well as in reports of survey research, that good looks, appropriate dress, and a cheerful personality all contribute to career success, and not only for women. The handsome guy goes further faster than the ugly one, even when, as usually true, the boss is male.

The last prerequisites for work in a corporate or bureaucratic setting (the former a subset of the latter), and by no means does this constitute a definitive list, are the imagination and intuition. Even in a lower management position or a clerical one, it is necessary to imagine more efficient ways to organize and perform tasks. In upper levels of management where policy and corporate directions are established, one must intuit the nature and direction of one's competition, the potential sales of a new product, and the coming stages of the business cycle, including Federal Reserve policy, interest-rate trends, and so on. Obviously, being well informed is necessary to this wide range of important tasks, but deciding what to do in light of information draws upon imagination and intuition.

What does the workplace require today? First is literacy, competent mental operations of various types, and special training. Second are social skills, a capacity for relationality, for empathy, for sensitivity. Third, one must redo oneself in order to be attractive or pretty, perhaps slightly less so now for women and more so now for men. Fourth is a cultivated imagination and intuition. Note that three of these four have been associated with women and only the first, training and mental acumen, have in the present century been associated with men. What women have lacked due to their location in the home—training and logical skills—they now receive.

In light of the corporate workplace, feminism can be regarded as a theoretical apparatus which allows women and men to accept (or at least understand) the necessity of women's entry into hitherto all-male domains, and the necessity of men's reformulation of masculinity, along more feminine lines. To suggest so is not to denigrate the courage and achievement of many individual women. Feminism has moved men quickly and in so doing aroused greater conservative reaction than it might have, due to the vision, brilliance, and bravery of many women. Even though the profitability of the corporate sector now depends upon women's participation and masculinization, and men's feminization, men are yet to realize it.

In fact, men have no theoretical apparatus, no parallel to feminism, to help them to understand what has happened and is happening to them. There are men's groups, but these are relatively uncommon and often superficial. Men experience the changed status of women, the changed nature of personality and physical requirements, and they have no male-gender specific theory to permit them to understand, accept, and legitimate these developments. The women's movement has left men often superficially compliant and inwardly resentful, and rape, pornography, and less obvious forms of misogyny continue at an astonishing rate. The increased visibility of male homosexuals provides small comfort for most men. I worry about men, especially so because there are so many gifted persons are already worrying about women.

So we have parallel developments in the economic sector, and in the family. In schools, themselves recent developments (as public or common schools), we see similar trends, with emphasis upon training, social skills, bureaucratized forms of learning and social interaction. In the family, what is feminine is what is familiar and what is masculine becomes, I think, increasingly stylized, based as it is in the traditional nuclear family, upon the imaginary. [There is a rapid breakdown of the nuclear family, including some experimentation with sex roles, with the father mothering the children while the mother works to support them, but the scope of this breakdown seems still relatively small.]

The relationship of art to other elements constituent of society such as the family, the workplace, the school, is by no means simple or self-evident. One view among others is that contemporary art expresses a subterranean reality of human life, those layers of semi- and unconscious material that are unacceptable in everyday social life, either for reasons of morality, custom, or efficiency. Art in this view expresses realities not socially realized in everyday life but nonetheless present. The immense shifts in gender identity I have sketched, due in large part to the changing requirements of the workplace, the changed psychological structure of the family and school, and due to the theoretical and political power of feminism, are reflected in some forms of contemporary music and musicians. For women there are many examples, such as Annie Lennox of the Eurhythmics. I think of the parody of traditional women in the music videos of the Go-Gos and the Waitresses. Even in a more traditional woman such as Stevie Nicks, there is an unmistakable power and self-assertion, qualities in sharp contrast to the Beaver's mild-mannered mother of the 1950s, let alone the easily fainting bourgeois hysteric of Freud's turn-of-the-century Vienna.

What of men? Michael Jackson is hardly John Wayne, or Mick Jagger, although Jagger is an androgynous character despite his sometimes sleazy heterosexuality. But it is Boy George who captures my attention as a kind of "cultural icon" who perhaps expresses, although in extreme terms, the direction of gender reformulation. I do not focus here on his music, which—and I hope I offend no one here—I find eclectic in an unexceptional way. It his is cultural meaning and power as an image—in his music videos, on network television accepting a Grammy ward—that makes him worthy of mention. He is, despite his self-characterization on the Grammy program, no ordinary drag queen. His makeup is extensive but it creates not the illusion of looking upon a woman; rather it somehow allows if not underscores his anatomical reality as a man. His smile carries the irony of a man turned in upon himself, who has made his own masculinity, buried it would seem, the object of his reflection and perhaps desire. In this respect he becomes both woman and man, and in one being sexual and personality attributes which in other individuals and in other times were bifurcated into two persons, are brought together (copulating perhaps?), in one.

The maximation of profits in our time requires greater efficiency, read greater imaginative and intuitive planning and organization of every aspect of corporate life: research and development, manufacture, marketing sales, personnel deployment, etc. In order to achieve this greater efficiency, the workplace demands a reformulation of traditional (i.e. common a generation or so ago) femininity and masculinity, specifically a masculization of women and a feminization of men, a movement toward androgyny, a movement whose political and social aspects are conceptualized and legitimated by several strands of feminist theory. Where are the signs? In the air, including the airwaves. Watch the music videos. Boy George heralds a new formulation of gender culture, a new—forgive me—culture club.

XI

Death in a Tenured Position
(1984)

Economic events, of course, are rarely only economic in nature and consequence. They are political and social and psychological as well. In fact, they seem to seep into most realms of human experience, regardless of how determined participants may be that their realm be quarantined. The American curriculum field has not been quarantined. Recent economic events have infected the field in discernible and not only economic ways, ways which influence not only the character of everyday academic life but the nature of the research and practice we conduct.

The recent past I want to describe is the past five years, roughly the tenure of Paul Volcher as Chairman of the Federal Reserve Board. This is the period of "monetarism" in the U.S. monetary policy, the view that rates of inflation are more closely tied to monetary growth than to federal government fiscal policy. The events we have lived through during this time have occurred disproportionately, especially during the administration of President Ronald Reagan. It is the impact of "monetarism" upon curriculum studies in the United States, including economic and psychological and political effects, which I want to sketch here.

Background

American capitalism worked well for the two decades following World War II. American military and economic pre-eminence, accompanied by passivity in the Third World and by tame domestic trade unions, all contributed to a warm climate for

American "free enterprise." In the 1960s America's dominance of international economic, political, and military matters was challenged. Suppliers of raw materials were less inclined to accept modest compensation for those supplies. On matters ranging from social welfare legislation to environmental protection, the domestic system of the 1950s was challenged. Disguised initially by the boom created by the Vietnam War, the American economy declined, and a series of familiar difficulties followed: rising prices, diminishing productivity gains, increasing unemployment—what came to be termed by John Kenneth Galbraith as "stagflation."

In what Galbraith characterizes as the "third postwar phase," beginning during the Carter years (1976-1980) and intensifying after Reagan's election, the corporate sector reacted to deflate the ballooning power of the unions and the citizenry. The device was monetarism. "Monetarists practice flawless common sense: those who have a lot of money generally benefit by keeping money scarce. Tight money can be rough for those who do not have enough" (Bowles, Gordon & Weisskopf, in Galbraith).

It is clear that monetarism is by no means a technical economic matter. It is hardly socially neutral. Monetarism favors the upper or monied classes at the expense of the poor and indebted middle class. The rationale for monetarism contains references to a shortage of investment funds for the modernization of plant. And so fiscal policy becomes "supply side," the argument being that cuts in taxes, proportionately higher cuts for the upper-middle and upper classes, free money for investment and attendant increases in productivity. Governmental taxes are held to be excessive, soaking up money that could be used for investment, research, and development. [Galbraith points out that West Germany and Sweden, where government is relatively more expensive than it is in the United States, have both enjoyed more stable economies than has the U.S.]

The problem, according to business leaders, is also a lack of motivation in the modern corporation workplace. Bowles et al. in Galbraith's "The Wealth of a Nation" comment: "Corporations have shown all kinds of interest in improving worker motivation, but they have shown even greater interest in preserving their centralized power and privileges. Forced to choose ... most corporations have preferred to forego greater worker effort rather than give up any management control." In his review of Bowles' book, Galbraith disagrees that ultimate power resides finally in capital and with the capitalists. While not denying the enormous influence of capital, Galbraith suggests "that far more of our present economic problems [can] be attributed to corporate bureaucratic tendency (than to calculated capitalist design).... We are far more in the grip of the undesigned dynamic of great organizations—a subservience that, it might be observed, we share in some measure with the socialist and communist world."

Foreground

This "Great Repression" (a term employed by Leonard Silk of *The New York Times*) has aggravated the economic problems of education schools, colleges and departments, already facing decreasing enrollments in most parts of the U.S. This occurs not only due to the oversupply of teachers (except in mathematics and science, and except in some areas of the American South), the increasing difficulties of the public schools, and the public's accurate perception that teaching is far from an easy or lucrative way to earn a living. The crisis within education schools and departments is intensified because the "Great Repression" is not economic only. It is political and psychological. Conservative forces in all domains have taken heart and strength from the Reagan-Thatcher-Kohl regimes. Within universities, conservatives in arts and sciences departments become more vocal and active in expressing their prejudices concerning the academic study of education, a tendency perhaps more pronounced in private colleges and universities than in public institutions, in more prestigious institutions than in less prestigious ones. Those with "cultural capital" attempt to make it less available to "borrowers" by demeaning applied fields such as education, the academic equivalent of the poor and the indebted.

Within schools of education, the politically ascendent departments—educational administration with its emphasis on finance, and educational psychology with its claims to knowledge of cognition and learning disabilities—continue to make gains against the vulnerable ones—educational foundations such as philosophy of education and curriculum, including teacher education and curriculum theory. Within curriculum departments, "back to basics" conservatives assert power; graduates of "cognate" or "parent" disciplines are hired. Deans and department chairpersons become obsessed with (not just watchful of) full-time student numbers, and collegial relations deteriorate as competition, suspicion, fear and resentment, never absent from the academic scene, intensify. Tenured faculty drink even a little more, and retire more aggressively into personal lives. Untenured junior faculty become more robotic, produce reams of articles (often mass produced with 2, 3, 4, or more collaborators) on increasingly safe subjects. [There are important exceptions to this trend I think, and some of these we publish in *The Journal of Curriculum Theorizing*.] What has been repressed during the past five years has not only been the money supply, not only economic activity in general and the hiring of curriculum specialists in particular, but also imagination, intellectual experimentation, and generosity, even the malefic kind.

The movement within the curriculum field known as the Reconceptualization has not been immune to these general developments. One of the most prominent Reconceptualists began, in the late 1970s, to characterize himself as a sociologist, not a curriculum theorist, and he began to promote his work not as curriculum theory but as social theory. Other socially and economically oriented curriculum specialists have followed his move, the academic equivalent of moving to the suburbs. Those of us who remain in the inner city that is the curriculum field are the autobiographers, the gender analysts, the feminists, and a younger generation of socially and economically oriented curriculum scholars who seem not as obsessed with status, with moving to the disciplinary suburbs. But as a movement within the curriculum field the Reconceptualizaion is no longer, even if a sense of community and purpose persists among the original participants. To an extent the Reconceptualization has occurred, as even a casual examination of the American Educational Research Association Division B (Curriculum and Objectives) annual program suggests. The scholarly field has indeed been reconceptualized from an atheoretical, ahistorical, pseudo-practical field of the late 1960s into a field that could congeal into a complex paradigm comprised of elements of social, economic, and gender analysis, methodologically influenced by not only Marxism, but by hermeneutics, phenomenology, and literary theory and methods, such as autobiography and poststructuralism. While the so-called traditionalists have hardly disappeared, no knowing observer of curriculum studies would characterize the field as Schwab (1970) or Huebner (1976) or Pinar (1978) have characterized it. The field is no longer moribund or arrested, but the signs of life and movement remain somewhat faint and the depression in the academic job market may still depress these signs of life to the brink of extinction.

What are these signs of life? While no longer strictly a reconceptualist journal, *JCT* finds a slowly-increasing number of readers. The *JCT*-organized conferences do exhibit a vitality and spontaneity of conversation not evident at the larger association-organized meetings such as AERA and ASCD (the Association for Supervision and Curriculum Development). There is Canadian work that articulates a phenomenological critique and vision, such as that of Aoki, Carson, and Jacknicke at the University of Alberta. In Quebec Clermont Gauthier and Jacques Daignault write puzzling and dazzling essays which reconceive even reconceptualized curriculum theory. In the U.S. a new generation of theorists such as James Sears, William Reynolds, Jo Anne Pagano, Madeleine Grumet, Janet Miller are but a very few of the recently graduated Americans who hold great promise for the advancement of curriculum theory and practice. But these individuals struggle to work under difficult conditions: low pay, temporary positions, excessive work loads, as well as the weight of a rarely appreciative older generation.

Despite these signs of life, on the whole I find it a time of decline, even a time of death. The sixties are dead, finally and completely. Hopes of adequate funding for education at all levels are dead, despite the recent promises of Mondale and other 1984 Democratic Presidential candidates. Amanda Cross's detective story—*Death in a Tenured Position*—unwittingly provides a symbolic characterization of the present moment.

The novel opens with the dilemma of Harvard's English
Department. The Department has been given a one-million
dollar gift provided that it be spent in the employment of a
woman scholar. Grudgingly the all-male department agrees,
hiring a mature, unmarried woman. The woman is later found
dead, seated inside a stall in the men's washroom. There is a
hint that the local lesbian community may be involved. While
the Cambridge police investigate, Kate Fansler, a professor of
English at one of New York's universities, an amateur sleuth,
investigates the apparent homicide herself. Eventually she discovers that neither the lesbians nor the English department
faculty is the murderer. The death is a suicide. The icy reception she received, not only at the beginning of her first year at
Harvard but throughout her brief tenure, coupled with a humil-
iating incident devised by the (male) English faculty, seems to
have been the cause for her despair and self-destruction.

Those of us who have worked to reconceptualize the curriculum field are like the unwelcome woman: our arrival brought
no applause, only an occasionally broken hostility which
expressed itself not always directly, but often obliquely in a myriad of ways that made professional life difficult and discourag-
ing. The warning this novel offers us, however, is that perhaps
the most dangerous "enemy" of those of us who work for profound transformation of education is not, at this time, primarily
individual administrators and colleagues. Nor is it the "ruling
class" or the structure of economic rewards or the nature of the
workplace, although each of these functions to sabotage our
efforts and our spirits. The danger at the present movement is
perhaps not murder, despite the fears of the Left upon the election of President Reagan that fascism was only a year or so
away. The danger now may not be murder, but suicide. The
crisis of the present time is thus not only political and economic. It is a crisis of the heart, of the spirit. Whatever forms
our aspiration and our work take, those forms require the
strength and wariness that might come from a continuing realization that the defeat of our project is threatened not only
from political and economic events but from personal ones as
well.

The site of struggle now

It is this "living through" the historical conjecture that is the present time, this crystallization of the historical moment in individual lives, which holds the greatest promise of movement in the short term. I am suggesting that it is not only the person who must be attended to in order to act effectively in the public domain. I am suggesting that for now the major arena of struggle, the "site" if you will, of the most intense struggle of conflicting historical forces, is in individual lives. It is not in the congealed and presently stagnant political, economic, and social realms. No longer can one reasonably argue for teachers to ally themselves with the labor movement, or look to socialism as the primary strategy for reforming North American education. The moment may come when it is advisable to do so, but that moment is not in the foreseeable future, and it is not now. The intense political struggles of the present time are being conducted on interpersonal, bureaucratic levels, and in this regard, Galbraith agrees. Here I do not mean the politics of the bureaucracy, although these must be conducted. But a single-minded belief in political triumph in bureaucratic politics may bring triumph, but defeat in the below-the-surface struggle. I regard as most intense that struggle not to succumb to the routinization of life, and to the attendant freezing over of the fluidity of individual life, the struggle not to succumb to role, to the robotic, to witness and by so witnessing to amplify our withering capacities to live outside the bureaucratic mainstream of "thought" and "action." Only authentic thought and action can occur—at the present time—outside the congealed, frozen, patterned thought-become-procedure that is bureaucratic regulation and the bureaucratic form of life. Mainstream social science itself is an abstracted form of this same historical tendency.

During the authoritarian present I have little hope that our capacity to live outside this mainstream tendency toward standardization, efficiency, routinization, for political conservatism celebrates these forms of death to the human spirit as morality and right living. But we can, and must, blow on the flame of human life, trying to keep some light shining in the present

darkness. The methodology can be self-inquiry, an amplifica-
tion of the self that exists outside bureaucratic definitions of it.
Autobiography as Grumet and others have practiced it can provide a device by which we might find crevices in the wall of our
self-estrangement, our self lost to social definition and bureaucratic role. Like a pick autobiography allows me to crawl
through the narrow spaces of accumulated internalizations into
the lava-flows of individual pre-histories. But the past three
years have shown that autobiography, however practiced, supplies no insulation from the pain of living in bad times, times
when the forces of what is dead-and-past triumph, when what is
ugly mars the landscape, when death fouls the air, and we the
living cringe, cry, and despair.

There is reason to hope. Some think Mondale's election
would fuel our efforts, with badly-needed money if nothing else.
There is life in curriculum studies, as witness the work we print
in *The Journal of Curriculum Theorizing.* But just now I cannot
feel this hope. I feel only the dark age around me, in me, and
pray for another time.

References

Cross, Amanda (1981). *Death in a Tenured Position*. New York: Ballantine.

Galbraith, John Kenneth. The Wealth of a Nation. *New York Review of Books*, vol. 30, no. 9, pp. 3-6.

Huebner, Dwayne (1976). The Moribund Curriculum Field: Its Wake and Our Work. *Curriculum Inquiry*, vol. 6, no. 2.

Pinar, William F. (1978). Notes on the Curriculum Field 1978. *Educational Researcher*, vol. 7, no. 8.

Schwab, J. J. (1970). *The Practical: A Language for Curriculum*. Washington, DC: National Education Association.

XII

Autobiography and an Architecture of Self
(1985)

Is there an authentic self? In Jungian terms, this concept is roughly equivalent to the religious concept of soul (Jung, 1939). In Jung's imagery of self, Self is the totality of which ego, personality, animus, anima, and so on, are constituent parts. Personality is that which is socially expressed and constituted; it merges and separates itself from Self.

In this movement of merging and separating can be situated issues of authenticity and inauthenticity. If the personality is disjunctive with self, i.e., represents a denial, distortion, or some other form of convolution of that Self, we can judge the self (personality) as inauthentic. "He does not know himself" is a judgment that suggests the person being observed in some way is veiled from himself, is in contradiction with himself. On the contrary, the person whose actions express the smoothness, indeed, peacefulness, of being congruent with the Self, can be said to be authentic. Heidegger sought this peacefulness, this pre-modern absence of angst and crisis, in much of his philosophical work. Because ideas of self and authenticity/inauthenticity are common, perhaps increasingly so as curriculum theory continues to borrow from continental philosophy and literary theory, they become appropriate subjects for scrutiny and theorizing—theorizing situated not in the parent disciplines in which they originated, but in contemporary curriculum discourses where we use them now.

An archeology of self

Imagery of sedimentation, social or individual, is a literary device, not data, as Foucault seems to say much of the time. Images provide a landscape, a way of describing, a point of view. For the moment, let us visualize the following.

Freud (1917), more importantly than Jung, has taught that "energy is neither created nor destroyed," that all that happens to us as infants and children remains, almost always hidden from view, but present nonetheless. These accumulations of experience, layers of sedimentation—social, private, of various modalities and categories—constitute a Self, and within the self, an ego, superego, and id. For Jung, the unconscious spheres or processes of these aspects of the individual are pre-individual, i.e., collective (as in species) as well as individual.

The issue of the private vs. social character of self formation is non-problematic here (Jacoby, 1975). Important are the social (including specifically class) determinants of family and individual. Gender and specifically political contents of self constitution are central as well. The issue problematic here concerns the implications of this complicated fact for those of us who work to understand curriculum and instruction. To move closer to the issue of implications, let us move now to illustrations of the above observations.

> ...and, being dashed
> From error on to error, every turn
> Still brought me nearer to the central truth.
> —E. B. Browning, *Aurora Leigh, Book First*

The central truth might well be who I have been conditioned to be, and its realization is living in accordance with it. There is a psychic symmetry to such an achievement, but it is not without its difficulties, difficulties in travelling there and once having arrived.

Of course, schools create constant diversions from this destination of authentic self. For most public and private school children, the models of "learner" presented to them clash with who they are and the identities encouraged at home (Pinar, 1975). Social and class dislocations occur concomitantly with psychological distortions. A capitalist economy, with its tendencies to commodify psycho-social processes, including personality constitution and identification, contributes to self-estrangement as well. At this time in capitalism, at this place-nation-state, within educational institutions, the prospects for "authentic being" and "authentic self-knowledge" are few. So it is that calls for a "return to things themselves," to the discovery of "authentic voice," have political as well as epistemological and pedagogical content. Such work involves a "bracketing" and distancing that makes psychologically possible a politico-cultural critique. Homileticians such as Troegger (see Pinar, 1988) see "authentic voice" as pre-condition for effective preaching; it is as well a precondition for other forms of pedagogy, in the present situation.

What does it mean to "be brought nearer the central truth"? For one who has been lost in a Heideggerean public world of false selves and false values, it means "returning home." For Heidegger, it meant literally staying home, refusing to accept university appointments in large, sophisticated cities such as Munich and Berlin. He preferred to remain in Freiberg, a city near his birthplace: "Philosophical work does not take its course as the aloof business of a man apart. It belongs in the midst of the work of peasants. When the young peasant drags his heavy sledge up the slope, and then guides it, piled high with beech logs, down the dangerous descent to his house, when the herdsman, lost in the thought and slow of step, drives his cattle up the slope, when the peasant in his shed gets the countless shingles ready for his roof—then is my work of the same kind. It is intimately rooted in and related to the life of the peasants" (Heidegger, quoted in Megill, 1985).

Of course, for another, returning home might mean a city. The geographical move (or remaining) contributes variably to the psychological journey; it is the latter which is pertinent. Returning home means being relatively conscious of origins, being "open" to the disclosure of unconscious material (through dreams, waking fantasy and so on) and integrating those origins with present circumstances. Remaining near the place of one's birth may make such a process more possible, although this is only possibility, and Heidegger's reverence for home and birthplace can be regarded as nostalgic (Megill, 1985). For many, returning home means moving far away.

Once "home," is the issue resolved? The issue of authenticity may be, but the educational issue remains. What do I make of what I have been made? Put differently, what is to be the relation of the knower to the known? What if who I have been conditioned to be is a homophobe, a racist, a misogynist? Experiencing this racism may lead to psychological healing and self-acceptance momentarily, but even a partially conscious individual understands this posture is unacceptable. One must then work against this particular legacy, perhaps through logic, perhaps through prayer and other religious means, perhaps through study. The point is this: as significant as self-knowledge and authenticity are, as important as it is now for teachers to exemplify as well as know these modes' psychological end-states, they set the stage for asking: what attitudes and actions are appropriate given this self-knowledge?

For Foucault, this question must be answered through identification with marginalized groups: the so-called insane, the impoverished—loathed groups of various categories (Megill, 1985). For Sartre such an answer meant writing that was both philosophical and political in nature, as well as conventional political action, such as street activism (Cohen-Solal, 1987). Foucault acknowledges no such division; writing *is* political action. Theory *is* practice. Politics is the power competition among various discourses (world-views, world representations) and so the struggle over discourse is inescapably political.

This choice to identify with marginalized social groups can be made intra-psychically, and illustrates the order of thought and action implied by an "architecture of self". Of course there is no one-to-one correspondence between social group and intra-psychic elements, nor can the suffering of the former be compared to the repression of the latter. Acknowledging the onto-logical incommensurability one accepts still that political action can and ought to occur within the individual character structure, as well as across character types or groups. Reich (1961) and others (Lasch, 1984) have sketched associations between "character structure" and political orientations. While such associations are more suggestive than descriptive (repressed liberals are hardly uncommon for instance), they do point to the appropriateness of linking the two spheres of concern, however complicated that might be.

Lasch adds a third element to this analysis: historical moment. In his 1984 study of what he terms *The Minimal Self*, he argues that two twentieth-century events—the Holocaust (and the present threat of nuclear annihilation) and the development of an imagistic (read non-linear, and momentary) culture—have eroded the self's sublimated relationship to the public sphere (and all objects within it, including human beings). The self is so receded it becomes self-involved or narcissistic, a developmental turn of events which makes for presentism (either solipsism or symbiosis, two sides of the same psychological coin) and political passivity. It also makes for anomie in the schools, where an antiquated curriculum (read non-imagistic compounded by excessive linearity) insures the atrophied capacity for sublimation withers further. Without a cultural and characterological basis for academic work, school officials and parents must resort to external rewards and (more commonly during the Reagan Restoration) punishments (Lasch, 1984). Returning home, finding the "central truth,"discovering oneself, however, is only a beginning.

> "The things one says
> are all unsuccessful attempts
> to say something else."
> —Bertrand Russell, letter to Lady Ottoline Morrell,
> August, 1918

Psychoanalysis is a systematic method for uncovering that which one does not say, does not know, who one was once but is not (exclusively or consciously) now. Psychoanalysis has scientific origins, although its scientific status is a well-worn subject of dispute. Scientific or not, it is a system, and that may represent what for Gadamer is the wholly inappropriate movement of scientific method into human and cultural spheres. Rejecting Romanticist as well as scientific world views, Gadamer argued for a constructive (not in a Piagetian sense), aesthetic epistemology. It is a theory of knowing that takes creation more seriously than discovery.

Nietzsche attacks the very idea of a system, whether philosophical or scientific (Nietzsche, 1974). "The will to a system is a lack of integrity," he writes in *Twilight of the Idols*. He views systems of thought as veils of maya, functioning to protect us from the harsh and chaotic nature of human existence. The distance that reflection and system-building creates between the individual and the turbulence and fluidity of everyday life is the distance of Apollonian dreaming. As such dreaming comforts us with "the healing balm of blissful illusion," it provides us a "splendid illusion that would cover dissonance with a veil of beauty" (Nietzsche, 1974).

Nietzsche contrasts the Apollonian movement with the Dionysian impulse, an interest in piercing the veil created by theorizing and system-building, or the illusion of a stable, fixed, "authentic reef." Such stability is undermined by the Dionysian quest for an "intoxicated reality." While such a quest does yield closer contact with a "truer" experience of reality than can Apollonian dreaming, Nietzsche acknowledges as well that unrestrained, this impulse quickly leads to excess and frenzy (Megill, 1985).

Nietzsche's poles or orientations of contrast represent a very simple self system; they correspond (only in a limited sense) with Freud's imagery of id and super ego, although the Apollonian interest is less punitive than it is stability-seeking. It may be that in each historical period different impulses ascend, and others recede, according to class, ethnicity, and of course according to individuals within each class and ethnic grouping. For Lasch, the contemporary (male) self is undermined by the breakdown in the Apollonian illusion of constancy and fixed identity, and thus at the mercy of Dionysian inconstancy (a major symptom of which includes narcissism, i.e. self denied or fused). Interesting in this regard is Nietzsche's description of Dionysian impulses in language very close to Lasch's account of symbiosis, that form of narcissism which projects self onto world, denying the independent existence (or identity) of each. Dionysus seeks to discover the "Mothers of Being," who lead the way to "the mysterious primordial unity." In object relations theory, such language suggests the yearning of the over-determined (male) ego, excessively distanced from its pre-oedipal identification with the mother, now stranded in a world of atomized items, whirling about without meaning or solace (Chodorow, 1978). It is the isolation and impotence of Lasch's solipsist.

One imagines the proliferation of the contemporary American school during times of cultural fluidity. Immigration was of sufficient magnitude during the period 1890-1930 that some believed the fixed identity of the nation to be threatened. Racist groups attempted to influence mainstream educational groups such as the National Education Association (Selden, 1988). Perhaps at the height of this Dionysian development the curriculum field was born, conceived by the parents of management/business and educational administration, brought up to ensure standardization. Its cultural function was to wean immigrants' children away from their parents (and from their parents' origins), to create for them a fixed American identity, one overdetermined (i.e., excessively patriotic), stereotypic, and thus reliable. The emphasis of the curriculum was language, manners (including the range of cultural expectations and standards—dress, courtesy, etc.), preparation for mass labor, and arithmetic for business.

Curriculum as enculturation, as political socialization is, in Nietzschean terms, a metaphysical expression of the human will to power. In this sense, curriculum is the human hubris to make order out of the chaotic, knowledge out of mystery. Nietzsche: "It is an eternal phenomenon; the insatiable will always find a way to detain its creatures in life and compel them to live on, by means of an illusion spread over things" (Nietzsche, 1956). The scholar, the theorist, the intellectual believe they gain privileged points of view, by virtue of information unearthed, imaginatively interpreted, and convincingly argued. For Nietzsche, this belief is illusion. Academics and others who live "the life of the mind" are simply men and women also struggling to balm the "wound of existence." The Piagetian developmental achievement of formal operations is another statement of this evasion. For Nietzsche, human abstract thought is "wretched, transitory, purposeless, forceful." Human thought is a falsification of reality. Nietzsche: "Every concept originates through equating the unequal." The Nietzschean world is without order, made up of atomized bits of matter and circumstance, incapable of yielding to generalization or conclusion. Science is the contemporary religion that denies and distorts this reality. The Christian God may be dead, Nietzsche asserts, but "He" is replaced by another God: Science. Scientists are the high priests of the modern period. They give hope of a better life after the present one, a life free of disease, toil, and ignorance. For Nietzsche these promises are no different than those offered by ecclesiastical officials: incapable of final substantiation, they lead only to tithing.

What is the function of human cognition in this "scheme" (anti-scheme)? In short, concepts cannot be said to represent true, genuine knowledge of reality. On the contrary, they are bare schemata that rob reality of its multiplicity, richness, and vitality (Megill, 1985).

Where does Nietzsche leave us? In a world of Dionysian immediacy and sensuality? Yes and no. While he desires both, he acknowledges that only by transcending immediacy and sensuality into abstraction do human beings achieve some degree of humanness. Megill observes on this point that: "...Nietzsche envisages not the destruction of the conceptual world but rather...its deconstruction—that is its transportation into a realm of aesthetic illusion and play" (Megill, 1985, p. 53).

As artistic creation, as myth-maker, science is praised. In his *Human, All-Too-Human*, Nietzsche endorses "the spirit of science," "scientific knowledge," "scientific methods," the "clear thinking of reason," "rigorous thought, cautious judgment, and logical conclusions," and "the spirit of enlightenment" as opposed to "Romanticism." Further, as Megill (1985) explains:

> Artists, he [Nietzsche] suggests, are intellectual lightweights. The artist "does not stand in the front rank of enlightenment and civilization of humanity," for he remains a child or youth throughout his life, his development having been arrested "at the point where he was overcome by his artistic impulse." Artists are "always of necessity *epigoni*." They lighten the burdens of life, but their healing is only temporary, and in the meantime it has the unfortunate effect of discouraging men "from working toward a genunie improvement in their conditions." Their backward, childish condition leads to a belief in gods and demons, to a spiritualization of nature, to a hatred of science. (p. 67)

Yet this apparently "positivistic" voice makes clear that science—like art—is also a fiction. What is praiseworthy about science is that which is praiseworthy about art: the capacity of fiction to make order out of the universe, to serve as a "vital lie," to function as myths and as means by which myths can be created, destroyed, and reformulated. For Nietzsche the evil of contemporary science is its destruction of myth, and the creation of a Western culture that is rationalistic and obsessively skeptical. This, in Nietzsche's view, is a disaster. For Nietzsche believes myth to be absolutely essential to the health of a culture: "Without myth every culture loses the healthy power of its creativity: only a horizon defined by myths completes and unifies a whole cultural movement. Myth alone saves all the posers of the imagination and of Apollonian dream from their aimless wanderings.... The problem, then, is to recover myth, and thus to restore the lost vitality of culture" (Megill, 1985, p. 75).

Cultural myths are, of course, intertwined with personal myths. In one sense the architect of self works with the material of myths, especially its literary subgenre, stories. We tell stories about our families, our school history, etc., and in so doing interpret experience, creating fictions. Our personal stories occur in cultural stories, sometimes coinciding with the latter, sometimes told in opposition or denial of them. The point is that in a Nietzschean sense the self is fictive; it is an aesthetic creation, and the means by which the self is planned and "built" are story-telling and myth-making.

Curriculum which denies teachers' and students' interpretations, or accords them a marginal status, functions to either collapse the self into the subject material (as in the prototype of the obedient teacher or student who might display an encyclopedic memory but has few ideas of his or her own) or drive the self away, withdrawn into itself (as in the prototypical case) of the estranged student, ego intact—if not overly determined and congealed—but incapable and unwilling to ever merge with material enough to acquire it. The possible educative functions of curriculum, including its conceptualization as building material for the architect of self, are inseparable from the processes of myth-making and storytelling.

> "Reason... is the most stiff necked
> adversary of thought."
> —Heidegger

The image of an architecture of self might suggest a fixed plan, a stable identity, a true or false self; in either case, it suggests an enduring and boundaried identity. While it is true that the image does imply fixity, it is also true that a plan can be altered. Indeed, a plan or an extant structure (although less easily) is an act of creation, an aesthetic event in the Nietzschean sense (regardless of its beauty). What is planned and constructed can be deconstructed.

In the architecture of self both moments are present, perhaps not simultaneously, but present nonetheless. Which moment to consciously cultivate depends upon the character of the existing structure. Lasch's minimal self, obsessed with itself (whether the obsession takes an obvious turn toward the self as in contemporary interests in health clubs or a less obvious one when it is fused with the "other," and obsesses over the "earth"), would seem to recommend a conscious attention to building a stable identity, an identity which stretches from a "private" or psychological self to the "public" or social and political self. For the excessively socialized individual, the over-determined self, the inflated ego of the (often male) corporate personality, the deconstructive moment is to be sought. Only via deconstruction can a reformulation of self begin, a self not frozen and overly fixed psychologically or socially, but capable of perceiving and processing new information according to constantly adjusting notions of reality, the future and past.

The scientization of the study of human life, particularly those forms evident in mainstream social science, accompanied two important historical developments in the West: the concerted effort toward cultural homogeneity in the face of mass immigration and the rise of mass production, with a corresponding homogeneity in the work force, both "blue" and "white" collar. The personality "produced" paralleled the structure of these developments: stable, predictable, common. The "minimal self", while inherently unstable, indeed driven by often unconcealed anxiety, still seeks culturally homogeneous forms. The schools still organize themselves as if cultural standardization were the main agenda item. In general, however, in the most parts of the United States, cultural standardization has been achieved.

While social science, as science, has enjoyed limited success, the cultural myth that scientific generalization about human life is possible has been successfully propagated, especially by disciplines such as psychology and sociology (Bauman, 1978). Heidegger opposed the scientization of the study of humankind precisely because he perceived its depersonalizing and anti-intellectual consequences. Within the academy, he understood that the questions asked would become smaller and smaller, confined by mathematized methods of inquiry. He opposed what he saw as the tendency of contemporary scholarship toward methodological standardization and trivialization (Megill, 1985).

The character of cognition itself changes, he observed. Cognition becomes calculative, only interested in its own results and conclusions. Knowledge rather than that mode of relation to experience which is knowing, is esteemed. Heidegger was concerned with the act of thinking, not its conclusions. His thought is a "passionate thinking," a meditative rather than calculative thinking. The latter is one heritage of the scientization of contemporary thought, the replacement of ethics with engineering, morality with social science. We moderns dwell not in interior lives, but rather in public ones. Megill (1985) comments: "[Heidegger] is saying that the banal and superficial life that we lead when, in the broadest sense, we are our 'meeting the public' conceals from us the knowledge that we are alienated beings and makes us feel 'at home' within the world" (p. 118).

Heidegger's work has been said to exhibit a nostalgia for an earlier period, a time unmarred by inauthenticity, manipulation, and fabricated, public selves. To re-experience this earlier time, developmentally as well as historically, means "going home" to a "place" that is more primal. In this sense, Heidegger anticipates the symbiotic agenda of Lasch's minimal self, an agenda in which rationalism, artifice, and industrial and post-industrial economics are suspect. Megill (1985) comments: "In short, Heidegger's nostalgia can be read as a longing for the immediate Dionysian presence of the origin, from which all division, all separation, all difference is excluded" (p. 125).

Being, one presumes, is profoundly non-personal experience, and individuality, self, disappear. While such experience and knowledge merit our respect, they must be brought back to the public sphere if they are to gain our everyday practical interest. As a moment or series of moments in the deconstruction of an overly-determined public (probably male) ego, this Heideggerean regression to a pre-individual and pre-oedipal merging with the Source is developmentally useful, perhaps even necessary. Only via destruction of false self can the buried, authentic self be revealed. Laing (1960) understood that breakdown, even madness, can represent necessary means to sanity in some cases. For the architect of self, should he judge his current edifice obscuring its foundation in ways that keep him ignorant of himself, such a study is advised. For the already broken-down, another order of work is appropriate.

The kind of body society needs

Foucault has studied institutional productions of personality. In prisons, psychiatric hospitals, and in schools, particular versions of reality are breathed into life, other versions choked. For Foucault, however, it is not an authentic self that is obscured and distorted in these institutional forms of the impulse to "discipline" and "punish." There is no home to where one might return, no possibility of congruence with an already formed, imprinted personality. What one has been and is always "contains" what one has not been, and is not now. And what has been rejected or repressed defines or can define the self as completely as what one accepts and integrates consciously. The participation of self in personality, the entire process and possibility suggested by the imagery of an architecture of self, is at every moment a political choice. Certain impulses are permitted expression, accorded status; others are not. Foucault observes that power "conceals," "masks," "censors," and "abstracts." It also "produces; it produces reality; it produces domains of objects and rituals of truth."

Power becomes form through discourse and language. In fact, for the Foucault of *The Order of Things*, all that exists is language, is discourse. The world is language, and vice versa. Theory, for instance, is practice. "Theory does not express, translate, or serve to apply practice: it is practice" (Megill, 1985, p. 195). The surveillance of language by the psychiatric and educational establishments functions to perpetuate the repression of excluded groups and possibilities. Foucault seems to assume the cause of excluded groups, implying that their struggle keeps alive human possibility in any form.

The construction of self, including its relational bonding with others and with objects, requires exclusion. The exclusion construction requires is denied at the cost of stasis and arrest. The architect imagines reforming even as he aspires for stability. The point is to suspend that which is excluded, not obliterate it. In suspension, marginalized elements are kept alive. Alive, they sustain the life of accepted elements. Obliterating madness by medicalization, situating its experience in formal codifications, "thrusts into oblivion all those stammered, imperfect words without fixed syntax in which the exchange between madness and reason was made" (quoted in Megill, 1985, p. 199). If I insist on public precision or matter-of-factness in all my relationships, I annihilate the "inner speech" that foreshadows futures for which I cannot plan at present.

Foucault allies himself with possibilities, exclusions, repressions. He does so in language and discourse. If reality is fundamentally discursive, then reality can be transformed discursively. Theory is practice. His motive is to demonstrate the arbitrariness of the extant order and the exclusions it contains. Foucault's alliance with the mad, the imprisoned, the sexually deviant, is provisional, however:

> One can thus imagine him turning against the discourse of homosexuality if that discourse becomes dominant, for far from ushering in the millenium, any such rise to dominance will merely provide the occasion for erecting new systems of exclusion. It is thus not surprising that Foucault's attitude toward the various so-called "action groups" with which he has been associated is peculiarly double-edged and ironical. He is willing to ally himself with these groups insofar as they are able to mount challenges to the existing order, attacking that order at one or another of its weak points. But insofar as they are committed to estab-

lishing new, allegedly liberating orders, he remains highly suspicious of
them. For what Foucault has articulated is an instrument of systematic
suspicion toward any order whatsoever—an analytical weapon that can
be used against any and all "discursive productions" even those with
which Foucault has for the moment aligned himself (Megill, 1985, p.
239).

His political stance is a subversive one. If the social (or self)
order is always arbitrary, the role of the intellectual is to represent the exclusions, whatever they may be. The kind of
body—physical body, personality, political body—society needs is
the kind of body Foucault wishes to seduce, to pervert, to redo
with excluded and marginalized material. His interest in
schools would not be in what we term the hidden curriculum
(he would say it is obvious, only unstated), but those realities
and possibilities of language and relationality that, at first blush,
are unimaginable. These might include, for instance, the
mediative rather than the calculative, the intuitive rather than
the rationalistic, the imagistic rather than the conceptual. A
Foucauldian perspective might place the arts at the curricular
center of schools—not science and mathematics. The excluded
and marginalized elements become central, and the discursive
formation that is the political present is perverted.

Commodified subjectively—the kind of psychological body
society needs—would be unravelled. The self might become
dazed, not focused—immersed in lived time not appointment
minutes. It might experience itself as a body, as a being among
physical objects, on the shore of Being. The manipulation of
self for effect, for task completion, and the accompanying
exchange quality of relationships—these would be attacked,
seduced, made over in a Foucauldian architecture of self. The
pleasures of expressivity—without an eye to their effect, loyalty,
devotion, (or rancor and revenge) toward each other, regardless their consequence for career or romance—these contrary
de-commodified, exchange-defiant forms of self might typify a
Foucaudian self. Such a self intends provocation not program,
and its architecture requires both construction, and deconstruction, sometimes simultaneously.

More so than Foucault, Derrida is an ironist, at times a paro-
dist. He makes no argument, carefully assembling evidence to

prove a point, to persuade a reader. At times he does not mean what he writes; at other times, he means what he does not write. Megill (1985) notes: "Every stance Derrida articulates has both its 'pro' and its 'anti' aspects; every portion that he adopts is immediately rendered nugatory" (pp. 261, 266). Like Foucault, Derrida perceives no phenomenological essence, no definitive ground of being, no authentic self. There are truths that are so only because arbitrary exclusions and emphases obtain. Derrida attacks the nostalgic motifs in Heidegger's thought, although he requires Heidegger in order to do so. Megill (1985) explains: "Heidegger envisages destroyed a tradition in order to get back to an original, unconcealed meaning. In Derrida the 'destruction' becomes a 'deconstruction,' a simultaneous smashing down and building up, with no privilege granted to origin and with the tradition retained, though not in historicist form" (pp. 269-270).

In one sense, Derridean thought, in its intrinsic instability and dynamism, resembles Nietzsche's visions or reality as chaotic, without meaning. In another sense, however, Derrida supplies a method of thinking, and a method of participating in the architecture of self, that makes complex an ever-shifting order of Nietzschean chaos. It is an order that deconstructs as it constructs, decommodifies and commodifies, and so on. Derrida uses the Hegelian concept of dialectic, but adds a fourth moment. After synthesis is deconstruction. There is nothing inevitably progressive in Derridean thought and history, and yet we are not stuck at some imagined stasis point, like Camus' Sisyphus. There is movement in the Derridean universe as there is stasis; there is intoxication as there is sobriety; there is profundity and humor, each undermining, indeed perverting, the other. The process is, of course, political as well as epistemological, and Derrida seems to support, like Foucault, the marginalized—not due to their intrinsic worthiness (or indeed superiority)—but rather because they are marginalized. In this regard, Jews are for Derrida what homosexuals are for Foucault (Megill, 1985).

Certain orders of discourse have been marginalized as well. Derrida appears to believe that writing has been demeaned or "abased" over the course of Western history. Speech has been valued more. For Derrida speech suggests immediacy, intelligibility, the experience and expression of truth, "transcendence signified." Writing denotes secondariness, distance, abstraction. Derrida: "Writing, the sensible inscription, has always been considered by Western tradition as the body and matter external to the spirit, to breath, to speech, and to the logos." Megill (1985) notes that speech is regarded as presence; writing is the denial of presence. The voice disappears immediately upon its being said; writing is a mediation. It separates itself from its origins and preserves itself even when those origins are lost (pp. 285, 287). Derrida: "[Writing is] a mediation and the departure of the logos from itself.... Writing is the dissimulation of the natural, primary, and immediate presence of sense to the novel within logos" (quoted in Megill, 1985, p. 287).

Whereas Nietzsche and Heidegger portray abstraction as distortions of and distractions from the lebenswelt, Derrida portrays the mediation of experience and being as intrinsic to the apprehension of reality at all. While speech may obscure the indelible mark and function of mediation and in so doing reduce the distance between the sensory and the discursive, it does not replace the space. Foucault and Derrida point to the duality of this epistemology of mediations. They observe that all human forms represent such mediations. For instance, the shape, play, and coupling of bodies are discursive forms. Foucault and Derrida deny the nostalgia of biologism which, for instance, implies that particular forms of love-making are "natural" while others are not. The judgment and experience of "naturalness" are discursively located and represent mediations of politics, economics, culture, and history. The coupling of specific anatomical parts and aversion of others, the very contours of the anatomy itself (fat versus thin for a non-subtle example) represent discursive mediations.

Autobiography and the architecture of self

Writing in the Derridean sense becomes a kind of architecture, that space and those movements of mediation which give and take form to formlessness. A kaleidoscope of impulses, instincts, memories, and dreams are visualized, theorized, told as a story. Autobiography takes this task seriously. It is the task of self formation, deformation, learning, and unlearning. Speech, like poetry and music, can hover close to the Heideggerean "ground of Being;" but writing, and in particular, the craft of autobiography, can soar, and from the heights, discern new landscapes, new configurations, especially those excluded by proclamations of Government, State and School (Megill, 1985).

Lasch suggests that the (appropriate) terror of living in a present shadowed by Holocaust past and every moment possibly the last, has minimalized the self into political passivity, thus making more likely the occurrence of what is dreaded. Minimalized, the self hovers close to presentistic psychological experience, obsessing over its "condition," constantly seeking to maintain or improve the health the political world threatens to annihilate. Minimalized, the self flees from itself into the mystical—read imagined— fusion with the earth, precisely that world from which—in fact— it has receded. The loss of relatedness to the public sphere, the extension of private to public self, implies the space of mediation, the secondariness of writing, the identification and empathy with the excluded or marginalized. Lasch points us back to the Judaic-Christian tradition (Lasch, 1984). In as far as this movement supports an architecture of self connected (in relation) to the "public" sphere, and not a movement toward ideological submersion in a tradition Nietzsche rightly named as rancor disguised as sweetness, it is a movement toward "maximalization" and not inflation.

Autobiography can serve as a method for enlarging, occupying and building the space of mediation. It enlarges the space by pushing back the edges of memory, disclosing more of what has been "forgotten," suppressed and denied. In order to do so the stories one tells must not be the ones we save for fellow airplane travellers or colleagues we meet annually at AERA. They are not stories to embellish and disguise the past and present, for an imagined effect. Rather, that autobiography which makes the self's architecture more complex moves below the surface of memory, requiring the dismantling of self-defenses. It retrieves sensory experience, and in so doing does not portray the past from the point of view of the present. Instead it undermines the stories we tell for comfort or amusement's sake, and allows (to a variable extent) a re-entry into the past, a re-experience of the past moment now somewhat present in its multidimensionality and orderlessness. Now, the edges of memory pushed back, the water and air of experience seep in, making the pool of memory larger, deeper, more complete.

One danger of autobiography is further reification of these processes, and the construction of an unchanging edifice, a skyscraper proudly proclaiming its owner and occupants. Norman Holland's (1980) work may succumb to this danger as it insists that a unity resides in the reader. He suggests there is no textual unity, objectivity; however, there is unity in the biographic theme of the reader. Regardless, the literary text (and read text here as curriculum) is a Rorschach test onto which the lived themes of readers are projected. There is no textual unity; the illusion of sameness is created by the projection onto texts of the unity inherent in life themes.

Of course there are such themes; there are true (and false) selves. What Holland's work may obscure, however, is that the truth in these themes inheres through their exclusion of others. The exclusions and absences are also true. By denying the partiality and arbitrariness of one's life theme(s), one substitutes a false stability and unity of self for a false unity of text.

Autobiography is not interesting because it supplies us a wealth of data. Such a preoccupation could represent another form of self commodification and reification. Autobiography is interesting when its telling enlarges and complicates the telling subject, and the listening subject. We are not the stories we tell as much as we are the modes of relation to others our stories imply, modes of relation implied by what we delete as much as by what we include.

Derrida's sense of speech as presence, writing as absence, suggests Lacan's view of self as the "empty subject," a subject defined by its relationships, incapable of thematic unity (Lacan, 1977). For Lacan the self is an empty space, an intersection of multiple functions, possibilities, voices, "answers" (questions) to the "questions" (answers) that constitute the Other.

Is there a true voice? A true self? Speaking of text, denying that text (or self) can ever be a plenitude, a configuration of elements patterned in themselves and pointing only to themselves, to the text, Derrida (1981) observes:

> Every element...is contributed from the trace it bears in itself of the other elements in the chain or system. This interweaving results in each "element"—phoneme or grapheme—being constituted on the basis of the trace within it of the other elements of the chain or system. This interweaving, this textile, is the text produced only in the transformation of another text. Nothing, neither among the elements nor within the system, is anywhere ever simply present or absent. There are only, everywhere, differences and traces of traces (p. 26).

Autobiography as alternately sublimated and desublimated modalities of self-self, self-other, and self-object relations, is itself an exclusion, an absence, in schools and in the public sphere generally. To engage oneself and others autobiographically reconnects the minimalized, psychological self to the public, political sphere as it de-commodifies interpersonal relations. Such engagement risks debasement if performed exclusively or primarily through speech, that presence of immediacy which recapitulates the momentariness of mass culture. Through the "secondariness" of writing, solitarily, in a Kierkegaardian "soliloquy with oneself," can the architect construct (and deconstruct) one's presence to oneself and to others in the world. Like Nietzsche's Zarathrustra, one might reconfigure elements of oneself, contradicting: "...with every word, this most affirmative of all spirits; all opposites are in him bound together in a new unity" (Nietzsche, 1979). The architecture of self is the construction of an authentic humanity; in this sense autobiography becomes reformulation of History as well as of life history. As Nietzsche imagines:

> Anyone who manages to experience the history of humanity as a whole as his own history will feel in an enormously generalized way all the grief of an invalid who thinks of health, of an old man who thinks of the dreams of his youth, of a lover deprived of his beloved, of the martyr whose ideal is perishing, of the hero on the evening after a battle that has decided nothing but brought him wounds and the loss of his friends. But if one endured, if one could endure this immense sum of grief of all kinds while yet being the hero who, as the second day of battle breaks, welcomes the dawn and his fortune, being a person whose horizon encompasses thousands of years past and future, being the heir of all the nobility of all past spirit—an heir with a sense of obli-

gation, the most aristocratic of old nobles and at the same time the first
of a new nobility—the like of which no age has yet seen or dreamed of,
if one could burden one's soul with all of this—the oldest, the newest,
losses, hopes, conquests, and victories of humanity? If one could finally
contain all this in one's soul and crowd it into a single feeling—this
surely would have to result in a happiness that humanity has not known
so far: the happiness of a god full of power and love, full of tears and
laughter, a happiness that, like the sun in the evening, continually
bestows its inexhaustible riches, pouring them into the sea, feeling
richest, as the sun does, only when even the poorest fisherman is still
rowing with golden oars! This godlike feeling would then be called-
humanness (Nietzsche, 1979).

The curriculum is not comprised of subjects, but of Subjects,
of subjectivity. The running of the course is the building of the
self, the lived experience of subjectivity. Autobiography is an
architecture of self, a self we create and embody as we read,
write, speak and listen. The self becomes flesh, in the world.
Even when authentic and learned, it is a self we cannot be con-
fident we know, because it is always in motion and in time,
defined in part by where it is not, when it is not, what it is not.
The self who welcomes the dawn is a self constantly expanding
to incorporate what it fears and resists as well as what it desires.
The self who rows with golden oars is a self constantly contract-
ing, losing its gravity so it may rise, expansive toward the sky.
Full of tears and full of laughter may we teach and may we
learn; may we become gods of own lives, servants to others.
Mais oui.

References

Bauman, Z. (1978). *Hermeneutics and social science.* New York: Columbia University Press.

Chodorow, N. (1978). *The reproduction of mothering.* Berkeley: University of California Press.

Cohen-Solal, A. (1987). *Sartre: A life.* Trans. Anna Concogui. New York: Pantheon.

Derrida, J. (1981). *Positions.* Chicago: University of Chicago Press.

Foucault, M. (1973). *The order of things.* New York: Vintage.

Freud, S. (1917). *Introductory lectures on psychoanalysis,* SE, Vols. 15 & 16, pp.3-476. London: Hogarth.

Holland, N. (1980). In S. R. Suleiman and I. Crossman (eds.), *The reader in the text.* Princeton: Princeton University Press.

Jacoby, R. (1975). *Social amnesia.* Boston: Beacon Press.

Jung, C. K. (1939). *The integration of personality.* New York: Farrar & Rinehart.

Lacan, J. (1977). *Ecrits: A selection.* London: Tavistock.

Laing, R. D. (1960). *The divided self.* New York: Patheon.

Lasch, C. (1984). *The minimal self.* New York: Norton.

Megill, A. (1985). *Prophets of extremity.* Berkeley: University of California Press.

Nietzsche, F. (1956). *The birth of tragedy.* Trans Francis Golffing. Garden City, N.Y.: Doubleday.

Nietzsche, F. (1974). *Twilight of the idols, in the complete works of Friedrich Nietzsche.* Oscar Levy (ed.). New York: Gordon Press.

Nietzsche, F. (1979). *Ecce homo.* Trans. R. J. Hollingsdale. New York: Penguin.

Nietzsche, F. (1979). *The gay science.* Trans. Walter Kaufman. New York: Penguin.

Nietzsche, F. (1984). *Human, all too human*. Trans. & intro. by Marion Faber with Stephen Lehmann. Lincoln: University of Nebraska Press.

O'Hara, D.T. (n.d.) The prophet of our laughter: or Nietzsche as educator. *Boundary* 2, pp. 1-79.

Pinar, W. (1975). Sanity, madness and the school. In W. Pinar (ed.), *Curriculum theorizing: The reconceptualists* (359-383). Berkeley: McCutchan.

Pinar, W. (1988).   Time, place, and voice: Curriculum theory and the historical moment. In W. Pinar (Ed.). *Contemporary curriculum discourses* (264-278). Scottsdale, AZ: Gorsuch, Scarisbrick.

Ray, W. (1984). *Literary meaning: From phenomenology to deconstruction*. New York: Basil Blackwell.

Reich, W. (1961). *Character analysis*. New York: Noonday Press.

Sartre, J-P. (1974). *Between existentialism and marxism*. New York: Pantheon.

Selden, S. (1988). Biological determinism and the normal school curriculum. In W. Pinar (ed.), *Contemporary curriculum discourses* (50-65). Scottsdale, AZ: Gorsuch Scarisbrick.

Wexler, P. (1988). Body and soul: Sources of social change and strategies of education. In W. Pinar (Ed.), *Contemporary curriculum discourses* (201-222). Scottsdale, AZ: Gorsuch, Scarisbrick.

Wilder, A. (1975). Lacan and the discourses of the other. In J. Lacan, *The language of self*, ed. & trans. by A. Wilder. New York: Delta.

XIII

A Reconceptualization of Teacher Education
(1988)

The theoretical apparatus is now in place for a curricular reconceptualization of teacher education. If schools are to be a "second site" of reconceptualization, teacher education will be an important instrument. Consideration of political and curricular issues accompanying such a reconceptualization is the subject of this paper.

The Reconceptualization of curriculum studies began in a critique of the traditional field [see Pinar, 1975], a field largely identified with the Tyler Rationale (1949). After a decade of declining enrollments and a national curriculum reform movement led not by curriculum generalists but by disciplinary specialists, the field was vulnerable to critique (Pinar & Grumet, 1988). In 1969 Joseph Schwab delivered the first of a decade-long series of critiques, one consequence of which was to accelerate the breakdown of the Tylerian "paradigm" (Brown, 1988). In its place surfaced an effort to understand curriculum as well as develop it. The effort was informed by history, political theory, aesthetic theory, phenomenology, gender research, autobiography and feminist theory. During the 1970s the curriculum field became absorbed with the complex of ways that culture and individuals reproduced and transformed themselves via public institutions, particularly the school and specifically school knowledge or curriculum. The Reconceptualization had twin emphases: the school as microcosm of society and the school as experienced by the individual. The Reconceptualization has ended as a social and intellectual movement within curriculum studies. Indeed, within curriculum theory, the Reconceptualization has occurred (Pinar, 1988a).

The forms this multifaceted, complex, and evolving understanding of curriculum would take in teacher education programs vary according to external influences (such as the political climate of the local schools) and internal influences, including the perspectives of those involved most closely, even if these individuals were all "reconceptualists." This paper sketches qualities of one possible version of a "reconceptualist" teacher education program. This version makes use of the controversial Holmes Group proposals, proposals which, in modified form, can advance teacher education significantly. The three most interesting Holmes proposals are (a) eliminating the undergraduate major in education, (b) reconceptualizing teacher education coursework, and (c) linking teacher education programs to the schools.

In our interest

Politically, the Holmes proposals are in the political best interests of education faculties. They represent a way of claiming defeat as victory, that is if we act decisively and take reconceptualization seriously. Now education faculties are given the blame for the perceived failure in schools. We know that is only partly true, but the public perception is not going to be corrected soon or easily, and certainly not by the accused. Shifting the responsibility for undergraduate learning to our colleagues in arts and sciences also shifts the political responsibility for the quality of those students who graduate from their disciplines and enter ours. Creating clinical faculty from colleagues in the schools to teach methods courses and supervise student teachers or interns helps shift political responsibility to existing teachers. Reducing the number of coursework hours we have teacher education students reduces the liability of teacher educators.

Despite its dangers, the differentiated staffing idea is smart politically and economically. The major problem will involve keeping internal bureaucratic politics minimal so that the more intelligent and professional of teachers are those who are promoted to the highest category and thus earn the highest salaries. If intelligent, well-trained, and dedicated people are appointed to the promotion boards which make these decisions, there is a chance. If behavioristic schemes are used, mostly by existing administrators, especially principals, one can be less sanguine. Even the creation of an instructor class, those with bachelors degrees in arts and sciences disciplines but no or little education coursework, is a risk worth taking in the short term. If significant amounts of new money are not forthcoming, a reasonable assumption for most school districts, then keeping entry-level salaries low will help free monies to create higher-paying, "career professional" positions. The Rochester, New York, top salary of approximately $70,000 is one with which all districts ought to compete. Most districts will see not the absolute increases in their budgets Governor Cuomo provided New York State districts, and so starting salaries must be considerably below the Rochester ones of nearly $30,000. If, for example, a history major were paid $20,000 to begin a teaching career, then experienced, educated, intelligent teachers could be paid considerably more. Unless this monetary incentive is built in the system soon, all reform efforts will be undermined. And the public will be unwilling to provide additional monies unless discernible (if not dramatic) reform is underway.

From a political point of view, then, the Holmes proposals provide a diversification of responsibility for the quality of teachers, thus reducing the liability for education faculties. They ensure fundamental educational experience in the basic arts and sciences disciplines anterior to the study of teaching and curriculum. Finally, a reduction in the number of coursework hours available to teacher education faculties requires those faculties to reconceptualize those courses those courses along more academically rigorous and complex lines. The curricular sketch which follows points toward one such reconceptualization.

Liberal arts education

Undergraduate education majors do not sufficiently study the arts and sciences. No matter how sophisticated it may be, and at many institutions it is hardly sophisticated, the study of teaching, learning, and curriculum always derives, to an extent, from the arts, humanities, and sciences. These disciplines constitute orders of information and experience that are epistemologically anterior to the rigorous study of curriculum and teaching. Curriculum is always, in a fundamental sense, an extrapolation from arts, humanities, and sciences disciplines. To reduce prospective teachers' arts, humanities, and sciences work is to reduce the knowledge a teacher can bring to elementary and secondary school students.

Exemplary teaching is hardly universal in arts and sciences disciplines. Vocationalism, an orientation which views undergraduate work as primarily preparatory to graduate work, is common, especially in research universities. A bachelor's degree in the arts, humanities, and sciences in no way guarantees expertise in working with children and young adults. And the differentiated staffing proposal does pose the possibility of creating a permanent "underclass" of teachers in the "instructor" category. However, students whose undergraduate experience has been limited to methods and foundations courses (often courses not academically rigorous or as idea-rich as arts, humanities, and sciences courses) sometimes cannot pass minimal competency tests imposed by some states, nor are they perceived by the public as having succeeded with the nation's schoolchildren. Indeed, the Holmes, Carnegie, and NCATE reports are responses to a widespread judgment of academic bankruptcy for our schools. While the reasons for this bankruptcy are complex, and responsibility belongs to no one group such as education faculties or teachers, the point is that a fundamental reorganization of the teacher preparation process is politically required. Even if this judgment of bankruptcy were false, as many mainstream teacher educators seem to believe, the public believes it by and large, the politicians believe it, and most others in the higher education community believe it also.

Coursework for preservice teachers

Tom (1987) expresses a well-grounded skepticism regarding "the knowledge base of teaching" mentioned in the Holmes proposals. Efforts to develop a science of teaching have indeed failed. One would hope that reconceptualist scholarship had laid to rest this false ambition. It rests on a mechanical view of humankind which, if accurate, would not then require a technology of teaching, given that human behavior would then be manipulable and predictable (Pinar, 1988b). Pseudo-scientific, "practice-oriented" teacher preparation emphasizes a narrow vocationalism over the cultivation of professional judgment.

The cultivation of professional judgment and wisdom, provided they are grounded in serious study in the arts, humanities, and sciences and in curriculum theory, is an appropriate aspiration. This general and important distinction between academic vs. vocational or technical curriculum is well expressed in the following catalogue statement, taken from the University of Michigan Law School announcement.

> [T]he Law School is very much a professional school. But it is distinctly not a vocational school. Students are not trained to perform many, or even most, of the tasks that its graduates may be called upon to perform as lawyers, and should not expect to be fully prepared to deliver a wide range of legal services on the day of graduation. [S]tudents may acquire or begin to develop some practical or technical skills and may gain confidence in their ability to perform as lawyers. Our practice-oriented courses and clinics provide, however, only an introduction to skills and a framework for practice which can only be defined through years of experience. The majority of our graduates join law firms where numerous opportunities exist for skill development under supervision of experienced practitioners who share with the novitiate responsibility for the quality of service rendered. Michigan, more than many other law schools, seeks to provide students with the intellectual and theoretical background with which an attorney can undertake a more reflective and rewarding practice. *It is felt that too much haste or emphasis on vocational skills, without a broader and more critical view of the framework on which lawyering occurs, runs the risks of training technicians instead of professionals* (p. 15; emphasis added).

The production of technicians is ill-advised also because it polarizes the undergraduate experience and professional training. Graduate study in education must not be severed from the undergraduate liberal arts curriculum; rather it must enhance and surpass the experiences and understandings that students have accumulated during these pre-education years. A "curriculum theory" M.A. preservice year would intersect but not coincide with undergraduate experience. It would grasp and extend that experience. What a curriculum theory informed fifth year can offer students is an analysis of arts and sciences knowledge grounded in curriculum and suggested by specializations such as the history of science (mathematics, etc.), the sociology of knowledge (including science), gender analyses of the disciplines, phenomenology of educational experience, aesthetic ways of knowing, and the politics of school knowledge. The graduate of such a curriculum is more likely to be a "transformative intellectual" than a technician and bureaucratic functionary (Giroux, 1988).

These affiliated areas can be taught in several courses with interdisciplinary content. For instance, rather than the conventional child developmental psychology course, an "Experience of Childhood" course drawing upon undergraduate knowledge in arts and social science disciplines could be developed. It would include readings in developmental psychology, but also in the history and phenomenology of childhood, in fictional accounts (both novels and poems) of growing up, as well as political and economic analyses of the family, children, and schooling. Other interdisciplinary courses might include the "Nature of Knowledge," including characteristic ways of knowing from arts, sciences, and the humanities, with particular attention to teaching exemplifications of each tradition of knowing. Non-European knowledge as well as material from marginalized classes and groups must be included.

While thematic organization of knowledge are hardly novel (Barnes, 1987), teacher preparation informed by contemporary curriculum theory would explicitly occupy the intersections between undergraduate study of the liberal arts and institutional demands of practitioner performance. These courses could be taught, if economy required, in large lecture sections. Intense small-group workshop experiences could accompany them. These courses must be rigorous academic experiences constructed to integrate undergraduate knowledge in the various disciplines with knowledge of curriculum and instruction. Considerations of practice are best left to the methods courses that would be taught in the program by Ph.D. students in interdisciplinary curriculum theory programs or by clinical faculty, who, under ideal circumstances, would be graduates of such programs. Clinical faculty trained in such programs would be more likely to provide continuity between classroom work and teaching experience.

The early courses would be intensely academic experiences; later experiences would be intensely practical. That is, methods courses could be taught in the schools by working teachers who have already undergone a thoroughly theoretical preparation. Supervision of student teaching ought to include sponsor teachers and at least one university person. Testimonial material from students, parents, and administrators ought be included in a candidate's portfolio. This material ought to be used in a reflective supervisory practice, as this permits the student critically to analyze his or her performance (Garman, 1986). Standardized instruments are best avoided, as they force a mechanization of teaching. Versions of Eisnerian "aesthetic" evaluation are preferable. Student teaching sites ought to be multiple, and include public and private schools, as well as demographically diverse settings.

During a student's M.A. year, he or she should maintain a journal in order to address phenomenological and gender-related experience (Grumet, 1988). Each M.A. student might be assigned to a faculty member or to an advanced Ph.D. student who would meet weekly with the student throughout the program. This person, trained in autobiography and journal work, would help the student reflect upon and analyze the experience. This person would also serve as an advocate for the student, but not necessarily be in a grade-conferring position. After student teaching, this "advisor" would be included in the committee judgment regarding conferral of the Master of Arts degree.

Schools

The Holmes Group calls for more closely linking education faculties with schools and for reorganizing schools. Clinical faculty who would have offices in educational faculty buildings and who would interact with education faculty will help link education faculties to schools. So-called "professional development schools," sites where collaborative training and research projects might be formulated and pursued, will permit closer ties between schoolteachers and university professors. Preferably, not only education faculties will be involved, but education schools will facilitate arts and science faculties involvement on part-time bases.

Closer links to the schools ought not to be viewed uncritically. The powerful press of daily life in the school can function as a kind of "black hole" into which theory disappears. Survival can come to mean coinciding uncritically with situations as they are (Baldwin, 1987). While we are friends with our colleagues in the schools—they are our former students—we must maintain a respectful distance from them. We cannot advise or educate those with whom we have thoroughly identified. For teacher educators, the school must remain an object of study as well as a site for success (Pinar & Grumet, 1988).

A caution

There is a fear that Holmes Group reforms will make more difficult the recruitment of minority teacher candidates [see, for example, Martinez, 1988]. This fear must be taken seriously but must also be situated in a larger economic context. Minority students will return to teaching if and when it becomes lucrative and respected. This is, in large measure, a market-driven matter. Making the field more prestigious and more appropriately compensated should make it easier to recruit minority students. Accommodations in admission criteria will have to be made on occasion, especially when GRE scores or other culturally narrow and standardized instruments are an essential factor in admissions decisions (Barone, 1987). Retention of minority teacher candidates might be made more likely by incorporating appropriate cognitive "styles" (Anderson, 1988). Acknowledgement of and support for cultural, class, and specifically ethnic variabilities in modes of cognition are important aspects of a curriculum-theory inspired teacher preparation program.

The diversity of teacher education institutions would probably be reduced (Tom, 1987), and that is not necessarily unfortunate. Most nonresearch universities, including many small colleges, have very limited resources for teacher education. Common to many small colleges is an education department of two to five overworked faculty with one hundred or more students among them. With little time or institutional support to keep abreast of current scholarship or to attend annual professional meetings, these faculty, despite their intelligence, strong training, and commitment cannot offer what research universities can offer prospective teachers.

Conclusion

The Holmes proposals represent concession portrayed as victory, and curriculum theorists must claim the victory as partially their own, as we have been critical of the vacuous pseudo-science that has sometimes characterized mainstream teacher education in the past. Behavioral objectives, instruction inter-action analyses, and standardized forms of evaluation have contributed to the "deskilling" and "dis-empowerment" of educators and to the deterioration of American public education. The Holmes proposals, by promising increased teacher autonomy and higher salaries, intersect with the curriculum theory agenda. Vigorous intervention on behalf of women and minorities—in recruitment and in curriculum content—is an essential item of a curriculum theory-Holmes proposal.

The real battle is not over whether a reconceptualization of teacher education will occur. That battle is over, lost in the perceptions of politicians and the public. The battle concerns the content of fifth-year or extended programs and whether that content will remain or become even more standardized, behavioristic, and technological or whether it will reflect the critical and reflective content and goals of the recent Reconceptualization of curriculum studies. Curriculum theorists can enter the battle in the professional journals, in their own faculty meetings, and in legislative sessions, arguing for a reconceptualization that will authorize truly interdisciplinary and critically rigorous teacher preparation programs.

Acknowledgement

I wish to thank Tony Whitson for bringing the University of Michigan Law School announcement to my attention.

References

Anderson, J. A. (1988). Cognitive styles and multicultural populations. *Journal of Teacher Education*, 39 (1), 2-9.

Baldwin, E. E. (1987). Theory vs. ideology in the practice of teacher education. *Journal of Teacher Education*, 38 (1), 16-19.

Barnes, H. L. (1987). Conceptual bases for thematic teacher education programs. *Journal of Teacher Education*, 38 (4), 13-18.

Barone, T. E. (1987). Educational platforms, teacher selection, and school reform. *Journal of Teacher Education*, 38 (2), 12-17.

Brown, T. (1988). How fields change: A critique of the "Kuhnian" view. In W. Pinar (Ed.), *Contemporary curriculum discourses* (16-30). Scottsdale, AZ: Gorsuch, Scarisbrick.

de Martinez, B. (1988). Political and reform agenda' impact on the supply of black teachers. *Journal of Teacher Education*, 39 (1), 10-13.

Garman, N. (1986). Reflection, the heart of supervision. *Journal of Curriculum and Supervision*, 2 (1), 1-24.

Giroux, H. A. (1988). Liberal arts, teaching, and critical literacy. In W. Pinar (Ed.), *Contemporary Curriculum Discourses* (243-263). Scottsdale, AZ: Gorsuch, Scarisbrick.

Pinar, W. (Ed.) (1975). *Curriculum theorizing: The reconceptualists.* Berkeley, CA: McCutchan.

Pinar, W. (1988a). Introduction. *Contemporary Curriculum Discourses* (1-13). Scottsdale, AZ: Gorsuch, Scarisbrick.

Pinar, W. (1988b). "Whole, bright, deep with understanding:" Issues in qualitative research and autobiographical method. In W. Pinar (Ed.), *Contemporary Curriculum Discourses* (134-154). Scottsdale, AZ: Gorsuch, Scarisbrick.

Pinar, W. & Grumet, M. (1988). Socratic caesura and the theory-practice relationship. In W. Pinar (Ed.), *Contemporary Curriculum Discourses* (92-100). Scottsdale, AZ: Gorsuch, Scarisbrick.

Tom, A. (1987). *How should teachers be educated? An assessment of three reform reports.* Bloomington, IN: Phi Delta Kappa Education Foundation.

Tyler, R. (1949). *Basic principles of curriculum and instruction.* Chicago: University of Chicago Press.

University of Michigan Law School Announcement (1986-7). Ann Arbor: University of Michigan.

XIV

"Dreamt into Existence by Others:" Curriculum Theory and School Reform
(1991)

Perhaps every man knows he is being conceived by others; a sense in which he likewise dreams others into existence as husband/father to places and times, as Fool to every ghost-child he entertains or hunts for with pitiful, pitiless ambition. A sense in which every revolution of the hunt, every religion of the sexes, is related to potentiality for child-bearing, ghost-bearing, capsules of ambition—the unborn child/ghost of hope for some, the never-to-be-born child/ghost of aborted future for others. Related therefore to a ceremony of expectations and of silent mourning concealed perhaps from oneself but active in every career night and day as fate (Harris, 1975, p. 44).

A ceremony of expectations

The pressure upon us is enormous. Students, teachers, administrators, and education professors have all been called to work even harder, to achieve even more. While this political pressure includes calls for increased teacher autonomy, it also may bring standardized examinations by which national academic standards will then be said to be established. Schools will be said to be able to be compared. Such efforts at increased standardization will undermine any movement toward increased teacher autonomy, i.e., academic freedom. The "bottom line" in the pressure we feel today is performance in an economic sense. We might say that what is operative is an accountant's concept of education, higher figures (in our case, higher test scores) to indicate accumulation, in this instance, of cultural capital, which is supposed to translate into increased gross national product.

Of course, the bipartisan campaign to link the United States' deteriorating economic position internationally with the failures of public education is only partially sincere. Particularly on the right, it is also a cynical effort to deflect blame from the private sector, whose failures include the widely reported policy of U.S. corporations to direct their efforts for short-term profits, excessive salaries and benefits for top management, and inadequate investment in so-called human capital, including the tendency to "lay off" loyal employees at the first sign of downturns.

Blaming the schools for American economic difficulties also functions to shield those Republican policies (including income tax reductions and massive defense spending increases) that resulted in the so-called "debt binge" of the 1980s, which now wreaks havoc with the balance sheets of banks and insurance companies, has created [summer 1991] a "credit-crunch" for all industrial, corporate, and private borrowers, and has "squeezed" the middle class particularly (Uchitelle, 1991). Teachers—historically the prototypical "good sports" of society— have been like sitting ducks.

There is much wrong with the U.S. public school system. For 70 years and more, curriculum specialists have been complaining about inaccurate curricula, inadequate teacher preparation, inappropriate evaluation, and dysfunctional administrators. Problems internal to the American public school system do contribute to the nation's economic problems, but the schools are hardly the major culprit. Corporate and political practices— as well as international developments quite beyond U.S. control (e.g., interest rates in Japan and Germany, natural disasters, difficulties in negotiating international trade agreements)— appear to be more implicated (than schools) in what is widely perceived as a deteriorating economic position in the United States, especially vis-a-vis Japan and Germany (Frontline, 1991).

Perhaps due to the multiple motives for contemporary school reform, we are experiencing enormous pressure to produce higher test results, possibly greater than we have witnessed since the 1957 Sputnik launching persuaded another Republican administration to search for a scapegoat. Then it was not just the right wing that insisted schools were the reason the U.S.S.R. had moved ahead of the U.S. in space exploration; massive curriculum reform efforts were launched by the liberal Kennedy and Johnson administrations in the 1960s.

This time, new programs are few, as money (for domestic programs at least) is said to be scarce. As Lasch (1984) has observed, the recent strategy of the right wing has been psychopolitical, "superego" in nature. "Just say no!"—not just to drugs but to pleasure generally—would appear to be the simple answer to complex economic and cultural questions. Among the initiatives proposed or under way are more homework, lengthening the school year, more frequent and often more quantified evaluation of teachers and students, and teacher education reform, including "professional development schools," wherein education professors will assist in reform school practices (Pinar, 1989).

Despite the disguised political motives for the current school reform movement and the "bottom line" character of reform, this is a time of genuine opportunity. I applaud those (such as Sizer, 1984) who embrace this time of opportunity and work with the schools, determined to help realize the educational ideals of teachers, teacher educators, and students. I believe some measure of educationally sound reform can be made at this time. If the conservative reaction in schools of the past 20 years can be cracked—reversing it is too optimistic given its continuation in the country generally and give that the current school reform movement received its impetus from political conservatives—we would know that our labor was justified. Perhaps teachers will be granted greater discretion over instructional method, although greater discretion over curriculum strikes me as less likely, given the preoccupation with test scores. A change as modest as a return to electives and flexible scheduling would constitute a remarkable advance, even if it represents only an "advance" back to the 1960s.[1]

Any change at all might seem exhilarating, so complete seems the suffocation and stasis of the past 20 years. One must qualify: change might seem exhilarating to those of us who study the schools from the universities. For many teachers, current school reform might feel like being yanked around yet one time more. In the nearly 25 years I have observed and studied the schools, never have I seen so many teachers defeated. Not that teachers mope, mind you. A few still wear smiles, although they appear to be cynical smiles of defiance rather than those of pleasure and satisfaction.

Many teachers seem hardened, sullen, brittle, easily indignant. It is as if long ago they lost hope for significant change in the schools. It is as if long ago they lost hope they could teach all children. If that is true, one might say that the times defeated them, not just the massive retreat from the innovations of the 1960s, but also changes in the youth culture (hardly a one of which seems to make for increased enthusiasm for school) and changes in the profession (still less public respect for teaching, more salary ground lost vis-a-vis other professionals, more of the "best and brightest" studying business, law, medicine, and other subjects outside of education).

The academic characteristics of prospective teachers tend to place them near the bottom of the university hierarchy while grade inflation in education courses fools few as to their actual academic accomplishment. Whether or not teacher education reform such as those directed by the Holmes Group will make a significant difference in the quality of teacher candidates and programs is unclear, although the promise of improvement seemed to warrant a qualified endorsement (Pinar, 1989). Market conditions (salary and working conditions generally) will probably undermine university efforts to improve the academic quality of prospective teachers. In the tradition of the Peace Corps, only a relative few—arts and sciences majors from the first-tier colleges and universities—volunteer to "teach for America."

In general, then, it is a somewhat grim situation in which current reforms are under way. Even so, one finds hope; in specific individuals and in specific places one observes occasional excitement. Reform will occur; how fundamental and progressive it will be is unclear. If the current wave of reform is judged a failure, what will the consequences be? It is unlikely that this time the nation will enjoy the order of economic growth characteristic of the 1960s which could function to make politicians and the public forgiving. If our critics are unforgiving, then there is a possibility the public system will break up, which might then allow the dismantling of university-based teacher education in favor of less expensive school-system based internships. Whether such a break-up would provide conditions to support fundamental and progressive reform is also unclear.

Grounding curriculum thought

The American public schools were created over 100 years ago to prepare citizens for jobs in an industrial economy. The private sector did want to pay for this job preparation; they persuaded the public sector to pay. On this issue, little has changed in the last 100 years. The schools are still assumed to exist for the sake of job preparation, despite continuing if empty rhetoric linking education with democracy and a politically-engaged citizenry.

While schools have not changed much, the economy they were designed to support has. The consensus view is that the American economy is more "service oriented," strongly "information based," much less industrial than even 30 years ago. It is said to be international or global in character. Rather than the assembly line of the early automobile plant, the major contemporary mode of economic production is semiotic (i.e. production of signs, symbols, and other information) [see Wexler, 1987], and occurs in committees and in front of computer screens in corporate offices. Schools, however, still tend to be modeled after the assembly-line factory. Modeling schools after contemporary corporations would represent an improvement. So-called "smart schools" (Fiske, 1991) tend to be versions of the corporate model. The economic function of schools remains unchallenged, however, and the modes of cognition appropriate to even corporate schools are fewer and narrower than intelligence broadly understood (Gardner, 1983).

Because the organization and culture of the school are linked to the economy, the school is not ideal "ground" for curriculum thought. For the foreseeable future, teachers will trained as "social engineers," directed to "manage" learning that is modeled after corporate work stations. Certainly some segment of the curriculum field will devote itself to assist in the design of the corporate school curriculum. However, those of us who labored to reconceptualize the atheoretical, ahistorical field we found in 1970 (Pinar, 1975) have always seen a more complex calling for the curriculum field (Pinar, 1991). The theoretical wing of the reconceived field aspires to ground itself not in the pressured everyday world of the classroom but in worlds not present in schools, in ideas marginal to the maximization of corporate profits, and in lived experience that is not exclusively instrumental and calculative.

These "worlds apart" from the pressure and instrumentality of the daily classroom may seem valueless to the harassed teacher, pressed to raise the test scores of students who may not have eaten that morning or slept the night before. As much as we feel pulled to help our school colleagues, true help may involve more than the provision of practical answers to everyday problems. Our presence may prove more valuable in the longer term if we continue to point to other worlds, worlds that might enable our school colleagues to achieve sufficient distance from the daily pressure to make a separate peace, while devising creative and self-affirmative strategies for teaching.

If theory does not exist to provide practical solutions to everyday problems, why does it exist? Ten years ago Madeleine Grumet and I tried to answer this question. After reviewing the three major moments in the theory-practice relationship in the West—ancient Greek, Christian, and scientific—we acknowledged that:

> Too often, curriculum theory has been tainted with the self-conscious complexity of academic work, disdaining practical activity in order to maintain the class privilege that clings to the abstract in order to aggrandize its status. Although the field situation provides a context where curriculum theory and practice confront one another, our object ought not to be to resolve their differences, reducing one to the dimensions of the other.... Rather, let us play theory and practice against each other so as to disclose their limitations, and in so doing enlarge the capacity and intensify the focus of each (Pinar & Grumet, 1988, p. 991; 1981, pp, 37-38).

We espoused the ancient Greek notion of contemplation while repudiating the employment of the sexism and slavery by which that contemplation was supported economically. We agreed that contemplation must not be reserved for the privileged; indeed, it must function to dissolve privilege. Theory must create spaces apart from the pressurized sphere of practical activity, spaces in which the demands of the state and of the principal, parents, and students can be viewed, understood and reframed as questions posed to oneself. By living in worlds apart from the everyday and the take-for-granted, we might participate in the daily world with more intensity and intelligence.

School reform that moves us from the factory or the assembly-line model of schooling to a corporate model will probably produce welcomed if incremental improvements in test scores and in the quality of life in schools. These would be genuine accomplishments, well worth our labor. However, more profound issues of identity, politics, and experience will tend to be ignored unless theory stays out of bed with practice, continues to wait in other rooms while policymakers and politics wrestle with the excitement, pleasure, and frustration of the programmatic conception. We theorists must continue to create separate rooms of our own in which we try to see past the corporate model, to not-necessarily economic forms of human organization, intelligence, and experience. We must not do so with arrogance but with the humility that accompanies the knowledge that we too are conceived by others.

Conceived by others

In its press for efficiency and standardization, the factory model tends to reduce teachers to automata. In designing and teaching the curriculum in units that presumably "add up" to a logical even disciplinary "whole" (like products on an assembly line), the factory-model school achieves social control at the cost of intelligence, intelligence understood as including problem solving, critical thinking, and creativity as well as memorization and calculation. Those students who tolerate the routinized, repetitious nature of instruction that is teacher centered and relies upon memorization sometimes are able to perform reasonably well on similar tasks, although the "transferability" of these task-specific skills has remained a problem for the factory model.

The corporate model accepts learning the "basics" as the goals of the school. However, this model permits a variety of instructional strategies to be employed in its attainment. Peer teaching, other forms of so-called cooperative learning, even minor curriculum changes are permitted to allow students and teachers to find their own ways of learning. Moreover, the corporate model tends to acknowledge that intelligence is multiple in nature and function and includes aesthetic, intuitive, and sensory elements as well as linear, logical, narrowly cognitive ones. The social character of intelligence is also acknowledged (relatively speaking) as corporate classroom organization often permits use of dyadic and small-group activities. The teacher in this scheme is a manager or, in Sizer's (1984) image, a "coach." These images are considerably less authoritarian than that of the teacher in the factory school.

Even in the corporate model, the goal of instruction—the acquisition of that knowledge and the cultivation of that intelligence deemed necessary for economic productivity in a post-industrial period—is not in question. Intelligence is viewed as a means to an end, the acquisition of skills utilizable in the corporate sector. The maximation of profit remains the "bottom line" of the corporation as well as that of its earlier version, the factory. I am not suggesting that schools should not keep an eye on the relationship of its activities to the economy. Contemporary capitalism does require knowledge and intelligences the corporate model of schooling is more likely than the factory model to produce. Nor am I suggesting that we could have publicly supported schools that might have non-economic goals, at least for the imaginable future. What I do want to remind us is that for intelligence to be cultivated in fundamental ways, it must be set free of even corporate goals. Such an approach hardly excludes instrumental reason, calculation, and problem-solving as major modes of cognition. Intellectual freedom would allow, however, for meditative, contemplative modes of cognition, and for exploring subjects—those associated with progressive forms of the arts, humanities, and social sciences—that have no immediate practical pay-off and might not be evaluated by standardized examinations.

Intelligence is made more narrow, and thus undermined, when it is reduced to answers to other people's questions, when it is only a means to achieve a preordained goal. This calculative concept of intelligence, while useful to the present form of economic organization—the corporation—is less helpful in investigations of more basic questions of human experience, experience that might not lead directly to economic development and increased productivity. To study these questions is not to seek answers to questions comprising a school test. Rather, it is to "ride" intelligence to destinations perhaps not listed in the present economic agenda. As noted, it is the aspiration of what in science is termed basic research, wherein destinations are not known in advance. In education, it would be theoretical research freed of the taken-for-granted demands of everyday problems in schools. To illustrate one form such research might take, let us discuss briefly an emergent category in curriculum theory. This category—identity—has emerged in debates over multiculturalism, but it promises to take us other places as well, including investigations of what it means educationally to be conceived by others.

Identity

The category of identity organizes investigations of politics, race, gender, and experience around questions of self. This self is not the bourgeois individual decried by the various Marxisms and embraced by conservatives but rather the vortex of psychosocial and discursive relations theorized by Lacan, Freud, and Foucault. The study of identity enables us to portray how the politics we had thought were located "out there," in society, are lived through "in here," in our bodies, our minds, our everyday speech and conduct. Politics are not simply "reproduced," of course. Even when we resist social trends and political directives, we are reconstructing ourselves in terms of those trends and debates and our resistance to them. In studying the politics of identity, we find that who we are is invariably related to who others are, as well as to who we have been and want to become.

Currently, the teacher's identity is being reconceived from factory supervisor to corporate manager. It *is* a promotion. However, if loyal to the cultivation of intelligence, teachers still face the challenge to become more than they have been conceived and conditioned to be. If we are submerged in identities conceived by others, the cultivation of intelligence is necessarily restricted and undermined. Of course, we teachers must meet contractual obligations regarding curriculum and instruction. However, we need not necessarily believe them or uncritically accept them. Curriculum theorists might assist teachers to avoid the disappearance of their ideals into the maelstrom of daily classroom demands. We might support teachers' identities apart from those of the professionalized role by proclaiming the existence of other ways of conceiving education, non-instrumental ways of speaking and being with children (van Manen, 1991). Autobiography remains one important means to investigate the "subject" of education [see "Biography and life history, 1990].

To investigate the politics of identity enables one to reconceive the social relations that are curriculum and instruction. For instance, what has been taken for granted as the canon, our literary and intellectual heritage, can be understood as a debate over national identity. That is, we can rethink curricular issues implicated in the debate over multiculturalism in terms of the politics of identity. To do so, let us, briefly, consider the identity of the "civic" individual, the American citizen. If we link the debates over the canon, over multiculturalism, to questions of identity, we begin to understand apparently practical issues as questions concerning who we are and who we wish to become. Further, if we understand ourselves as conceived by others, the question "who am I?" becomes "whose am I?" Answers might illustrate a value of theory for those practitioners who wish to understand the question "what do I do on Monday? as a theoretical (and in the instance of multiculturalism, a racial) as well as practical question.

Curriculum as social psychoanalysis

We say "we are what we know." But, we are also what we do not know. If what we know about ourselves—our history, our culture—is distorted by deletions and denials, then our identity —as individuals, as Americans—is distorted. We can think of this distorted self as a repressed self, an exhibiting a partial, fictionalized identity. Such a self lacks open access to itself and and to the world. Repressed, one's capacity for intelligence, for informed action, for simple functional competence, is limited. In capsule form, this is another way to grasp the current clashes over multiculturalism. It is also another way to frame the current educational crisis.

The conservatives' insistence upon the traditional school curriculum, an Eurocentric curriculum, can be understood as not only a denial of self to African-Americans but to European-American students as well. "White" students fail to understand that the American self—in historical and cultural senses—is not exclusively an European-American self. It is inextricably African-American. One refers not only to widely reported demographic trends but to American history and to contemporary American popular culture. In very large measure, the American nation was built by African-Americans. African-American elements of American culture are multiple and fundamental. For European-American students to understand who they are, they must understand that their existence is predicated upon, interrelated to, and constituted in inextricable ways by African-Americans (Goldberg, 1990).

The absence of African-American knowledge in the curriculum of many American schools is not mere oversight. Its absence represents an academic instance of racism. Just as African-Americans have been denied their civil rights in society generally, they have been denied access to their history and culture—we might say their curricular rights—in schools. However, not only African-Americans have been denied. By teaching incomplete and distorted versions of American history and culture, we have misrepresented the American nation to European-American students as well. Such denial of the truth seems to occur almost unconsciously. Understanding curriculum as social psychoanalysis implies that the progressive revelation of the past transforms the present. Knowledge is not static, not deposits in a cognitive bank account or skills to be employed at work sites; knowledge enables us to see who we are and what the world is and might become.

During the past decade the American self-image—at least for mainstream American popular culture—was the business executive. The prototypical American was white and male: Lee Iacocca, Donald Trump, Michael Milken. White, male, shrewd, adaptive, adjusting to "reality" in self-profiting ways, this version of the American self projected African-Americans as the Other: pleasure-seeking, accomplished in athletics and the arts. The trouble with society, Republicans taunted, was that everyone was not like Milken. President and Mrs. Reagan declared war on drugs (just say "no"), on laziness ("do more homework!"), on the poor (as governmental programs were reduced), and on women, children, and gays. Once more, the right wing fantasized, the United States is a "white" place, a "white" male place, and those who were not—women, children, minority groups, and gays—were marginalized. Such repression of the "other" can be conducted only by the self-repressed.

The truth is that European-Americans and African-Americans are two sides of the same cultural coin, two interrelated narratives in the American story, two inseparable elements of the American identity. Projected as "other" and repressed, African-Americans' presence in the American, indeed, Western self has been understood compellingly by Frantz Fanon (1963, 1967, 1970). Like James Baldwin (1971, 1985), Fanon understood that "white" is a fabrication made by the construction of the concept "black." There can be no "black" without "white" and vice versa. One cannot understand the identity of one without appreciating how it is "co-dependent" upon the other.

So it is that European-Americans cannot hope to understand themselves unless they are knowledgeable and knowing of those they constructed as "different," as "other." The sequestered, suburban "white" students are uninformed unless they come to understand how, culturally, they are also—in the historical cultural, indeed psychological sense—African-American. Because

"white" does not exist part from "black" the two co-exist, intermingle, and the repression of this knowledge deforms us all,
especially those who are white.   All Americans are racialized
beings; knowledge of who we have been, who we are, and who
we will become is a story or text we construct.   In this sense
curriculum—our construction and reconstruction of this knowledge for conversation with the young—becomes a form of social
psychoanalysis [see Kincheloe & Pinar, 1991].

Child/Ghost of an aborted future

Understood from a social psychoanalytic perspective, we teachers are conceived by others, by the expectations and fantasies of
our students and the demands of parents, administrators, policy
makers, and politicians, to all of whom we are sometimes the
"other." We are formed as well by their and our own internalized histories. These various spheres or levels of self-constitution require investigation. Locating the process of knowing in
the politics of identity suggests escaping the swirling waters created by the demands and pressure of others. The capacity to
stand calmly in a maelstrom can come only with knowledge of
other worlds, with living in other realities, not split off or dissociated from the world of work. "Separate but connected" permits us to enter the work world larger, more complex than the
roles prescribed for us, making less likely that we will collapse
upon the social surface, reduced to what others make of us.

   We might then model to our children how we can live in this
society without succumbing to it, without giving up our dreams
and aspirations for education. Teachers can become witnesses
[in a theological sense; see Pinar, 1988] to the notion that intelligence and learning can lead to other worlds, not just the successful exploitation of this one. Knowledge need not be
regarded as a sacralized text as in fundamentalist religion or an
inviolate procedure as on the assembly line; nor is it only the
more complex, sometimes even creative means to an end as it
is in the corporate model. Rather, knowledge and intelligence
as free exploration become wings by which we take flight, visit
other worlds, returning to this one to call others to futures
more life affirmative than the world we inhabit now. When we

sink, submerged in those professionalized roles conceived by others, we become aborted possibilities, unable to realize in everyday life, in our relations with others, the politics of our individual and civic identities, the dynamics of creation and birth.

What value is theory to the practitioner? To those teachers hardened by 20 years of conservative reaction, it will seem pointless. To the novice teacher eager to earn "merit" salary increases by effective problem-solving in the corporate school, it will seem fanciful, perhaps interesting, to be reserved for later, much later. The constituency of theorists may not be in schools at this time. However, if we can teach, if we can make friends with our colleagues struggling in the schools, build bridges between the realms of theory and practice, create passages—to borrow Daignault's phrase—to travel from here to there and back again, broadened, deepened, enlivened by the voyage, then we theorists might participate with subtlety and acumen in school reform. Being a theorist, after all, does not mean being dissociated or inefficient. Being a theorist does not mean being a celibate in terms of everyday practice. It does not mean one cannot function successfully in the corporate school, providing advice and assistance. Being a theorist does mean that contemporary curriculum organization and the modes of cognition it requires can be bracketed, situated in history, politics, and ourselves. Such theory might allow us to participate in school reform in ways that do not hypostatize the present, but rather, allow our labor and understandings to function as do those in psychoanalysis, to enlarge the perception and deepen the intelligence of the participants.

Conclusion

Despite the conservative origins of the current wave of school reform, genuine educational progress can be made at this time. The transformation of the school from the factory model to a corporate one is under way. Under the corporate model, the "mode of production" becomes more semiotic and less industrial. The role of teacher is reconceived from factory supervisor to corporate manager. Despite the improvements this promotion will bring, the school—and the modes of cognition it requires—remains linked with the economy. While major segments of the curriculum field will be deployed to participate in this reform, it remains ill-advised to ground all curriculum theory in the everyday reality of schools.

Theory must stay out of bed with current reform in order to remain free to theorize modes of knowing and knowledge linked with neither the factory nor the corporate model. While harassed practitioners may find such theory not immediately translatable into practical action, they may find that such theory, in underlining the arbitrariness of current practice, provides a lived distance sufficiently apart from the everyday to support self-affirmative, critical, and creative curriculum and teaching.

To illustrate how theory unmarried to practice might prove of value, we looked briefly at the concept of identity. The potential value of identity for reconceptualizations of the professional role of teachers is implied by employing the term to rethink a contemporary curriculum debate, i.e., multiculturalism.

Theory that is free of classroom constraints is not an exotic phenomenon; it is parallel to a concept of basic research in the sciences. The insistence that all intellectual activity in education schools and departments bear an explicit link to school reform must itself be critiqued and understood historically. An enlarged and intensified sphere of theory can support a more intelligent and intensified sphere of practice.

Notes

1. Other aspects of the current reform movement distinguish it from that of the 1960s. The current movement is rationalized by international economic competition and relies on the metaphor of the corporation. The 1960s movements employed references, on the right, to international military competition and, on the left, to democratization and liberation. Other differences between the current movement and that of the 1960s include the current importance of computers in the classroom and certain organizational proposals, such as "school-based management" and "school choice."

References

Baldwin, J. (1971). Author's notes, in Blues for Mister Charlies. In J. Glassner & C. Barnes (eds.), *Best American Plays* (49-50). New York: Crown.

Baldwin, J. (1985). White man's guilt. In J. Baldwin, *Price of the Ticket* (409-414). New York: St. Martin's/Marek.

Biography and life history in education. [Special issue.] (1990). *Cambridge Journal of Education*, 20 (3).

Fanon, F. (1963). *The wretched of the earth*. New York: Grove Press.

Fanon, F. (1967). *Black skin, white masks*. New York: Grove Press.

Fanon, F. (1970). *A dying colonialism*. Harmondsworth: Pelican.

Fiske, E. (1991). *Smart schools, smart kids*. New York: Simon & Schuster.

Frontline (1991, November 19). Public Broadcasting Service (television), 9 p.m.

Gardner, H. (1983). *Frames of mind*. New York: Basic books.

Goldberg, D. T. (1990). *Anatomy of racism*. Minneapolis: University of Minnesota Press.

Harris, W. (1975). *Companions of the day and night*. London: Faber & Faber.

Kincheloe, J. & W. Pinar (1991) (Eds.). *Curriculum as social psychoanalysis*. Albany: State University of New York Press.

Lasch, C. (1984). *The minimal self: Psychic survival in troubled times*. New York: Norton.

Pinar, W. (1975 (Ed.). *Curriculum theorizing: The reconceptualists*. Berkeley, CA: McCutchan.

Pinar, W. (1988). Time, place, and voice: Curriculum theory and the historical moment. In W. Pinar (Ed.). *Contemporary curriculum discourses* (264-278). Scottsdale, AZ: Gorsuch, Scarisbrick

Pinar, W. (1989, January-February). A reconceptualization of teacher education. *Journal of Teacher Education*, 50, 9-12.

Pinar, W. (1991). The white cockatoo: Images of abstract expressionism in curriculum theory. In G. Willis & W. Schubert (Eds.), *Reflections from the Heart of Educational Inquiry* (244-249). Albany: State University of New York Press.

Pinar, W. & M. Grumet (1988, 1981). Socratic caesura and the theory-practice relationship. In W. Pinar (Ed.), *Contemporary Curriculum Discourses* (92-100). Scottsdale, AZ: Gorsuch, Scarisbrick. Earlier version printed as Theory and practice and the reconceptualization of curriculum studies. In L. Barton & M. Lawn (Eds.), *Rethinking curriculum studies* (20-42). New York: Halsted Press.

Sizer, T. (1984). *Horace's compromise*. Boston: Houghton Mifflin.

Utchitelle, L. (1991, November 17). Trapped in the impoverished middle class. *The New York Times*, section 3, pp. 1-10.

van Manen (1991). *The tact of teaching*. Albany: State University of New York Press.

Wexler, P. (1987). *Social analysis of education*. London: Routledge.

XV

The Lost Language of Cranes: Windows and Mirrors in the Regressive Phase of *Currere*
(1992)

"Is that what your dissertation is about?"
Philip asked. "Lost languages?"
Jerene shrugged and smiled at him.
"More or less," she said. "More or less."
—David Leavitt (1986, p. 52).

To tell you the truth, I took this title while in Jo Anne Pagano's study (the window of which has a lovely view of the surrounding upstate New York countryside). Jo Anne, Janet Miller, Liz Ellsworth, Wen-Song Hwu and I were meeting to plan this (the 1992 Bergamo) conference. We noticed that "cranes" showed up in two proposals that we accepted. What a beautiful bird, I thought. The crane. Right then, I wanted a crane in my title, too. So, my title comes, not exactly out of mischief, but, maybe from some reproductive urge, i.e. wanting to multiply cranes. How lovely I thought: cranes, at Bergamo. You can see I was enthusiastic. I even proposed to Jo Anne and Janet that we put a crane on the cover. Well, at least, I pointed out, it wasn't about collaboration, which seemed to be the topic of the year, and about which I teased Janet, whose book, I accused her, started this whole, well, orgy of collaboration.

Cranes. Whooping cranes. Cranes from the East. My friend Wen-Song says that in Chinese culture the crane symbolizes long life. It also symbolizes marriage, he says, since two cranes remain together for the duration of their lifetime. He says they usually die together. And so the crane symbolizes marriage, union, and long life. Cranes. The language of cranes.

While the occasion for my title was the meeting of the Bergamo Conference Planning Committee last July at Jo Anne Pagano's house, it is borrowed from David Leavitt's 1986 novel, published by Knopf in New York. Leavitt's novel is entitled *The Lost Language of Cranes*. An abbreviated and revised version of the novel was shown by American public television last summer. The novel is about a family: a son, a father and a mother. The son is grown (in his early 20s) and living in his own place. His name is Philip, and he works as an editor for a publishing house that turns out romance novels. When the novel opens, he is, in fact, in love. With Eliot, who, it turns out, is not in love with him. In a while Eliot leaves Philip.

Philip's father Owen has a Ph.D. in English, but after a brief career in academe, he moved to a fancy private school where he is director of admissions. Owen experiences homosexual desire, but he has kept that a secret, until he is prompted to face his desire when his own son "comes out."

Philip's mother and Owen's wife Rose is a restrained, disciplined woman who doesn't want to know too much, who believes in boundaries and distance. This restraint, admirable I would say in our time of talk-show confessionals, costs her certain information, however, that is important for her to know, namely that her husband is gay. Rose wants her world to stay as it is, but it won't. She and Owen are on the verge being evicted from their apartment, their home of many years ... it's going co-op. Her son, to her dismay, is gay. Speaking to her son who wants to tell her more about his sexual life than she cares to hear, Rose says: "Keeping certain secrets is important to—the general balance of life ..." (p. 173). Also illustrative of her restraint is an exchange that occurs in the middle of the night between her and her husband who has just returned home after being with man. Despite the late hour, Rose does not demand to know where he has been or whom he has been with. Instead she tells him: "I'm not going to ask any questions.... I don't want to know anything. But I want you to promise me one thing. I want you to promise me that the next time you go out until two-thirty in the morning, you will call and warn me so I won't worry myself to death wondering if you're dead. You're right, honey," Owen said. "I'm sorry. I will" (pp. 241-242). Rose even maintains a certain distance from herself, leaving herself open to a surprise self-encounter. Returning home one day "... she ... caught a glimpse of her face in a store window— the face of a worried, older woman, someone she might pass on the street and feel sorry for, someone, at an easier time in her life, she might have felt grateful not to be" (p. 220).

While Rose is not too curious, her husband is not especially forthcoming. Owen has hidden himself from her for the sake of their marriage, well not all of himself, of course, but the part he thought would go away, but which did not. This is the part he expresses during his Sunday afternoon walks, which include visits to a gay movie house. Perhaps this "Sunday-afternoon part" is what he gave to his son, a son who is not interested, however, in keeping secrets.

In keeping his desire quarantined, Owen seems to have deteriorated psychologically over the years. He becomes chronically anxious, as if he were a caged man. The narrator tells us:

> For years he had felt safe only in his apartment, only with Rose. But now everything had turned around. The apartment was the place where he was afraid. Unidentifiable dangers lurked in the corners, waiting to spring. Static electricity clung to the walls, the bedspread, the sofa. He could not touch his fingers to any surface without risking a tiny shock. Worst of all, the threat was obscure. It hid like a coward, refused to show its face. He could not name it. He grew so anxious he had to flee into the open placelessness of the city, where, if not safety, he found at least the company of other scared strangers. There was a brotherhood of middle-aged men who wandered on Sunday afternoons, looking at each other gravely across streets, never nodding (pp. 20-21).

Rose, the restrained one, perhaps afraid to look, to ask, and Owen, the anxious, withholding one: these two are married, husband and wife. But this is a marriage in which restraint and secrets have left each afraid and separate, looking across at each other from a distance. The narrator tells us: "At night they lay awake, far apart, each clinging to the extreme edge of the bed, and assumed the other to be sleeping" (p. 11).

That's the trouble, isn't it, with uninterrupted restraint, with withholding uninterrupted by giving: one's left clinging to the extreme edge of the bed, assuming the other to be asleep. For the son, no clinging to edges for him. Philip wants to be in the center of the bed, he wants to hold, and to be held, by his loved one. For Philip, no desire suspended or quarantined. Indeed, his desire has been set free, and it spreads through his life like ... well, like mice freed from an overturned truck. Riding in a taxi one night, Philip and Eliot notice that a truck, carrying mice to Columbia University for research purposes, has overturned in the winter, snow-covered street.

> Then Philip looked out the window and saw that the intersection was full of white mice. Thousands of them. They swarmed in the street in panicked hordes, like tiny indistinguishable sufferers in a fourteenth-century vision of hell. They cascaded over the sidewalk curbs and plunged after each other into gutters. Against the new snow they were nearly invisible, small quakings of motion (pp. 29-30).

Small quakings of motion. Like electric shocks in one's apartment, like quivering quietly so as not to awaken the awake sleeping spouse. Small quakings of motion, like furtive sex acts in dimly lit theaters. A twentieth-century vision of hell.

My son, my father

I think I have always tried to avoid the position of the father. I loved my father, mind you, perhaps too much. But I hated his position. The rule-maker. Husband to my mother. He talked too long at the dinner table, repeating the same stories over and over, interrupting my mother, who eventually fell silent. I became a father in my twentyninth year, and that was a problem. Loving her, loving him, hating my position. So I tried to leave. I left my home a second time. My son grew up with his mother in California, and my visits there were limited to summers at first, then every month, and for a time—when People's Express flew coast-to-coast for $99—each week. Under these circumstances the position of father seemed pretty nice. The week-end, summer Dad. His escape from Mom.

Then, two years ago, Mike came to live with me. When my son moves in, so does my father. I had buried Dad in June

1988, but now here he is, resurrected, in me. With my son in my house, my father comes spilling out of me. I edit his voice, of course; I do not want my son to have the childhood I had. But I am filled with the lost language of my father, my mother, the child I was. There I am, in Baton Rouge, Louisiana, with my fourteen year old California son, pulled back into my own Ohio childhood, as I try to figure out how to negotiate the end of Mike's childhood with him. Parenting, like teaching, is an opportunity to recover lost languages, to speak again, even if silently, from one's own childhood.

The real discomfort was to begin the second year, when Mike turned fifteen, old-enough in Louisiana to drive, and drive off he did. An adolescent in the tradition of his father, he did not drive off quietly; he screeched the tires as loudly as it would take to bring on his father's screeching. So, my life strategy—to avoid the position of the father—failed. It turns out one can't have a son without being a father. It turns out one cannot leave one's family, neither the one that one's parents made, nor the one in which we children are the parents. There is no sense pretending each other is asleep.

This past August I was in London for a week. One Sunday night, I felt like eating in, and so I went to what turned out to be an empty hotel restaurant. Behind the bar was a handsome young man, in his mid-twenties, the same age of the fictional Philip, and this young man, named Michael, was quite friendly, happy, I suppose, to see at least to see one customer in the place. The more I drank the friendlier we became. Michael grew up in New Zealand, he tells me, and after secondary school, he decided to work his way around the world. He had been in London several months now. As we talked longer, he began, slowly, well, to strut. He became erect. Yes, his posture was sexually charged, but the charge was sublimated and expressed verbally as competence and male independence, and in his posture, which as I mentioned, was quite erect. He was supporting himself in London, no money needed from parents, and furthermore, he was having a very fine time. I could not find my voice right away. At the time I thought it was my own dishonesty undermining me, pretending to be only friendly but finding him appealing. He was unfazed by my bumbling, as if he knew the scene. How many middle-aged men, I wondered, had taken an interest in him, there, standing behind the bar, strutting, bragging a little? Finally, liquored enough, I talked normally. What struck me the next day was that I noticed plainly and exactly when my titillation at him converted to concern for him. In one discernible moment the sexual charge I had experienced changed to parental concern. It was a relief; a taboo (an older gay man interested in younger straight man) traded for a socially acceptable relationship (a father interested in his son). Rather than ask questions, at that point I began to chide him for not calling his mother in New Zealand. I became a bit forceful, in a gentle way, but clearly, now, in a sublimated way, I was "entering" him, embracing him. He felt it; he blushed with pleasure and I think some guilt. For me to speak of his father in Australia seemed to become too obvious, me being the stand-in, and he being my own Michael. So I asked no questions about the father, gave no advice, and about him he was silent. He became increasingly open—drugs were mentioned—and I emphasized my parental posture: take care of yourself I told him. It was so clear to me then, the sexual sublimated becomes the parental. To put it differently, parental love lives on the sublimated side of incest. Sublimated, that's a relief, I agree. But I do think that stripped of the erotic altogether, by that I mean that without a certain teasing, maybe we can even say a certain seductive element, the parental posture risks becoming merely power-seeking and power-wielding, at times, good old fashioned authoritarianism. Ever vigilant to keep anything remotely seductive out of my relationship with my own son, I sank, at times, during that second year of his stay with me in Baton Rouge, into authoritarianism, which my son rejected, at times brazenly, but to which, when I was son to my own father, I think I succumbed.

In always being very careful with Mike to be sure that in my actions, especially my expressions of affection, conveyed to him no part of myself he might not want, I was unprepared to be playful with him when he became the angry adolescent in his fifteen year. Stripped of any teasing, of sublimated sexuality, our encounter drifted toward simple confrontation. Ah, oedipus. Even though we knew he was returning to California for his final two years of high school—David Duke's campaign for the Louisiana governorship was intolerable, unforgivable—we could not seem to find our way out of what felt at times like a death struggle.

A near death on the west-coast provided a passage. It was the Rodney King beating. I stayed shocked that Thursday night, but Mike was on the phone organizing a walk-out at his high school. He asked me for my blessing, and my wallet, so he could photocopy walkout announcements. I asked him not to do it. We argued. I pointed out that the school administration would respond harshly. His rage at the beating in California merged with his oedipal rage at me. Then, my father beside me, I forbade him to do it. His rage increased. A smart boy, he pointed out, thunderingly, how he used to admire me, but that now maybe my political ideals had been traded, well, for what, he admitted, he had no idea. You get the picture. Actually, the picture I then recalled was a television screen. There I was, it was 1968, in Columbus, Ohio, and I am screaming at my father while we watched the Chicago police beat up my generation in Grant Park during the Democratic National Convention. Back in Baton Rouge twenty-four years later, I stood there, in our brightly lit kitchen, screaming at my father while my son screamed at me. I gave him the money, and poured another drink.

Mike led a walk-out the next morning. Knowing it was coming, the school administration had troopers on campus and threatened arrest. Thankfully my son and his fellow students returned to class after a brief confrontation. That wasn't the end of it, of course. When they figured out who had been the ringleader, the administration tried to expel Mike just before final exams, which would have cost him the entire second semester. At the expulsion hearing I watched the necks of the principal and assistant principal and school board representative turn red. The principal leaned forward to tell me, tersely: "I expected this kind of thing was going on all over the state. Nooo. This was the only walkout in the entire state of Louisiana." [Not bad, Mike, I thought to myself.] The superintendent, also a displaced Ohioian whom I had known in a friendly way when I served as chair of the department, intervened. We saved the second semester. In facing the rage of the school administration, we managed to refocus our own, and a hug outside the principal's office signalled, I hoped, the end of the father-son wars.

Mike returned to his mother this past summer, and I moved to the French Quarter. Talk about layers and lost languages (Spanish, French, and African in this case), and about regression. Echoes of my son, of the principal's office, of the PTA, and the band boosters, in the summer heat of a city living in its own past.

The French Quarter of New Orleans, you will recall, has three layers of European occupation, first Spanish, then French, now American. Well, only lightly European-American. New Orleans is African-American. But it feels as if the soul of this city is partly Caribbean. Caribbean not as a vacation spot, or as the ocean between North and South Americas, but as the center of African culture in the western hemisphere. It is as if, culturally, New Orleans faces the Caribbean, and its back is to the U.S. mainland. I live in Haiti on the mainland, an exaggerated but not a completely false association, given the French influence, the poverty, the Voodoo. I live amidst the black exuberance, the black suffering that are two poles of this American Haiti.

New Orleans is viewed as "the other" by many living elsewhere in the U.S., a place to visit (not live), get drunk, and do ... well, what respectable people would not do "back home." In this sense, the French Quarter is like a cultural unconscious of America; it is one place this country might turn to look for its own lost languages: Spanish, French, the languages of Africa. The French Quarter is a white gay ghetto in a Caribbean city, the sound of the blues, of jazz, and local rock bands fill the humid night air, while tourists stumble around drunk, bleary-eyed, not noticing the hustlers and hookers watching, walking the streets looking for their next trick, while a few blocks away in the projects another teenager gets snuffed out over maybe a drug deal gone sour. Always the sounds of sirens mixes with the blues, in this Haitian city on the mainland.

Peter and Clare are married

I mentioned earlier I was in London last summer. That was a week I vacationed alone before joining my close friends the Becks (Fran and Bill) and the Dolls (Mary and Bill) for Peter Taubman's wedding in Innshannon, Ireland. Peter married Clare O'Brien, a brilliant and beautiful young Irish woman, who works for a large legal firm in New York. Perhaps you saw her name in the news accounts (she was in the Baton Rouge newspaper, for instance) of the St. Patrick's Day Parade controversy in New York. An Irish gay group [ILGO] sued for the opportunity to march in that parade with signs, and Clare was their attorney. [They lost, but the case is on appeal.]

Friday afternoon August 7, 1992, in Innshannon was a breathtaking Irish afternoon, bright sun, and warm by Irish standards. Everyone but the Americans were in black in seemed; the color worn to funerals here is worn to weddings there. Peter you probably know from his important curriculum scholarship regarding gender and poststructuralism, and from his presence (not this year, however) at Bergamo. Close friends since our time together in Rochester in the late 1970s, Peter had asked me to participate in the wedding. Like others, I was to make a brief statement. A former theology student, I was doubly pleased: finally a moment in the pulpit. With their permission I repeat my August statement here. With Peter and Clare on my right, my friends the Dolls and the Becks seated amidst the black Irish in that old Catholic church, I tried to convey my affection for Clare and Peter:

> Matrimony is, we know, a holy state, blessed by God, embraced gratefully by a humankind caught in sufferings we often do not escape, but which we often can endure, in part thanks to the blessing and grace of God.
> Matrimony is holy, and worldly. They are not mutually exclusive states, of course. Indeed, one view of the Christian life is to enter the world fully, with faith and passion. As Bonhoeffer wrote: "To be a Christian does not mean to be religious in a particular way, to cultivate some particular form of asceticism ... but to be a [person in the world]. It is not a religious act which makes a Christian what he [or she] is, but participation in the suffering of God in the life of the world" (Bonhoeffer, 1953, pp. 166-167.)

Both Clare and Peter have so participated, both on behalf of victimized gender groups, Clare through her important legal work and Peter through his teaching and highly significant scholarship. Working from different vocations, as well as from different religious traditions and nationalities, Clare and Peter's participation in the world might be said to honor the Christian's conviction that "We are no longer Jews or Greeks or slaves or free men or even merely men or women, but we are all the same ..." (Galatians 3:28).

Different, but all the same. In this view apparent opposites like "man" and "woman" are fused, as well as separated, one depiction of the married state. We are invited here to take the marital union itself as an ideal for human relations in general. Thus, those whom I might construct as opposite to myself, for instance black to white, straight to gay, Protestant to Catholic, become in this view my spouse. To live in such spiritual union with others probably places one in a position of defiance—defiance of a world in which the sufferings of separation, isolation, racism, and sexism are everyday reality. Such defiance might express one version of the religious life today. With Moltmann we might say: "Those who hope in Christ can longer put up with reality as it is, but begin to suffer under it, to contradict it.... Peace with God means conflict with the world" (Moltmann, 1967. p. 21).

As Clare and Peter continue to live out their hopes for the world, a world someday united—as are they—by love, may their own union be blessed by the strength and peace of God. In Christ's name I pray for that. A men.

Love and happiness

All my friends are married. Well, just about all my friends. I feel married too, I suppose, in a way to them, in a way to me, in a parental sense to my son, and still a bit in the usual sense to his mother Denah, after all these years. To my work, and to the field—the social and intellectual, they are not clearly distinguishable in my life. I stand before you tonight a married man.

I confess that I have always preferred my sex outside of marriage. [And, for that matter, my learning outside of school.] Marge Piercy speaks for me in her poem "From Shadows of the Burning. Duir."

From Shadows of the Burning. Duir.

... Love is a downer we take,
love is a habit like sucking on death tit cigarettes,
love is a bastard art.

It is the romance I loathe, the swooning moon
of June which croons to the tune of every goon.

A succession of lovers like a committee
of Congress in slow motion put me back
together, a thumb under my ear, the ear
in an armpit, the head sprouting feet.

I cherish friendship and loving that starts
in liking but the body is the church
where I praise and bless and am blessed.
My strength and my weakness are twins
in the same womb, mirrored dancers under
water, the dark and light side of the moon.

Come step into the fire, come in,
come in, dance in the flames of the festival ...
Dance through me as I through you.
... Our cells are burning
each a little furnace powered by the sun
and the moon pulls the sea of our blood.
This night the sun and moon dance
and you and I dance in the fire of which
we are the logs, the matches and the flames (pp. 100-103).

In Christ's name I pray. Amen.

The crane child

A secondary character in David Leavitt's novel is named Jerene. Jerene is working on her dissertation, on lost languages it turns out. We are told, however, that she is stuck in her research. Working in the library one afternoon, skimming through psychoanalytic journals, looking for a "clue, a new grounding that would illuminate the way out of the ... unruly dissertation in which she was lost," Jerene came across an article about:

> A baby, a boy, called Michel in the article, [who] was born to a disoriented, possibly retarded teenager, the child of a rape. Until he was

about two years old, he lived with his mother in a tenement next to a construction site. Every day she stumbled in and around and out of the apartment, lost in her own madness. She was hardly aware of the child, barely knew how to feed or care for him. The neighbors were alarmed at how Michel screamed, but when they went to knock at the door to ask her to quiet him, often she wasn't there. Then one day, quite suddenly, the crying stopped. The child did not scream, and he did not scream the next night either. For days there was hardly a sound. Police and social workers were called. They found the child lying on his cot by the window. He was alive and remarkably well, considering how severely he appeared to have been neglected. Quietly he played on his squalid cot, stopping every few seconds to look at the window. His play was unlike any they had ever seen. Looking out the window, he would raise his arms, then jerk them to a halt; stand up on his scrawny legs, then fall; bend and rise. He made strange noises, a kind of screeching in his throat. What was he doing? the social workers wondered. What kind of play could this be?

Then they looked out the window, where some cranes were in operation, lifting girders and beams, stretching out wrecker balls on their single arms. The child was watching the crane nearest the window. As it lifted, he lifted; as it bent, he bent, as its gears screeched, its motor whirred, the child screeched between this teeth, whirred with his tongue.

They took him away. He screamed hysterically and could not be quieted, so desolate was he to be divided from his beloved crane. Years later, Michel was living in a special institution for the mentally handicapped. He moved like a crane, made the noises of a crane, and although the doctors showed him many pictures and toys, he only responded to the pictures of cranes, only played with the toy cranes. Only cranes made him happy. He came to be known as the "crane-child." And the question Jerene kept coming up against, reading the article, was this: What did it sound like? What did it feel like? The language belonged to Michel alone; it was forever lost to her. How wondrous, how grand those cranes must have seemed to Michel, compared to the small and clumsy creatures who surrounded him. For each, in his own way, she believed, finds what it is he must love, and loves it; the window becomes a mirror; whatever it that we love, that is who we are (pp. 182-183).

Conclusion

For Lacan, the infant is a chaotic, fragmented, pulsating field which congeals and finds unity as an ego in the gaze of the Other. This "mirror stage," as Lacan termed it, creates a self, or ego, which is at bottom alienated, since it is captured and given by another. With the introduction of the Symbolic, the subject is solidified as that ego, and gendered. Mistakenly, we take the alienated ego for the subject, when in fact the real subject lies in the unconscious. It is the question to the answer that is the crane.

Jerene also tells the story of "a woman [who] was committed to a mental hospital for something like forty-eight years because the doctors said she 'babbled.' And then it turned out she was a Ukrainian immigrant. No one at the hospital recognized that she was speaking Ukrainian" (Leavitt, p. 53). Perhaps we're a little like this woman, except the hospital in which we are incarcerated is our taken-for-granted ego.

The regressive phase of *currere* is about, in this sense, releasing the Ukrainian woman from the hospital, recognizing what might seem from the public and the everyday as madness, but which in fact is a language, a reality with its own integrity, its own history and meaning. The regressive phase of *currere* is not about wandering around in one's own house of mirrors, Narcissus-like, but remembering that the language we speak now derives from what and whom we saw through our windows as infants and children and young adults. Recalling these lost languages provides passages to our past, with silenced elements of ourselves, with the world we knew as children and which inhabits the world we know now as adults. Engagement with the world, pedagogical or legal or illegal, as in civil disobedience, keeps one eye looking out the window, where the worlds of past, present, and future collide in the chaos and order of the historical present.

Philip is the question to his own father's answer, his father's resolve to hold himself in. His son is out. Philip's gayness is in this sense his invitation to his father to love his son, a love perhaps Owen withheld as he suppressed his capacity to love homosexually. Philip becomes gay to bring his father out, to elicit his father's love, to provide the presence Owen's resolve kept absent. As Madeleine Grumet (1988) first pointed out fifteen years ago, each generation contradicts the "curriculum" of the preceding one. Our children express our own collective unconscious, often those parts of ourselves we repudiated, well, tried to repudiate. All we did was pass it on. Further, we tell them what we meant to tell Him and Her. We must seem like Michel to our children, speaking languages that, for them, must seem mechanical, unintelligible. The unjust, suffering world provides us with common ground.

Beginning the regressive phase of *currere*, by which I mean re-entry to the past and its conscious reincorporation into the present, can begin in Jo Anne Pagano's study, noticing two Bergamo presentations on cranes. From an arbitrary excitement, one can move associatively, to a symbolic expression of what appears to be a momentary interest. From Jo Anne's study and the cranes of the Bergamo program I moved to a novel, a curricular material may I say, in which the characters and their situations seem to both mirror and distort my own, although that is not clear initially. Reading the novel pulls me outward to the imaginary world that is the novel, at the same as it moves me back into a past recently lived but not reflexively grasped. After reading the novel I am returned from its imaginary world to my world, my present son, my absent father. Through my son I see my father resurrected, and in trying to bury him again I meet my son on other side of our own death struggle, thanks to Rodney King and a world whose injustice redirects our rage from each other back to the public world.

A Protestant in a Catholic Church on an Irish afternoon. I thee wed. Peter and Clare, thee wed. The world is where they met and married; the world is the "other," the turbulent presence of which draws them outward, intensifying, perhaps, their private love as they labor on others' behalf. Outside the window of the hotel where the wedding reception is a held is a beautiful shallow river. Someone is standing in the river, fishing. The sun shines through my martini, as I watch Clare's friend Jane speak from her Ilse of Wight. We return from the riverbank to eat, drink, and listen to testimonials. Congratulations, Peter and Clare. Love and happiness, in the midst of hate and suffering. "The body is the church where I praise and bless and am blessed." Later that night, dancing with Fran, dancing with Mary, I celebrate our friendship and Peter and Clare's union.

The past is not a language lost to the present, not a language sealed off in the unconscious, forever buried. It is here, and now, in the son I try to father, the friends I cherish, the students with whom I work, the books I read, the papers I write.

In this sense autobiographical studies are windows which permit us to see again that which we loved before, and in so doing, see more clearly what and whom we love in the present. The regressive phase of *currere* asks us to speak again in the lost language of cranes, to see again what was outside our windows, and to become married—that is, in unison—with ourselves and with those around us, by renewing our vows to those who are past, exchanging vows with those who are present, and dancing our way until the morning dawns.

References

Bonhoeffer, D. (1953). *Prisoner for God*. Edited by Eberhard Bethge. Trans. by R. H. Fuller. New York: Macmillan Co.

Grumet, M. (1988). *Bitter milk*. Amherst: University of Massachusetts Press.

Leavitt, David (1986). *The Lost Language of Cranes*. New York: Knopf.

Moltmann, J. (1967). *Theology of hope*. Trans. J. W. Leitch. New York: Harper & Row.

Piercy, Marge (1984). Shadows of the Burning. Duir. In M. Percy, *The Moon is Always Female* (100-103). New York: Knopf.

Name Index

Alexander, William, 79
American Educational Research
    Association [AERA], 4, 64, 65,
    78, 124, 194, 195, 217
Anderson, J., 230
Aoki, Ted, 195
Apple, Michael, 66, 67, 82, 111
Association for Supervision and
    Curriculum Development
    [ASCD], 64, 65, 124, 195
Australia, 4
Ayers, William, 2

Baldwin, E., 230
Baldwin, James, 246
Barnes, H., 228
Barone, Thomas, 230
Bauman, Z., 211
Beauchamp, George, 86
Beck, Frances, 262, 266
Beck, William, 261
Beckett, Samuel, 1
Berlin, Isaiah, 72
Bernstein, Richard, 77, 78, 83, 89,
    92, 93
Bonhoeffer, D., 261
Bourdieu, Pierre, 163
Bowles, Samuel, 192, 193
Boy George, 3, 4, 188, 189
Browning, Elizabeth Barrett, 202
Brown, Theodore, 223
Buber, Martin, 17
Butt, Richard, 2

Cambridge Journal of Educa-
    tion, 1
Camus, Albert, 215
Carson, Terry, 195
Carter, Jimmy, 192

Chodorow, Nancy, 154, 155, 184,
    207
Clandinin, D. Jean, 2
Cohen-Solal, A., 204
Colgate-Rochester Divinity
    School, 3
Columbia University, 256
Connelly, F. Michael, 2
Cooper, David, 131
Cremin, Lawrence, 46
Cuomo, Mario, 225

Daignault, Jacques, 195
Deleuze, Gilles, 161
Derrida, Jacques, 214, 215, 216,
    218, 219, 248
Dewey, John, 17, 46, 47, 48, 49,
    50, 51, 52, 55, 118
Dickens, Charles, 184
Doll, Mary A., 261, 266
Doll, Ronald, 79
Doll, Jr., William, 261
Dreisier, Theodore, 184
Duke, David, 259

Earle, William, 43, 44, 46, 104,
    105
Edwards, Jonathon, 119, 122
Eisner, Elliot, 229
Ellsworth, Elizabeth, 253
Erikson, Erik, 47

Fanon, Frantz, 246
Faulkner, William, 17
Figgins, Margo, 2
Fiske, Edward, 1, 239
Foucault, Michel, 129, 202, 204,
    212, 213, 214, 215, 216, 243

Freire, Paulo, 65, 90, 110, 111
Freud, Sigmund, 17, 88, 91, 92,
    161, 171, 172, 173, 188, 201,
    202, 206, 243

Gadamer, Hans-Georg, 205
Galbraith, John Kenneth, 192,
    193, 197
Gardner, Howard, 239
Garman, Noreen, 229
Gauthier, Clermont, 195
Giroux, Henry, 228
Gouldner, Alvin, 38
Graham, Robert, 2
Gramsci, Antonio, 163
Greene, Maxine, 1
Grumet, Madeleine, 1, 90, 91,
    127, 152, 165, 169, 170, 176,
    195, 198, 229, 230, 240, 265
Guattari, Felix, 161

Habermas, Jurgen, 67, 77, 78, 84,
    86, 87, 88, 91, 92, 93, 118, 129,
    148
Harris, W., 235
Harvard University, 196
Hegel, Georg W. F., 49, 72, 92
Heidegger, Martin, 201, 202, 210,
    211, 212, 215, 216, 217
Hobbes, Thomas, 84, 93
Hocquenghem, Guy, 161, 164,
    172, 173, 174
Holland, Norman, 218
Holmes Group, 3, 224, 225, 229,
    230, 238
Huebner, Dwayne, 1, 63, 67, 82,
    85, 195
Husserl, Edmund, 46, 69
Hwu, Wen-Song, 253

Iacocca, Lee, 246
ILGO, 261
Iroquois, 141

Jacknicke, Ken, 195
Jackson, Michael, 188

Jagger, Mick, 188
Johnson, Maurtiz, 64, 66
Joyce, James, 17
Journal of Curriculum Theorizing
    (JCT), 194, 195, 198
Jung, Carl, 17, 39, 52, 53, 54, 56,
    90, 201, 202

Kafka, Franz, 2, 29, 30, 42, 169
Kierkegaard, Soren, 7, 17, 41, 48,
    73, 94, 219
Kincheloe, Joe, 4, 247
King, Rodney, 259, 266
Kliebard, Herbert, 67, 83
Klohr, Paul, 1, 139
Kohl, H., 193
Kuhn, Thomas, 123

Lacan, Jacques, 218, 243, 264
Laing, R. D., 17, 38, 131, 212
Langer, Suzanne, 51
Lao Tze, 117
Lasch, Christopher, 184, 204, 205,
    206, 207, 210, 211, 217, 237
Leavitt, David, 254, 263, 265
Lennox, Annie, 188
Lessing, Doris, 131
Louisiana State University, 3

Macdonald, James, 1, 63, 82
Marcuse, Herbert, 131
Marx, Karl, 92, 163
McNeil, John, 80
McQueen-Mason, Jane, 266
Mead, Margaret, 8
Megill, A., 204, 207, 209, 211,
    213, 215, 216, 217
Merleau-Ponty, M., 69
Merton, Robert, 81
Milken, Michael, 246
Miller, Janet, 1, 195, 253
Mondale, Walter, 195, 198

Nicks, Stevie, 188
Nietzsche, Friedrich, 17, 41, 206,
    207, 208, 209, 215, 216, 219

O'Brien, Clare, 261, 262, 266
Ohio State University, 121
Olney, James, 55, 56, 58

Pagano, Jo Anne, 195, 253, 254,
    266
Philosophy of Education Society,
    68
Piaget, Jean, 104, 205
Piercy, Marge, 262
Pollock, Jackson, 2, 4, 7, 9
Proust, Marcel, 17

Raymond, Danielle, 2
Reagan, Nancy, 246
Reagan, Ronald, 185, 191, 192,
    193, 196, 205, 246
Reich, Wilhem, 204
Reid, William, 125
Reynolds, William, 2, 195
Rich, Adrienne, 161
Rochester Institute of
    Technology, 4

Sartre, Jean-Paul, 17, 20, 24, 102,
    129, 204
Saylor, Galen, 79
Schubert, William, 2
Schultz, Alfred, 69
Schwab, Joseph, 85, 125, 195, 223
Sears, James, 195
Selden, Steven, 207
Shores, Harlen, 79, 80
Silk, Leonard, 193
Sizer, Theodore, 237, 242
Slattery, Patrick, 2
Smith, B. O., 79
Socrates, 56

Spender, Stephen, 138
Stanley, William O., 79
Steinberg, Shirley, 4
Stratemeyer, Florence, 80

Taba, Hilda, 80
Tanner, Daniel, 80
Tanner, Laurel, 80
Taubman, Peter, 2, 261, 262, 266
Thatcher, Margaret, 193
Thoreau, Henry, 8, 9
Tolstoy, Leo, 55
Tom, Alan, 227, 231
Troegger, Thomas, 203
Trump, Donald, 246
Tyler, Ralph, 64, 79, 223

University of Alberta, 195
University of Michigan, 227
University of Rochester, 1, 3, 82
University of Virginia, 2

van Manen, Max, 244
Volcher, Paul, 191

Walker, Decker, 77, 78, 79, 95, 125
Westbury, Ian, 85
Wexler, Philip, 239
Whitson, Tony, 232
Willis, Paul, 159, 170
Woolf, Virginia, 2, 3, 13, 14, 15,
    16, 17, 57, 61, 127, 132, 135,
    138, 169

Zais, R., 80

Subject Index

Abortion, 101, 102
Absence, 218, 219
Adolescent, 258
Aesthetic theory, 223
Africa, 260
African-Americans, 245, 246, 260
Aging, 145
Anal eroticism, 172, 173
Anal intercourse, 162, 175
Anal repression, 175
Analytical, 25, 60
Anus, 172, 173, 174
Appollonian (the), 206, 209
Architect, 209, 212
Architecture, 201, 210, 214, 215, 216, 217
Arrest, 29, 31, 33, 36, 38, 39, 40, 42, 47, 51, 55, 57, 59, 95, 148, 195, 213
Art, 188, 209, 243, 246
Assembly line, 239, 241, 247
Athletics, 246
Authenticity, 201, 204, 215
Authoritarianism, 258
Authority, 171
Autobiography, 1, 2, 3, 4, 5, 43, 45, 52, 53, 58, 110, 111, 112, 122, 123, 130, 131, 133, 138, 148, 168, 194, 195, 201, 204, 217, 218, 219, 220, 223, 244, 267
Automata, 241
Avant-garde, 73

Basics, 242
Beauty, 210
Biographic agenda, 52
Biographic function, 48, 54, 109
Biographic issue, 125, 148, 149

Biographic movement, 20, 44, 47, 149
Biographic present, 128, 149
Biographic situation, 15, 19, 20, 54, 58, 60, 108, 128, 140, 148
Biographic theme, 218
Black, 246, 247, 262
Black radicals, 170
Blues (the), 260
Bureaucratization, 72, 161, 169, 187, 193, 197
Business, 238, 246

Canada, 195
Canon, 244
Capital, 193
Capitalists, 193
Capitalism, 130, 183, 191, 242
Caribbean, 260
Castration, 172
Catholic, 262
Celibate, 248
Character structure, 204
Childhood, 228
Chinese culture, 253
Christian, 240, 261
Circumcision, 159, 164, 176
Civil disobedience, 265
Civil rights, 245
Class analysis, 122
Classrooms, 124, 126, 170, 177, 240, 244
Class solidarity, 130, 131
Class struggle, 69
Cognition, 194, 208, 211, 242, 248
Cognitive development, 104
Collaboration, 253
Collaborative autobiography, 2
Commodification, 174, 203, 214, 218

Communist, 193
Community, 169
Competence, 245
Confrontation, 258, 259
Conscientizao, 110
Constructivist epistemology, 166
Contemplation, 241, 242
Cooperative learning, 242
Corporate model, 242, 247, 248, 249
Corporations, 1, 180, 192, 193, 236, 239, 242, 243
Cranes, 253, 254
Creativity, 241
Critical theory, 66, 83, 88, 121
Critical thinking, 241
Cultural capital, 103, 193, 235
Cultural homogeneity, 210
Cultural unconscious, 260
Currere, 19, 61, 91, 108, 111, 119, 148, 253, 265, 266, 267
Curricularists, 63, 123
Curriculum, 1, 2, 13, 16, 63, 67, 77, 78, 80, 81, 83, 86, 89, 95, 103, 107, 108, 109, 112, 121, 123, 124, 126, 151, 152, 158, 164, 166, 177, 185, 194, 207, 209, 220, 223, 225, 226, 228, 229, 237, 242, 244, 246, 247, 249, 265
Curriculum design, 85, 123, 124, 125, 126
Curriculum development, 79, 85, 94, 185
Curriculum discourses, 201
Curriculum field, 43, 63, 67, 68, 71, 77, 81, 82, 119, 122, 130, 192, 196, 223, 240, 249
Curriculum implementation, 79
Curriculum organization, 248
Curriculum reform, 80
Curriculum research, 82
Curriculum scholarship, 109, 122, 130
Curriculum theorist, 117, 118, 127, 148, 159, 194, 231, 244
Curriculum theory, 3, 13, 40, 71, 80, 82, 90, 152, 177, 194, 201, 227, 228, 231, 243, 249

Death, 57, 191, 195
Deconstruction, 208, 210, 212, 214, 215
Defiance, 262
Demasculinization, 167, 168, 169
Democratic National Convention, 259
Democracy, 239
De-oedipalization, 164
Deviant, 161, 213
Dialectical materialism, 163
Dialogical encounter, 65, 111
Dionysian (the), 206, 207, 208, 212
Discourse, 213
Dissertation, 263
Domain assumptions, 132
Drag queen, 188
Drugs, 246, 258

Earth, 210
Education, 16, 17, 19, 67, 70, 71, 90, 120, 122, 149, 193, 195, 196, 197, 227, 235, 236, 238, 239, 243, 244
Educational administration, 193, 207
Educational environment, 127
Educational experience, 25, 54, 91, 225, 228
Educational foundations, 194
Educational psychology, 77, 80, 193
Educational research, 15, 16
Educational researchers, 124
Educational theory, 46, 68
Efficiency, 241
Enculturation, 207
Ethics, 211
Ethnicity, 72, 167, 230
European-Americans, 245, 246, 260
Evaluation, 15, 85, 94, 236, 237
Examinations, 243
Exhibitionism, 163
Existentialism, 7, 17, 68, 122
Experimentalism, 118, 122

Factories, 1, 239, 241
Factory model, 242, 248, 249
Faith, 261
Fascism, 131, 196
Federal Reserve Policy, 186, 191
Fellatio, 162, 171
Femininity, 189
Feminism, 168, 183, 187, 188
Feminist man, 163
Feminist movement, 152, 168
Feminists, 194
Feminist struggle, 153
Feminist theory, 1, 3, 153, 189,
    223
Film, 7
Free enterprise, 192
Fundamentalist, 247

Gay, 152, 246, 254, 260, 262, 265
Gender, 151, 152, 153, 154, 166,
    167, 185, 187, 188, 194, 195,
    201, 223, 229, 243, 261
Germany, 236
Ghetto, 260
Grade inflation, 238
Guilt, 258

Haiti, 260
Happiness, 132, 133, 134, 144,
    149, 262, 266
Health clubs, 210
Hegemony, 103, 107, 131
Hell, 256
Hermeneutics, 86, 87, 169, 195
Heterosexuality, 152, 155, 156,
    160, 161, 162, 163, 165, 167,
    171, 175, 188
Historical conjuncture, 197
Holocaust, 67, 205, 217
Homework, 237, 246
Homicide, 196
Homiletics, 203
Homoerotic, 155
Homophobia, 175, 204
Homosexuality, 101, 156, 160,
    161, 164, 165, 166, 167, 174,
    176, 215, 254, 265

Hookers, 260
Hustlers, 260

Identity, 3, 36, 47, 50, 51, 55, 157,
    185, 187, 207, 210, 243, 244,
    245, 247, 248, 249
Ideology, 93, 122, 130, 160, 167,
    217
Immigration, 207
Imperialism, 120
Indoctrination, 111
Industrial, 248
Industrial economy, 239
Industrialization, 161, 184
Incest, 258
Instruction, 16, 67, 103, 107, 229,
    244
Intellectual development, 120,
    148
Intellectual movement, 149
Intelligence, 243, 244, 245, 247
Intoxication, 215

Japan, 236
Jazz, 260
Jews, 215, 262
Judaic-Christian tradition, 217

Law, 31, 36, 45, 161, 238
Laziness, 246
Learning disabilities, 194
Lebenswelt, 20, 216
Left wing, 101, 104, 151, 158,
    159, 196
Legal, 261, 262, 265
Lesbians, 196
Lesson plan, 7
Liberal arts, 226, 228
Liberals, 205
Liberation, 102, 111, 112, 113,
    129, 131
Life history, 37, 41, 91
Lived experience, 240
Love, 254, 262, 265, 266, 267
Love-making, 216

Macho, 162
Macho Marxist, 162, 163
Manhood, 160, 176
Manliness, 162
Marginalized, 215, 217
Marginalized classes, 228
Marginalized elements, 213
Marginalized groups, 204
Marginalized material, 214
Marriage, 254, 255
Married, 261, 262, 267
Marxian theory, 129, 130
Marxism, 68, 70, 93, 195, 243
Marxists, 3, 69, 93, 106, 110, 130
Masculinity, 168, 187, 189
Mass production, 210
Matrimony, 261
Matrisexuality, 169
Medicalization, 161
Medicine, 161, 238
Memory, 218
Men's groups, 187
Military, 171, 191, 192
Minority groups, 246
Minority students, 230
Mirrors, 253, 265
Misogyny, 204
Momentariness, 219
Monetarism, 191, 192
Money supply, 194
Morality, 211
Motherhood, 184
Multiculturalism, 244, 245, 249
Music videos, 188, 189
Myth, 209
Myth-making, 209

Narcissism, 108, 162, 206, 265
National Education Association, 207
Nazi, 102
Nineteen sixties (1960s), 237, 238
Nostalgia, 211, 212, 215

Objectives, 15, 231
Object relations, 170

Oedipus (theory), 152, 153, 154, 156, 158, 159, 160, 163, 165, 166, 172, 173, 176, 206

Painting, 7, 9
Parental, 258
Parents, 247
Passages, 248
Passion, 261
Paternity, 154, 158, 167
Patriarchy, 152, 159, 167, 168, 169, 170, 172
Peace Corps, 238
Peer teaching, 242
Penis, 165
Penis-envy, 172
Personal, practical knowledge, 2
Pervert, 214
Phallocentrism, 160, 162, 172
Phallus, 162, 163, 164, 171, 172, 173
Phenomenology, 1, 40, 68, 69, 70, 83, 88, 169, 195, 215, 223, 228, 229
Police, 259
Policemen, 171
Policymakers, 241, 247
Political socialization, 207
Political theory, 2, 84, 103
Politics, 129, 160, 161, 163, 204, 224, 241, 243, 244
Poor (the), 246
Post-industrial, 211
Poststructuralism, 3, 195, 261
Poverty, 260
Power, 162, 163, 172, 177, 192, 194, 213
Practice (the practical), 50, 67, 77, 78, 85, 86, 87, 92, 93, 95, 204, 213, 227, 241, 244, 248, 249
Pragmatic, 118
Prayer, 204
Pregnancy, 155
Praxis, 92, 110
Presence, 218, 219, 265
Privilege, 241
Problem-solving, 241, 242, 248

Professional development
schools, 230, 237
Professional judgment, 227
Progressive, 24, 59, 246
Protestant, 262
Psychoanalysis, 1, 15, 17, 20, 44,
55, 68, 70, 87, 88, 89, 90, 91,
120, 121, 148, 154, 205, 245,
246, 247, 248, 263
Psychotherapy, 157
PTA, 260
Public television, 254
Pulpit, 261

Quebec, 195

Race, 243, 247
Racism, 204, 245, 262
Racist groups, 207
Rape, 162
Reconceptualism, 70, 71
Reconceptualist, 71, 73, 78, 82,
89, 224, 227
Reconceptualization, 3, 4, 60, 63,
64, 66, 67, 68, 70, 71, 73, 89,
117, 169, 194, 223, 224, 225,
231, 249
Regressive, 21, 59, 253, 266
Regressive-progressive-analytic-
synthetic method, 19, 37, 44,
58, 60, 108
Relationship, 137, 147, 148, 149,
258
Reproduction theory, 109, 129,
151, 152, 158, 159, 170
Republicans, 236, 246
Resistance theory, 151, 152, 159
Right wing, 101, 104, 106, 109,
130, 246
Rock bands, 260
Romance, 254
Routinization, 197, 241

School reform, 4, 235, 236, 237,
241, 248, 249

Schools, 1, 2, 37, 66, 67, 104, 124,
152, 176, 193, 202, 211, 212,
214, 223, 224, 230, 235, 238,
239, 242, 243, 245, 248, 262
Scientization, 210
Seductive, 258
Self-encounter, 255
Semiotic, 248
Sensuality, 208
Sex acts, 256
Sexism, 168, 262
Sex-role expectation, 167
sex roles, 188
Sexuality, 90, 103, 141, 160, 161,
162, 172, 173, 176, 254, 258
Slaves, 262
Social control, 72
Socialism, 197
Socialist, 193
Social theory, 46, 194
Solipsism, 207
Soviet Union, 102, 108, 131, 237
Spiritual work, 146
Spouse, 262
Sputnik, 236
Standardization, 169, 197, 211,
241
Storytelling, 209
St. Patrick's Day, 261
Straight, 262
Student lore, 2
Students, 126, 209, 226, 235, 237,
242, 247
Student teachers, 224
Sublimated, 258
Suicide, 196
Surveillance, 213
Sweden, 192
Symbiosis, 156, 168, 170, 211
Synthetical, 26, 27, 60

Talk-show, 254
Taxes, 192
Teacher development, 2
Teacher education, 2, 4, 223, 224,
231, 237, 239
Teacher lore, 2

Teachers, 124, 125, 126, 127, 130,
   193, 209, 225, 235, 236, 237,
   238, 241, 242, 243, 247, 248,
   249
Teacher thinking, 2
Teaching, 7, 67, 121, 122, 152,
   193, 226, 227, 240, 249, 262
Technique, 34
Television, 188
Tests, 236
Theater, 1, 2
Theology, 3, 247, 261
Theory (the theoretical), 50, 78,
   79, 92, 93, 112, 204, 213, 230,
   240, 244, 248, 249
Tourists, 260
Trivialization, 211

Understanding, 39, 41, 42, 45, 50,
   54, 57, 59, 60, 71, 85, 88, 89,
   118, 122, 133, 148, 160, 177

Union (relationship), 254, 262
Union (spiritual), 262
Unions (trade), 191, 192

Victimized, 262
Vietnam War, 192
Vocationalism, 226, 227
Voodoo, 260
Voyeurism, 164

Wedding, 261, 266
West Germany, 192
White, 72, 246, 247
White students, 245
Windows, 253, 265, 267
World War II, 191
Youth culture, 238

Zen, 143, 144, 146